ROUTLEDGE–CAVENDISH
Core Statutes

Equity and Trusts

Equity and Trusts

2007-2008

D.G. Cracknell, LLB, of the Middle Temple, Barrister

 Routledge·Cavendish
Taylor & Francis Group
LONDON AND NEW YORK

Sixth edition published 2008 by Routledge-Cavendish
2 Park Square, Milton Park, Abingdon, Oxon, OX14 4RN
Simultaneously published in the USA and Canada
by Routledge-Cavendish
270 Madison Avenue, New York, NY 10016

Routledge-Cavendish is an imprint of the Taylor & Francis Group, an informa business

Previous editions published by Old Bailey Press
First edition   1994
Fifth Edition   2005

Typeset in Garmond

Printed and bound in Great Britain by Cromwell Press, Trowbridge, Wiltshire

British Library Cataloguing in Publication Data
A catalogue record for this book is available from the British Library

Library of Congress Cataloging in Publication Data
A Catalog record for this book has been requested

ISBN10: 0-415-45122-1 (pbk)
ISBN13: 978-0-415-45123-9 (pbk)

Equity and Trusts
2007-2008

Previously published by Old Bailey Press as the Cracknell's Statutes series, Routledge-Cavendish Core Statutes provide a comprehensive series of essential statutory provisions for the core subjects and major options on the LLB or GDL.

Each book in the series

- provides the precise wording of Acts of Parliament and is unnanotated, making it ideal for both course and exam use

- is updated annually to incorporate all of the latest legislation covered in most UK law syllabi

- features consolidated amendments, avoiding the need to cross-refer to amending legislation

- contains both alphabetical and chronological contents listings and is fully indexed

Douglas Cracknell was called to the Bar in 1957 and he is still in practice. Over the years, he has devoted much time to writing and editing textbooks for students and practitioners.

Routledge-Cavendish Core Statutes

New editions available for 2007-2008:

Constitutional and Administrative Law

Contract, Tort and Remedies

Criminal Law

English Legal System

Equity and Trusts

European Union Legislation

CONTENTS

PREFACE

Although the rules of equity, and the concept of trust, grew out of the relief of hard cases by the medieval Chancellor, 'the keeper of the King's conscience', in course of time many of these rules were embodied in, and amended by, Acts of Parliament.

Above all, it was Parliament which brought about, and subsequently confirmed, the 'fusion' of the rules of common law and equity and provided that, in the event of conflict or variance, it is the rules of equity which prevail.

This edition contains statutory provisions currently in force with which students may be required to be familiar. While the Charities Act 1601 has in fact been repealed, its preamble is included as it remains the cornerstone of charitable status – until the relevant provisions of the Charities Act 2006 are brought into force.

Statutes, and particular provisions of statutes, in force on 1 June 2007 have been taken into account. Accordingly, changes made by the Charities Act 2006 which were in force on that date have been covered in the text. Relevant changes which were not in force, or were only partly in force, on 1 June have been included in the Appendix and attention is drawn to those changes in appropriate places in the main text.

This edition also includes certain provisions in Part 2 of the Equality Act 2006 (Discrimination on grounds of religion or belief). These sections provide another example of the special treatment of charities in legislation of this kind. A note at the end of a statute indicates the source of any amendments – insertions, repeals or substitutions – which have been made to the sections included in the text.

Suggestions as to statutes, or provisions of statutes, which could helpfully be included in future editions would always be most gratefully received.

ALPHABETICAL TABLE OF STATUTES

STATUTES

CHARITIES ACT 1601
(43 Eliz 1 c 4)

Preamble
Whereas Lands, Tenements, Rents, Annuities, Profits, Hereditaments, Goods, Chattels, Money and Stocks of Money, have been heretofore given, limited, appointed and assigned, as well by the Queen's most excellent Majesty, and her most noble Progenitors, as by sundry other well-disposed Persons; some for Relief of aged, impotent and poor People, some for Maintenance of sick and maimed Soldiers and Mariners, Schools of Learning, Free Schools, and Scholars in Universities, some for Repair of Bridges, Ports, Havens, Causways, Churches, Sea-banks and Highways, some for Education and Preferment of Orphans, some for or towards Relief, Stock, or Maintenance for House of Correction, some for Marriages of poor Maids, some for Supportation, Aid and Help of young Tradesmen, Handicraftsmen and Persons decayed, and others for Relief or Redemption of Prisoners or Captives, and for Aid or Ease of any poor Inhabitants concerning Payments of Fifteens, setting out of Solders and other Taxes; which Lands, Tenements, Rents, Annuities, Profits, Hereditaments, Goods, Chattels, Money and Stocks of Money, nevertheless have not been employed according to the charitable Intent of the Givers and Founders thereof, by reason of Frauds, Breaches of Trust, and Negligence in those that should pay, deliver and employ the same …

WILLS ACT 1837
(7 Will IV & 1 Vict c 26)

1   Meaning of certain words in this Act
The words and expressions hereinafter mentioned, which in their ordinary signification have a more confined or a different meaning, shall in this Act, except where the nature of the provision or the context of the Act shall exclude such construction, be interpreted as follows: (that is to say,) the word 'will' shall extend to a testament, and to a codicil, and to an appointment by will or by writing in the nature of a will in exercise of a power, and also to an appointment by will of a guardian of a child and also to an appointment by will of a representative under section 4 of the Human Tissue Act Act 2004, and to any other testamentary disposition; and the words 'real estate' shall extend to manors, advowsons, messuages, lands, tithes, rents, and hereditaments, whether freehold, customary freehold, tenant right, customary or copyhold, or of any other tenure, and whether corporeal, incorporeal, or personal, and to any estate, right, or interest (other than a chattel interest) therein; and the words 'personal estate' shall extend to leasehold estates,

and other chattels real, and also to moneys, shares of government and other funds, securities for money (being not real estates), debts, choses in action, rights, credits, goods, and all other property whatsoever, which by law devolves upon the executor or administrator, and to any share or interest therein; and every word importing the singular number only shall extend and be applied to several persons or things as well as one person or thing; and every word importing the masculine gender only shall extend and be applied to a female as well as a male.

9   Signing and attestation of wills
No will shall be valid unless –

    (a) it is in writing, and signed by the testator, or by some other person in his presence and by his direction; and

    (b) it appears that the testator intended by his signature to give effect to the will; and

    (c) the signature is made or acknowledged by the testator in the presence of two or more witnesses present at the same time; and

    (d) each witness either –

        (i)   attests and signs the will; or

        (ii) acknowledges his signature,

in the presence of the testator (but not necessarily in the presence of any other witness), but no form of attestation shall be necessary.

15   Gifts to an attesting witness to be void
If any person shall attest the execution of any will to whom or to whose wife or husband any beneficial devise, legacy, estate, interest, gift, or appointment, of or affecting any real or personal estate (other than and except charges and directions for the payment of any debt or debts), shall be thereby given or made, such devise, legacy, estate, interest, gift, or appointment shall, so far only as concerns such person attesting the execution of such will, or the wife or husband of such person, or any person claiming under such person or wife or husband, be utterly null and void, and such person so attesting shall be admitted as a witness to prove the execution of such will, or to prove the validity or invalidity thereof, notwithstanding such devise, legacy, estate, interest, gift, or appointment mentioned in such will.

25   A residuary devise shall include estates comprised in lapsed and void devises
Unless a contrary intention shall appear by the will, such real estate or interest therein as shall be comprised or intended to be comprised in any devise in such will contained, which shall fail to be void by reason of the death of the devisee in the lifetime of the testator, or by reason of such devise being contrary to law or otherwise incapable of taking effect shall be included in the residuary devise (if any) contained in such will.

As amended by the Statute Law Revision (No 2) Act 1888; Statute Law Revision Act 1893; Statute Law (Repeals) Act 1969; Administration of Justice Act 1982, s17; Children Act 1989, s108(5), Schedule 13, para 1; Trusts of Land and Appointment of Trustees Act 1996, s25(2), Schedule 4; Human Tissue Act 2004, s56, Schedule 6, para 1.

APPORTIONMENT ACT 1870
(33 & 34 Vict c 35)

2   Rents, etc to be apportionable in respect of time

All rents, annuities, dividends, and other periodical payments in the nature of income (whether reserved or made payable under an instrument in writing or otherwise) shall, like interest on money lent, be considered as accruing from day to day, and shall be apportionable in respect of time accordingly.

5   Interpretation

In the construction of this Act –

The word 'rents' includes rent service, rentcharge, and rent seck, and also tithes and all periodical payments or renderings in lieu of or in the nature of rent or tithe.

The word 'annuities' includes salaries and pensions.

The word 'dividends' includes (besides dividends strictly so called) all payments made by the name of dividend, bonus, or otherwise out of the revenue of trading or other public companies, divisible between all or any of the members of such respective companies, whether such payments shall be usually made or declared, at any fixed times or otherwise; and all such divisible revenue shall, for the purposes of this Act, be deemed to have accrued by equal daily increment during and within the period for or in respect of which the payment of the same revenue shall be declared or expressed to be made, but the said word 'dividend' does not include payments in the nature of a return or reimbursement of capital.

7   Nor where stipulation made to the contrary

The provisions of this Act shall not extend to any case in which it is or shall be expressly stipulated that no apportionment shall take place.

As amended by the Statute Law Revision (No 2) Act 1893.

MARRIED WOMEN'S PROPERTY ACT 1882
(45 & 46 Vict c 75)

17   Questions between husband and wife as to property to be decided in a summary way

In any question between husband and wife as to the title or possession of property, either party may apply by summons or otherwise in a summary way to the High Court or such county court as may be prescribed and the court may, on such an application (which may be heard in private), make such order with respect to the property as it thinks fit.

In this section 'prescribed' means prescribed by rules of court and rules made for the purposes of this section may confer jurisdiction on county courts whatever the situation or value of the property in dispute.

24   Interpretation of terms

The word 'property' in this Act includes a thing in action.

As amended by the Statute Law (Repeals) Act 1969 and the Matrimonial and Family Proceedings Act 1984, s43.

PARTNERSHIP ACT 1890
(53 & 54 Vict c 39)

1   Definition of partnership

(1) Partnership is the relation which subsists between persons carrying on a business in common with a view of profit.

(2) But the relation between members of any company or association which is –

    (a)   registered as a company under the Companies Act 1862 or any other Act of Parliament for the time being in force and relating to the registration of joint stock companies; or

    (b)   formed or incorporated by or in pursuance of any other Act of Parliament or letters patent, or Royal Charter;

is not a partnership within the meaning of this Act.

4   Meaning of firm

(1) Persons who have entered into partnership with one another are for the purposes of this Act called collectively a firm, and the name under which their business is carried on is called the firm-name. …

10   Liability of the firm for wrongs

Where, by any wrongful act or omission of any partner acting in the ordinary course of the business of the firm, or with the authority of his co-partners, loss or injury is caused to any person not being a partner in the firm, or any penalty is incurred, the firm is liable therefor to the same extent as the partner so acting or omitting to act.

11   Misapplication of money or property received for or in custody of the firm

In the following cases; namely –

    (a)   Where one partner acting within the scope of his apparent authority received the money or property of a third person and misapplies it; and

    (b)   Where a firm in the course of its business received money or property of a third person, and the money or property so received is misapplied by one or more of the partners while it is in the custody of the firm;

the firm is liable to make good the loss.

13   Improper employment of trust-property for partnership purposes

If a partner, being a trustee, improperly employs trust-property in the business or on the account of the partnership, no other partner is liable for the trust property to the persons beneficially interested therein:

Provided as follows –

(1) this section shall not affect any liability incurred by any partner by reason of his having notice of a breach of trust; and

(2) nothing in this section shall prevent money from being followed and recovered from the firm if still in its possession or under its control.

20   Partnership property

(1) All property and rights and interests in property originally brought into the partnership stock or acquired, whether by purchase or otherwise, on account of the firm, or for the purposes and in the course of the partnership business, are called in this Act partnership property, and must be held and applied by the partners exclusively for the purposes of the partnership and in accordance with the partnership agreement.

(2) Provided that the legal estate or interest in any land … which belongs to the partnership shall devolve accordingly to the nature and tenure thereof, and the general rules of law thereto applicable, but in trust, so far as necessary, for the persons beneficially interested in the land under this section.

(3) Where co-owners of an estate or interest in any land … not being itself partnership property, are partners as to profits made by the use of that land or estate, and purchase other land or estate out of the profits to be used in like manner, the land or estate so purchased belongs to them, in the absence of an agreement to the contrary, not as partners, but as co-owners for the same respective estates and interests as are held by them in the land or estate first mentioned at the date of the purchase.

29 Accountability of partners of private profits

(1) Every partner must account to the firm for any benefit derived by him without the consent of the other partners from any transaction concerning the partnership, or from any use by him of the partnership property name or business connexion.

(2) This section applies also to transactions undertaken after a partnership has been dissolved by the death of a partner, and before the affairs thereof have been completely wound up, either by surviving or by the representatives of the deceased partner.

30 Duty of partner not to compete with firm

If a partner, without the consent of the other partners, carries on any business of the same nature as and competing with that of the firm, he must account for and pay over to the firm all profits by him in that business.

45 Definitions of 'court' and 'business'

In this Act, unless the contrary intention appears, –

The expression 'court' includes every court and judge having jurisdiction in the case:

The expression 'business' includes every trade, occupation, or profession.

46 Saving for rules of equity and common law

The rules of equity and of common law applicable to partnership shall continue in force except so far as they are inconsistent with the express provisions of this Act.

As amended by the Statute Law (Repeals) Act 1998, s1(1), Schedule 1, Pt X.

LIMITED PARTNERSHIPS ACT 1907
(7 Edw 7 c 24)

3 Interpretation of terms

In the construction of this Act the following words and expressions shall have the meanings respectively assigned to them in this section, unless there be something in the subject or context repugnant to such construction: –

'Firm', 'firm name', and 'business' have the same meanings as in the Partnership Act 1890:

'General partner' shall mean any partner who is not a limited partner as defined by this Act.

4 Definition and construction of limited partnership

(1) Limited partnerships may be formed in the manner and subject to the conditions by this Act provided.

(2) A limited partnership must consist of one or more persons called general partners, who shall be liable for all debts and obligations of the firm, and one or more persons to be called limited partners, who shall at the time of entering into such partnership contribute thereto a sum or sums as capital or property valued at a stated amount, and who shall not be liable for the debts or obligations of the firm beyond the amount so contributed.

(3) A limited partner shall not during the continuance of the partnership, either directly or indirectly, draw out or receive back any part of his contribution, and if he does so draw out or receive back any such part shall be liable for the debts and obligations of the firm up to the amount so drawn out or received back.

(4) A body corporate may be a limited partner.

5 Registration of limited partnership required

Every limited partnership must be registered as such in accordance with the provisions of this Act, or in default thereof it shall be deemed to be a general partnership, and every limited partner shall be deemed to be a general partner.

6 Modifications of general law in case of limited partnerships

(1) A limited partner shall not take part in the management of the partnership business, and shall not have power to bind the firm:

Provided that a limited partner may by himself or his agent at any time inspect the books of the firm and examine into the state and prospects of the partnership business, and may advise with the partners thereon.

If a limited partner takes part in the management of the partnership business he shall be liable for all debts and obligations of the firm incurred while he so takes part in the management as though he were a general partner.

(2) A limited partnership shall not be dissolved by the death or bankruptcy of a limited partner, and the lunacy of a limited partner shall not be a ground for dissolution of the partnership by the court unless the lunatic's share cannot be otherwise ascertained and realised.

(3) In the event of the dissolution of a limited partnership its affairs shall be wound up by the general partners unless the court otherwise orders.

(5) Subject to any agreement expressed or implied between the partners –

    (a) Any difference arising as to ordinary matters connected with the partnership business may be decided by a majority of the general partners;

    (b) A limited partner may, with the consent of the general partners, assign his share in the partnership, and upon such an assignment the assignee shall become a limited partner with all the rights of the assignor;

    (c) The other partners shall not be entitled to dissolve the partnership by reason of any limited partner suffering his share to be charged for his separate debt;

    (d) A person may be introduced as a partner without the consent of the existing limited partners;

    (e) A limited partner shall not be entitled to dissolve the partnership by notice.

7 Law as to private partnerships to apply where not excluded by this Act

Subject to the provisions of this Act, the Partnership Act 1890 and the rules of equity and of common law applicable to partnerships, except so far as they are inconsistent with the express provisions of the last-mentioned Act, shall apply to limited partnerships.

As amended by the Companies (Consolidation) Act 1908, s286, Schedule 6, Pt I; Statute Law Revision Act 1927; Banking Act 1979, ss46(b), 51(2), Schedule 7; Regulatory Reform (Removal of 20 Member Limit in Partnerships, etc) Order 2002, art 3.

TRUSTEE ACT 1925
(15 & 16 Geo 5 c 19)

PART II

GENERAL POWERS OF TRUSTEES AND PERSONAL REPRESENTATIVES

12   Power of trustees for sale to sell by auction, etc

(1) Where a trustee has a duty or power to sell property, he may sell or concur with any other person in selling all or any part of the property, either subject to prior charges or not, and either together or in lots, by public auction or by private contract, subject to any such conditions respecting title or evidence of title or other matter as the trustee thinks fit, with power to vary any contract for sale, and to buy in at any auction, or to rescind any contract for sale and to re-sell, without being answerable for any loss.

(2) A duty or power to sell or dispose of land includes a duty or power to sell or dispose of part thereof, whether the division is horizontal, vertical or made in any other way.

(3) This section does not enable an express power to sell settled land to be exercised where the power is not vested in the tenant for life or statutory owner.

13   Power to sell subject to depreciatory conditions

(1) No sale made by a trustee shall be impeached by any beneficiary upon the ground that any of the conditions subject to which the sale was made may have been unnecessarily depreciatory, unless it also appears that the consideration for the sale was thereby rendered inadequate.

(2) No sale made by a trustee shall, after the execution of the conveyance, be impeached as against the purchaser upon the ground that any of the conditions subject to which the sale was made may have been unnecessarily depreciatory, unless it appears that the purchaser was acting in collusion with the trustee at the time when the contract for sale was made.

(3) No purchaser, upon any sale made by the trustee, shall be at liberty to make any objection against the title upon any of the grounds aforesaid.

(4) This section applies to sales made before or after the commencement of this Act.

14   Power of trustees to give receipts

(1) The receipt in writing of a trustee for any money, securities, investments or other personal property or effects payable, transferable, or deliverable to him under any trust or power shall be a sufficient discharge to the person paying, transferring, or delivering the same and shall effectually exonerate him from seeing to the application or being answerable for any loss or misapplication thereof.

(2) This section does not, except where the trustee is a trust corporation, enable a sole trustee to give a valid receipt for –

    (a)   proceeds of sale or other capital money arising under a trust of land;

    (b)   capital money arising under the Settled Land Act 1925.

(3) This section applies notwithstanding anything to the contrary in the instrument, if any, creating the trust.

15   Power to compound liabilities

A personal representative, or two or more trustees acting together, or, subject to the restrictions imposed in regard to receipts by a sole trustee not being a trust corporation, a sole acting trustee where by the instrument, if any, creating the trust, or by statute, a sole trustee is authorised to execute the trusts and powers reposed in him, may, if and as he or they think fit –

    (a) accept any property, real or personal, before the time at which it is made transferable or payable; or

    (b) sever and apportion any blended trust funds or property; or

    (c) pay or allow any debt or claim on any evidence that he or they think sufficient; or

    (d) accept any composition or any security, real or personal, for any debt or for any property, real or personal, claimed; or

    (e) allow any time of payment of any debt; or

    (f) compromise, compound, abandon, submit to arbitration, or otherwise settle any debt, account, claim, or think whatever relating to the testator's or intestate's estate or to the trust;

and for any of those purposes may enter into, give, execute, and do such agreements, instruments of composition or arrangement, releases, and other things as to him or them seen expedient, without being responsible for any loss occasioned by any act or thing so done by him or them if he has or they have discharged the duty of care set out in section 1(1) of the Trustee Act 2000.

16   Power to raise money by sale, mortgage, etc

(1) Where trustees are authorised by the instrument, if any, creating the trust or by law to pay or apply capital money subject to the trust for any purpose or in any manner, they shall have and shall be deemed always to have had power to raise the money required by sale, conversion, calling in, or mortgage of all or any part of the trust property for the time being in possession.

(2) This section applies notwithstanding anything to the contrary contained in the instrument, if any, creating the trust, but does not apply to trustees of property held for charitable purposes, or to trustees of a settlement for the purposes of the Settled Land Act 1925, not being also the statutory owners.

17   Protection to purchasers and mortgagees dealing with trustees

No purchaser or mortgagee, paying or advancing money on a sale or mortgage purporting to be made under any trust or power vested in trustees, shall be concerned to see that such money is wanted, or that no more than is wanted is raised, or otherwise as to the application thereof.

18   Devolution of powers or trusts

(1) Where a power or trust is given to or imposed on two or more trustees jointly, the same may be exercised or performed by the survivors or survivor of them for the time being.

(2) Until the appointment of new trustees, the personal representatives or representative for the time being of a sole trustee, or, where there were two or more trustees of the last surviving or continuing trustee, shall be capable of exercising or performing any power or trust which was given to, or capable of being exercised by, the sole or last surviving or continuing trustee, or other the trustees or trustee for the time being of the trust.

(3) This section takes effect subject to the restrictions imposed in regard to receipts by a sole trustee, not being a trust corporation.

(4) In this section 'personal representative' does not include an executor who has renounced or has not proved.

19   Power to insure

(1) A trustee may –

    (a) insure any property which is subject to the trust against risks of loss or damage due to any event, and

    (b) pay the premiums out of the trust funds.

(2) In the case of property held on a bare trust, the power to insure is subject to any direction given by the beneficiary or each of the beneficiaries –

    (a) that any property specified in the direction is not to be insured;

    (b) that any property specified in the direction is not to be insured except on such conditions as may be so specified.

(3) Property is held on a bare trust if it is held on trust for –

    (a) a beneficiary who is of full age and capacity and absolutely entitled to the property subject to the trust, or

    (b) beneficiaries each of whom is of full age and capacity and who (taken together) are absolutely entitled to the property subject to the trust.

(4) If a direction under subsection (2) of this section is given, the power to insure, so far as it is subject to the direction, ceases to be a delegable function for the purposes of section 11 of the Trustee Act 2000 (power to employ agents).

(5) In this section 'trust funds' means any income or capital funds of the trust.

20   Application of insurance money where policy kept up under any trust, power or obligation

(1) Money receivable by trustees or any beneficiary under a policy of insurance against the loss or damage of any property subject to a trust or to a settlement within the meaning of the Settled Land Act 1925 shall, where the policy has been kept up under any trust in that behalf or under any power statutory or otherwise, or in performance of any covenant or of any obligation statutory or otherwise, or by a tenant for life impeachable for waste, be capital money for the purposes of the trust or settlement, as the case may be.

(2) If any such money is receivable by any person, other than the trustees of the trust or settlement, that person shall use his best endeavours to recover and receive the money, and shall pay the net residue thereof, after discharging any costs of recovering and receiving it, to the trustees of the trust or settlement, or, if there are no trustees capable of giving a discharge therefore, into court.

(3) Any such money –

    (a) if it was receivable in respect of settled land within the meaning of the Settled Land Act 1925, or any building or works thereon, shall be deemed to be capital money arising under that Act from the settled land, and shall be invested or applied by the trustees, or, if in court, under the discretion of the court, accordingly;

    (b) if it was receivable in respect of personal chattels settled as heirlooms within the meaning of the Settled Land Act 1925, shall be deemed to be capital money arising under that Act, and shall be applicable by the trustees, or, if in court, under the direction of the court, in like manner as provided by that Act with respect to money arising by a sale of chattels settled as heirlooms as aforesaid;

    (c) if it was receivable in respect of land subject to a trust of land or personal property held on trust for sale, shall be held upon the trusts and subject to the powers and provisions applicable to money arising by a sale under such trust;

    (d) in any other case, shall be held upon trusts corresponding as nearly as may be with the trusts affecting the property in respect of which it was payable.

(4) Such money, or any part thereof, may also be applied by the trustees, or, if in court, under the direction of the court, in rebuilding, reinstating, replacing, or repairing the property lost or damaged, but any such application by the trustees shall be subject to the consent of any person whose consent is required by the instrument, if any, creating the trust to the investment of money

subject to the trust, and, in the case of money which is deemed to be capital money arising under the Settled Land Act 1925, be subject to the provisions of that Act with respect to the application of capital money by the trustees of the settlement.

(5) Nothing contained in this section prejudices or affects the right of any person to require any such money or any part thereof to be applied in rebuilding, reinstating, to repairing the property lost or damaged, or the rights of any mortgagee, lessor, or lessee, whether under any statute or otherwise.

(6) This section applies to policies effected either before or after the commencement of this Act, but only to money received after such commencement.

22   Reversionary interests, valuations and audit

(1) Where trust property includes any share or interest in property not vested in the trustees, or the proceeds of the sale of any such property, or any other things in action, the trustees on the same falling into possession, or becoming payable or transferable, may –

    (a) agree or ascertain the amount or value thereof or any part thereof in such manner as they may think fit;

    (b) accept in or towards satisfaction thereof, at the market or current value, or upon any valuation or estimate of value which they may think fit, any authorised investments;

    (c) allow any deductions for duties, costs, charges and expenses which they may think proper or reasonable;

    (d) execute any release in respect of the premises so as effectually to discharge all accountable parties from all liability in respect of any matters coming within the scope of such release;

without being responsible in any such case for any loss occasioned by any act or thing so done by them if they have discharged the duty of care set out in section 1(1) of the Trustee Act 2000.

(2) The trustees shall not be under any obligation and shall not be chargeable with any breach of trust by reason of any omission –

    (a) to place any distringas notice or apply for any stop or other like order upon any securities or other property out of or on which such share or interest or other things in action as aforesaid is derived, payable or charged; or

    (b) to take any proceedings on account of any act, default, or neglect on the part of the persons in whom such securities or other property or any of them or any part thereof are for the time being, or had at any time been, vested;

unless and until required in writing so to do by some person, or the guardian of some person, beneficially interested under the trust, and unless also due provision is made to their satisfaction for payment of the costs of any proceedings required to be taken:

Provided that nothing in this subsection shall relieve the trustees of the obligation to get in and obtain payment or transfer of such share or interest or other thing in action on the same falling into possession.

(3) Trustees may, for the purpose of giving effect to the trust, or any of the provisions of the instrument, if any, creating the trust or of any statute, from time to time (by duly qualified agents) ascertain and fix the value of any trust property in such manner as they think proper, and any valuation so made if the trustees have discharged the duty of care set out in section 1 of the Trustee Act 2000 shall be binding upon all persons interested under the trust.

(4) Trustees may, in their absolute discretion, from time to time, but not more than once in every three years unless the nature of the trust or any special dealings with the trust property make a more frequent exercise of the right reasonable, cause the accounts of the trust property to be examined or audited by an independent accountant, and shall, for that purpose, produce such

vouchers and give such information to him as he may require; and the costs of such examination or audit, including the fee of the auditor, shall be paid out of the capital or income of the trust property, or partly in one way and partly in the other, as the trustees, in their absolute discretion, think fit, but, in default of any direction by the trustees to the contrary in any special case, costs attributable to capital shall be borne by capital and those attributable to income by income.

24   Power to concur with others

Where an undivided share in any property is subject to a trust, or forms part of the estate of a testator or intestate, the trustees or personal representatives may (without prejudice to the trust affecting the entirety of the land and the powers of the trustees in reference thereto) execute or exercise any duty or power vested in them in relation to such share in conjunction with the persons entitled to or having power in that behalf over the other share or shares, and notwithstanding that any one or more of the trustees or personal representatives may be entitled to or interested in any such other share, either in his or their own right or in the fiduciary capacity.

25   Delegation of trustee's functions by power of attorney

(1) Notwithstanding any rule of law or equity to the contrary, a trustee may, by power of attorney, delegate the execution or exercise of all or any of the trusts, powers and discretions vested in him as trustee either alone or jointly with any other person or persons.

(2) A delegation under this section –

    (a)   commences as provided by the instrument creating the power or, if the instrument makes no provision as to the commencement of the delegation, with the date of the execution of the instrument by the donor; and

    (b)   continues for a period of twelve months or any shorter period provided by the instrument creating the power.

(3) The persons who may be donees of a power of attorney under this section include a trust corporation.

(4) Before or within seven days after giving a power of attorney under this section the donor shall give written notice of it (specifying the date on which the power comes into operation and its duration, the donee of the power, the reason why the power is given and, where some only are delegated, the trusts, powers and discretions delegated) to –

    (a)   each person (other than himself), if any, who under any instrument creating the trust has power (whether alone or jointly) to appoint a new trustee; and

    (b)   each of the other trustees, if any;

but failure to comply with this subsection shall not, in favour of a person dealing with the donee of the power, invalidate any act done or instrument executed by the donee.

(5) A power of attorney given under this section by a single donor –

    (a)   in the form set out in subsection (6) of this section; or

    (b)   in a form to the like effect but expressed to be made under this subsection,

shall operate to delegate to the person identified in the form as the single donee of the power the execution and exercise of all the trusts, powers and discretions vested in the donor as trustee (either alone or jointly with any other person or persons) under the single trust so identified.

(6) The form referred to in subsection (5) of this section is as follows –

'THIS GENERAL TRUSTEE POWER OF ATTORNEY is made on [*date*] by [*name of one donor*] of [*address of donor*] as trustee of [*name or details of one trust*].

I appoint [*name of one donee*] of [*address of donee*] to be my attorney [*if desired, the date on which the delegation commences or the period for which it continues (or both)*] in accordance with section 25(5) of the Trustee Act 1925.

[To be executed as a deed]'.

(7) The donor of a power of attorney given under this section shall be liable for the acts or defaults of the donee in the same manner as if they were the acts or defaults of the donor.

(8) For the purpose of executing or exercising the trusts or powers delegated to him, the donee may exercise any of the powers conferred on the donor as trustee by statute or by the instrument creating the trust, including power, for the purpose of the transfer of any inscribed stock, himself to delegate to an attorney power to transfer, but not including the power of delegation conferred by this section.

(9) The fact that it appears from any powr of attorney given under this section, or from any evidence required for the purposes of any such power of attorney or otherwise, that in dealing with any stock the donee of the power is acting in the execution of a trust shall not be deemed for any purpose to affect any person in whose books the stock is inscribed or registered with any notice of the trust.

(10) This section applies to a personal representative, tenant for life and statutory owner as it applies to a trustee except that subsection (4) shall apply as if it required the notice there mentioned to be given –

- (a) in the case of a personal representative, to each of the other personal representatives, if any, except any executor who has renounced probate;
- (b) in the case of a tenant for life, to the trustees of the settlement and to each person, if any, who together with the person giving the notice constitutes the tenant for life; and
- (c) in the case of a statutory owner, to each of the persons, if any, who together with the person giving the notice constitute the statutory owner and, in the case of a statutory owner by virtue of section 23(1)(a) of the Settled Land Act 1925, to the trustees of the settlement.

26   Protection against liability in respect of rents and covenants

(1) Where a personal representative or trustee liable as such for –

- (a) any rent, covenant, or agreement reserved by or contained in any lease; or
- (b) any rent, covenant or agreement payable under or contained in any grant made in consideration of a rentcharge; or
- (c) any indemnity given in respect of any rent, covenant or agreement referred to in either of the foregoing paragraphs;

   satisfies all liabilities under the lease or grant which may have accrued and been claimed up to the date of the conveyance hereinafter mentioned, and, where necessary, sets apart a sufficient fund to answer any future claim that may be made in respect of any fixed and ascertained sum which the lessee or grantee agreed to lay out on the property demised or granted, although the period for laying out the same may not have arrived, then and in any such case the personal representative or trustee may convey the property demised or granted to a purchaser, legatee, devisee, or other person entitled to call for a conveyance thereof and thereafter –

   (i) he may distribute the residuary real and personal estate of the deceased testator or intestate, or, as the case may be, the trust estate (other than the fund, if any, set apart as aforesaid) to or amongst the persons entitled thereto, without appropriating any part, or any further part, as the case may be, of the estate of the deceased or of the trust estate to meet any future liability under the said lease or grant;

(ii) notwithstanding such distribution, he shall not be personally liable in respect of any subsequent claim under the said lease or grant.

(1A) Where a personal representative or trustee has as such entered into, or may as such be required to enter into, an authorised guarantee agreement with respect to any lease comprised in the estate of a deceased testator or intestate or a trust estate (and, in a case where he has entered into such an agreement, he has satisfied all liabilities under it which may have accrued and been claimed up to the date of distribution) –

(a) he may distribute the residuary real and personal estate of the deceased testator or intestate, or the trust estate, to or amongst the persons entitled thereto –

(i) without appropriating any part of the estate of the deceased, or the trust estate, to meet any future liability (or, as the case may be, any liability) under any such agreement, and

(ii) notwithstanding any potential liability of his to enter into any such agreement; and

(b) notwithstanding such distribution, he shall not be personally liable in respect of any subsequent claim (or, as the case may be, any claim) under any such agreement.

In this subsection 'authorised guarantee agreement' has the same meaning as in the Landlord and Tenant (Covenants) Act 1995.

(2) This section operates without prejudice to the right of the lessor or grantor, or the persons deriving title under the lessor or grantor, to follow the assets of the deceased or the trust property into the hands of the persons amongst whom the same may have been respectively distributed, and applies notwithstanding anything to the contrary in the will or other instrument, if any, creating the trust.

(3) In this section 'lease' includes an underlease and an agreement for a lease or underlease and any instrument giving any such indemnity as aforesaid or varying the liabilities under the lease; 'grant' applies to a grant whether the rent is created by limitation, grant, reservation, or otherwise, and includes an agreement for a grant and any instrument giving any such indemnity as aforesaid or varying the liabilities under the grant; 'lessee' and 'grantee' include persons respectively deriving title under them.

27   Protection by means of advertisements

(1) With a view to the conveyance to or distribution among the persons entitled to any real or personal property, the trustees of a settlement, trustees of land, trustees for sale of personal property or personal representatives, may give notice by advertisement in the Gazette, and in a newspaper circulating in the district in which the land is situated, and such other like notices, including notices elsewhere than in England and Wales, as would, in any special case, have been directed by a court of competent jurisdiction in an action for administration, of their intention to make such conveyance or distribution as aforesaid, and requiring any person interested to send to the trustees or personal representatives within the time, not being less than two months, fixed in the notice or, where more than one notice is given, in the last of the notices, particulars of his claim in respect of the property or any part thereof to which the notice relates.

(2) At the expiration of the time fixed by the notice the trustees or personal representatives may convey or distribute the property or any part thereof to which the notice relates, to or among the persons entitled thereto, having regard only to the claims, whether formal or not, of which the trustees or personal representatives then had notice and shall not, as respects the property so conveyed or distributed, be liable to any person of whose claim the trustees or personal representatives have not had notice at the time of conveyance or distribution; but nothing in this section –

(a) prejudices the right of any person to follow the property, or any property representing the same, into the hands of any person, other than a purchaser, who may have received it; or

(b) frees the trustees or personal representatives from any obligations to make searches or obtain official certificates of search similar to those which an intending purchaser would be advised to make or obtain.

(3) This section applies notwithstanding anything to the contrary in the will or other instrument, if any, creating the trust.

28   Protection in regard to notice

A trustee or personal representative acting for the purposes of more than one trust or estate shall not, in the absence of fraud, be affected by notice of any instrument, matter, fact or thing in relation to any particular trust or estate if he has obtained notice thereof merely by reason of his acting or having acted for the purposes of another trust or estate.

31   Power to apply income for maintenance and to accumulate surplus income during a minority

(1) Where any property is held by trustees in trust for any person for any interest whatsoever, whether vested or contingent, then, subject to any prior interests or charges affecting that property –

(i) during the infancy of any such person, if his interest so long continues, the trustees may, at their sole discretion, pay to his parent or guardian, if any, or otherwise apply for or towards his maintenance, education, or benefit, the whole or such part, if any, of the income of that property as may, in all the circumstances, be reasonable, whether or not there is –

    (a) any other fund applicable to the same purpose; or

    (b) any person bound by law to provide for his maintenance or education; and

(ii) if such person on attaining the age of eighteen years has not a vested interest in such income, the trustees shall thenceforth pay the income of that property and of any accretion thereto under subsection (2) of this section to him, until he either attains a vested interest therein or dies, or until failure of his interest:

Provided that, in deciding whether the whole or any part of the income of the property is during a minority to be paid or applied for the purposes aforesaid, the trustees shall have regard to the age of the infant and his requirements and generally to the circumstances of the case, and in particular to what other income, if any, is applicable for the same purposes; and where trustees have notice that the income of more than one fund is applicable for those purposes, then, so far as practicable, unless the entire income of the funds is paid or applied as aforesaid or the court otherwise directs, a proportionate part only of the income of each fund shall be so paid or applied.

(2) During the infancy of any such person, if his interest so long continues, the trustees shall accumulate all the residue of that income by investing it, and any profits from so investing it from time to time in authorised investments, and shall hold those accumulations as follows –

(i) If any such person –

    (a) attains the age of eighteen years, or marries under that age or forms a civil partnership under that age, and his interest in such income during his infancy, or until his marriage or his formation of a civil partnership, is a vested interest; or

    (b) on attaining the age of eighteen years or on marriage, or formation of a civil partnership, under that age becomes entitled to the property from which such income arose in fee simple, absolute or determinable, or absolutely, or for an entailed interest;

the trustees shall hold the accumulations in trust for such person absolutely, but without prejudice to any provision with respect thereto contained in any settlement by him made under any statutory powers during his infancy, and so that the receipt of such persons after marriage or formation of a civil partnership, and though still an infant, shall be a good discharge; and

(ii) In any other case the trustees shall, notwithstanding that such person had a vested interest in such income, hold the accumulations as an accretion to the capital of the property from which such accumulations arose, and as one fund with such capital for all purposes, and so that, if such property is settled land, such accumulations shall be held upon the same trusts as if the same were capital money arising therefrom;

but the trustees may, at any time during the infancy of such person if his interest so long continues, apply those accumulations, or any part thereof, as if they were income arising in the then current year.

(3) This section applies in the case of a contingent interest only if the limitation of trust carries the intermediate income of the property, but it applies to a future or contingent legacy by the parent of, or a person standing in loco parentis to, the legatee, if and for such period as, under the general law, the legacy carries interest for the maintenance of the legatee, and in any such case as last aforesaid the rate of interest shall (if the income available is sufficient, and subject to any rules of court to the contrary) be five pounds per centum per annum.

(4) This section applies to a vested annuity in like manner as if the annuity were the income of property held by trustees in trust to pay the income thereof to the annuitant for the same period for which the annuity is payable, save that in any case accumulations made during the infancy of the annuitant shall be held in trust for the annuitant or his personal representatives absolutely.

(5) This section does not apply where the instrument, if any, under which the interest arises came into operation before the commencement of this Act.

32   Power of advancement

(1) Trustees may at any time or times pay or apply any capital money subject to a trust, for the advancement of benefit, in such manner as they may, in their absolute discretion, think fit, of any person entitled to the capital of the trust property or of any share thereof, whether absolutely or contingently on his attaining any specified age or on the occurrence of any other event, or subject to a gift over on his death under any specified age or on the occurrence of any other event, and whether in possession or in remainder or reversion, and such payment or application may be made notwithstanding that the interest of such person is liable to be defeated by the exercise of a power of appointment or revocation, or to be diminished by the increase of the class to which he belongs:

Provided that –

(a) the money so paid or applied for the advancement or benefit of any person shall not exceed altogether in amount one-half of the presumptive or vested share or interest of that person in the trust property; and

(b) if that person is or becomes absolutely and indefeasibly entitled to a share in the trust property the money so paid or applied shall be brought into account as part of such share; and

(c) no such payment or application shall be made so as to prejudice any person entitled to any prior life or other interest, whether vested or contingent, in the money paid or applied unless such person is in existence and of full age and consents in writing to such payment or application.

(2) This section does not apply to capital money arising under the Settled Land Act 1925.

(3) This section does not apply to trusts constituted or created before the commencement of this Act.

33 Protective trusts

(1) Where any income, including an annuity or other periodical income payment, is directed to be held on protective trusts for the benefit of any person (in this section called 'the principal beneficiary') for the period of his life or for any less period, then, during that period (in this section called the 'trust period') the said income shall, without prejudice to any prior interest, be held on the following trusts, namely –

(i) Upon trust for the principal beneficiary during the trust period or until he, whether before or after the termination of any prior interest, does or attempts to do or suffers any act or thing, or until any event happens, other than an advance under any statutory or express power, whereby, if the said income were payable during the trust period to the principal beneficiary absolutely during that period, he would be deprived of the right to receive the same or any part thereof, in any of which cases, as well as on the termination of the trust period, whichever first happens, this trust of the said income shall fail or determine;

(ii) If the trust aforesaid fails or determines during the subsistence of the trust period, then, during the residue of that period, the said income shall be held upon trust for the application thereof for the maintenance or support, or otherwise for the benefit, of all or any one or more exclusively of the other or others of the following persons (that is to say) –

(a) the principal beneficiary and his or her spouse or civil partner, if any, and his or her children or more remote issue, if any; or

(b) if there is no spouse or civil partner or issue of the principal beneficiary in existence, the principal beneficiary and the persons who would, if he were actually dead, be entitled to the trust property or the income thereof or to the annuity fund, if any, or arrears of the annuity, as the case may be;

as the trustees in their absolute discretion, without being liable to account for the exercise of such discretion, think fit.

(2) This section does not apply to trusts coming into operation before the commencement of this Act, and has effect subject to any variation of the implied trusts aforesaid contained in the instrument creating the trust.

(3) Nothing in this section operates to validate any trust which would, if contained in the instrument creating the trust, be liable to be set aside.

(4) In relation to the dispositions mentioned in section 19(1) of the Family Law Reform Act 1987, this section should have effect as if any reference (however expressed) to any relationship between two persons were construed in accordance with section 1 of that Act.

PART III

APPOINTMENT AND DISCHARGE OF TRUSTEES

34 Limitation of the number of trustees

(1) Where, at the commencement of this Act, there are more than four trustees of a settlement of land, or more than four trustees holding land on trust for sale, no new trustees shall (except where as a result of the appointment the number is reduced to four or less) be capable of being appointed until the number is reduced to less than four, and thereafter the number shall not be increased beyond four.

(2) In the case of settlements and dispositions creating trusts of land made or coming into operation after the commencement of this Act –

    (a) the number of trustees thereof shall not in any case exceed four, and where more than four persons are named as such trustees, the four first named (who are able and willing to act) shall alone be the trustees, and the other persons named shall not be trustees unless appointed on the occurrence of a vacancy;

    (b) the number of the trustees shall not be increased beyond four.

(3) This section only applies to settlements and dispositions of land, and the restrictions imposed on the number of trustees do not apply –

    (a) in the case of land vested in trustees for charitable, ecclesiastical, or public purposes; or

    (b) where the net proceeds of the sale of the land are held for like purposes; or

    (c) to the trustees of a term of years absolute limited by a settlement on trusts for raising money, or of a like term created under the statutory remedies relating to annual sums charged on land.

35   Appointments of trustees of settlements and trustees of land

(1) Appointments of new trustees of land and of new trustees of any trust of the proceeds of sale of the land shall, subject to any order of the court, be effected by separate instruments, but in such manner as to secure that the same persons become trustees of land and trustees of the trust of the proceeds of sale.

(2) Where new trustees of a settlement are appointed, a memorandum of the names and addresses of the persons who are for the time being the trustees thereof for the purposes of the Settled Land Act 1925 shall be endorsed on or annexed to the last or only principal vesting instrument by or on behalf of the trustees of the settlement, and such vesting instrument shall, for that purpose, be produced by the person having the possession thereof to the trustees of the settlement when so required.

(3) Where new trustees of land are appointed, a memorandum of the persons who are for the time being the trustees of the land shall be endorsed on or annexed to the conveyance by which the land was vested in trustees of land; and that conveyance shall be produced to the persons who are for the time being the trustees of the land by the person in possession of it in order for that to be done when the trustees require its production.

(4) This section applies only to settlements and dispositions of land.

36   Power of appointing new or additional trustees

(1) Where a trustee, either original or substituted, and whether appointed by a court or otherwise, is dead, or remains out of the United Kingdom for more than twelve months, or desires to be discharged form all or any of the trusts or powers reposed in or conferred on him, or refuses or is unfit to act therein, or is incapable of acting therein, or is an infant, then, subject to the restrictions imposed by this Act on the number of trustees, –

    (a) the person or persons nominated for the purpose of appointing new trustees by the instrument, if any, creating the trust; or

    (b) if there is no such person, or no such person able and willing to act, then the surviving or continuing trustees or trustee for the time being, or the personal representatives of the last surviving or continuing trustee;

may, by writing, appoint one or more other persons (whether or not being the persons exercising the power) to be a trustee or trustees in the place of the trustee so deceased, remaining out of the

United Kingdom, desiring to be discharged, refusing, or being unfit or being incapable, or being an infant, as aforesaid.

(2) Where a trustee has been removed under a power contained in the instrument creating the trust, a new trustee or new trustees may be appointed in the place of the trustee who is removed, as if he were dead, or, in the case of a corporation, as if the corporation desired to be discharged from the trust, and the provisions of this section shall apply accordingly, but subject to the restrictions imposed by this Act on the number of trustees.

(3) Where a corporation being a trustee is or has been dissolved, either before or after the commencement of this Act, then, for the purposes of this section and of any enactment replaced thereby, the corporation shall be deemed to be and to have been from the date of the dissolution incapable of acting in the trusts or powers reposed in or conferred on the corporation.

(4) The power of appointment given by subsection (1) of this section or any similar previous enactment to the personal representatives of a last surviving or continuing trustee shall be and shall be deemed always to have been exercisable by the executors for the time being (whether original or by representation) of such surviving or continuing trustee who have proved the will of their testator or by the administrators for the time being of such trustee without the concurrence of any executor who has renounced or has not proved.

(5) But a sole or last surviving executor intending to renounce, or all the executors where they all intend to renounce, shall have and shall be deemed always to have had power, at any time before renouncing probate, to exercise the power of appointment given by this section, or by any similar previous enactment, if willing to act for that purpose and without thereby accepting the office of executor.

(6) Where, in the case of any trust, there are not more than three trustees –

    (a) the person or persons nominated for the purpose of appointing new trustees by the instrument, if any, creating the trust; or

    (b) if there is no such person, or no such person able and willing to act, then the trustee or trustees for the time being;

may, by writing, appoint another person or other persons to be an additional trustee or additional trustees, but it shall not be obligatory to appoint any additional trustee, unless the instrument, if any, creating the trust, or any statutory enactment provides to the contrary, nor shall the number of trustees be increased beyond four by virtue of any such appointment.

(6A) A person who is either –

    (a) both a trustee and attorney for the other trustee (if one other), or for both of the other trustees (if two others), under a registered power; or

    (b) attorney under a registered power for the trustee (if one) or for both or each of the trustees (if two or three),

may, if subsection (6B) of this section is satisfied in relation to him, make an appointment under subsection (6)(b) of this section on behalf of the trustee or trustees.

(6B) This subsection is satisfied in relation to an attorney under a registered power for one or more trustees if (as attorney under the power) –

    (a) he intends to exercise any function of the trustee or trustees by virtue of section 1(1) of the Trustee Delegation Act 1999; or

    (b) he intends to exercise any function of the trustee or trustees in relation to any land, capital proceeds of a conveyance of land or income from land by virtue of its delegation to him under section 25 of this Act or the instrument (if any) creating the trust.

(6C) In subsections (6A) and (6B) of this section 'registered power' means a power of attorney created by an instrument which is for the time being registered under section 6 of the Enduring Powers of Attorney Act 1985.

(6D) Subsection (6A) of this section –
   (a) applies only if and so far as a contrary intention is not expressed in the instrument creating the power of attorney (or, where more than one, any of them) or the instrument (if any) creating the trust; and
   (b) has effect subject to the terms of those instruments.

(7) Every new trustee appointed under this section as well before as after all the trust property becomes by law, or by assurance, or otherwise, vested in him, shall have the same powers, authorities, and discretions, and may in all respects acts as if he had been originally appointed a trustee by the instrument, if any, creating the trust.

(8) The provisions of this section relating to a trustee who is dead include the case of a person nominated trustee in a will but dying before the testator, and those relative to a continuing trustee include a refusing or retiring trustee, if willing to act in the execution of the provisions of this section.

(9) Where a trustee is incapable, by reason of mental disorder within the meaning of the Mental Health Act 1983, of exercising his functions as trustee and is also entitled in possession to some beneficial interest in the trust property, no appointment of a new trustee in his place shall be made by virtue of paragraph (b) of subsection (1) of this section unless leave to make the appointment has been given by the authority having jurisdiction under Part VII of the Mental Health Act 1983.

37   Supplemental provisions as to appointment of trustees

(1) On the appointment of a trustee for the whole or any part of trust property –
   (a) the number of trustees may, subject to the restrictions imposed by this Act on the number of trustees, be increased; and
   (b) a separate set of trustees, not exceeding four, may be appointed for any part of the trust property held on trusts distinct from those relating to any other part or parts of the trust property, notwithstanding that no new trustees or trustee are or is to be appointed for other parts of the trust property, and any existing trustee may be appointed or remain one of such separate set of trustees, or, if only one trustee was originally appointed, then, save as hereinafter provided, one separate trustee may be so appointed; and
   (c) it shall not be obligatory, save as hereinafter provided, to appoint more than one new trustee where only one trustee was originally appointed, or to fill up the original number of trustees where more than two trustees were originally appointed, but, except where only one trustee was originally appointed, and a sole trustee when appointed will be able to give valid receipts for all capital money, a trustee shall not be discharged from his trust unless there will be either a trust corporation or at least two persons to act as trustees to perform the trust; and
   (d) any assurance or thing requisite for vesting the trust property, or any part thereof, in a sole trustee, or jointly in the persons who are the trustees, shall be executed or done.

(2) Nothing in this Act shall authorise the appointment of a sole trustee, not being a trust corporation, where the trustee, when appointed, would not be able to give valid receipts for all capital money arising under the trust.

38   Evidence as to a vacancy in a trust

(1) A statement, contained in any instrument coming into operation after the commencement of this Act by which a new trustee is appointed for any purpose connected with land, to the effect that a trustee has remained out of the United Kingdom for more than twelve months or

refuses or is unfit to act, or is incapable of acting, or that he is entitled to a beneficial interest in the trust property in possession, shall, in favour of a purchaser of a legal estate, be conclusive evidence of the matter stated.

(2) In favour of such purchaser any appointment of a new trustee depending on that statement, and any vesting declaration, express or implied, consequent on the appointment, shall be valid.

39   Retirement of trustee without a new appointment

(1) Where a trustee is desirous of being discharged from the trust, and after his discharge there will be either a trust corporation or at least two persons to act as trustees to perform the trust, then, if such trustee as aforesaid by deed declares that he is desirous of being discharged from the trust, and if his co-trustees and such other person, if any, as is empowered to appoint trustees, by deed consent to the discharge of the trustee, and to the vesting in the co-trustees alone of the trust property, the trustee desirous of being discharged shall be deemed to have retired from the trust, and shall, by the deed, be discharged therefrom under this Act, without any new trustee being appointed in his place.

(2) Any assurance or thing requisite for vesting the trust property in the continuing trustees alone shall be executed or done.

40   Vesting of trust property in new or continuing trustees

(1) Where by a deed a new trustee is appointed to perform any trust, then –

    (a) if the deed contains a declaration by the appointer to the effect that any estate or interest in any land subject to the trust, or in any chattel so subject, or the right to recover or receive any debt or other thing in action so subject, shall vest in the persons who by virtue of the deed become or are the trustees for performing the trust, the deed shall operate, without any conveyance or assignment, to vest in those persons as joint tenants and for the purposes of the trust the estate interest or right to which the declaration relates; and

    (b) if the deed is made after the commencement of this Act and does not contain such a declaration, the deed shall, subject to any express provision to the contrary therein contained, operate as if it had contained such a declaration by the appointer extending to all the estates interests and rights with respect to which a declaration could have been made.

(2) Where by a deed a retiring trustee is discharged under section 39 of this Act or section 19 of the Trusts of Land and Appointment of Trustees Act 1996 without a new trustee being appointed, then –

    (a) if the deed contains such a declaration as aforesaid by the retiring and continuing trustees, and by the other persons, if any, empowered to appoint trustees, the deed shall, without any conveyance or assignment, operate to vest in the continuing trustees alone, as joint tenants, and for the purposes of the trust, the estate, interest, or right of which the declaration relates; and

    (b) if the deed is made after the commencement of this Act and does not contain such a declaration, the deed shall, subject to any express provision to the contrary therein contained, operate as if it had contained such a declaration by such persons as aforesaid extending to all the estates, interests and rights with respect to which a declaration could have been made.

(3) An express vesting declaration, whether made before or after the commencement of this Act, shall, notwithstanding that the estate, interest or right to be vested is not expressly referred to, and provided that the other statutory requirements were or are complied with, operate and be

deemed always to have operated (but without prejudice to any express provision to the contrary contained in the deed of appointment or discharge) to vest in the persons respectively referred to in subsections (1) and (2) of this section, as the case may require, such estates, interests and rights are as capable of being and ought to be vested in those persons.

(4) This section does not extend –

    (a)   to land conveyed by way of mortgage for securing money subject to the trust, except land conveyed on trust for securing debentures or debenture stock;

    (b)   to land held under a lease which contains any covenant, condition or agreement against assignment or disposing of the land without licence or consent, unless, prior to the execution of the deed containing expressly or impliedly the vesting declaration, the requisite licence or consent has been obtained, or unless, by virtue of any statute or rule of law, the vesting declaration, express or implied, would not operate as a breach of covenant or give rise to a forfeiture;

    (c)   to any share, stock, annuity or property which is only transferable in books kept by a company or other body, or in manner directed by or under an Act of Parliament.

In this subsection 'lease' includes an underlease and an agreement for a lease or underlease.

(5) For purposes of registration of the deed in any registry, the person or persons making the declaration expressly or impliedly shall be deemed the conveying party or parties, and the conveyance shall be deemed to be made by him or them under a power conferred by this Act.

(6) This section applies to deeds of appointment and discharge executed on or after the first day of January, eighteen hundred and eighty-two.

PART IV

POWERS OF THE COURT

41   Power of court to appoint new trustees

(1) The court may, whenever it is expedient to appoint a new trustee or new trustees, and it is found inexpedient difficult or impracticable so to do without the assistance of the court, make an order appointing a new trustee or new trustees either in substitution for or in addition to any existing trustee or trustees, or although there is no existing trustee.

In particular and without prejudice to the generality of the foregoing provision, the court may make an order appointing a new trustee in substitution for a trustee who is incapable, by reason of mental disorder within the meaning of the Mental Health Act 1983, of exercising his functions as trustee, or is a bankrupt, or is a corporation which is in liquidation or has been dissolved.

(2) The power conferred by this section may, in the case of a deed of arrangement within the meaning of the Deeds of Arrangement Act 1914, be exercised either by the High Court or by the court having jurisdiction in bankruptcy in the district in which the debtor resided or carried on business at the date of the execution of the deed.

(3) An order under this section, and any consequential vesting order or conveyance, shall not operate further or otherwise as a discharge to any former or continuing trustee than an appointment of new trustees under any power for that purpose contained in any instrument would have operated.

(4) Nothing in this section gives power to appoint an executor or administrator.

42   Power to authorise remuneration

Where the court appoints a corporation, other than the Public Trustee, to be a trustee either solely or jointly with another person, the court may authorise the corporation to charge such remuneration for its services as trustee as the court may think fit.

43   Powers of new trustee appointed by the court

Every trustee appointed by a court of competent jurisdiction shall, as well before as after the trust property becomes by law, or by assurance, or otherwise, vested in him, have the same powers, authorities, and discretions, and may in all respects act as if he had been originally appointed a trustee by the instrument, if any, creating the trust.

44   Vesting orders of land

In any of the following cases, namely –

   (i)   Where the court appoints or has appointed a trustee, or where a trustee has been appointed out of court under any statutory or express power;
   (ii)   Where a trustee entitled to or possessed of any land or interest therein, whether by way of mortgage or otherwise, or entitled to a contingent right therein, either solely or jointly with any other person –
          (a) is under disability; or
          (b) is out of the jurisdiction of the High Court; or
          (c) cannot be found, or, being a corporation, has been dissolved;
   (iii) Where it is uncertain who was the survivor of two or more trustees jointly entitled to or possessed of any interest in land;
   (iv)   Where it is uncertain whether the last trustee known to have been entitled to or possessed of any interest in land is living or dead;
   (v)   Where there is no personal representative of a deceased trustee who was entitled to or possessed of any interest in land, or where it is uncertain who is the personal representative of a deceased trustee who was entitled to or possessed of any interest in land;
   (vi)   Where a trustee jointly or solely entitled to or possessed of any interest in land, or entitled to a contingent right therein, has been required, by or on behalf of a person entitled to require a conveyance of the land or interest or a release of the right, to convey the land or interest or to release the right, and has wilfully refused or neglected to convey the land or interest or release the right for twenty-eight days after the date of the requirement;
   (vii) Where land or any interest therein is vested in a trustee whether by way of mortgage or otherwise, and it appears to the court to be expedient;
the court may make an order (in this Act called a vesting order) vesting the land or interest therein in any such person in any such manner and for any such estate or interest as the court may direct, or releasing or disposing of the contingent right to such person as the court may direct:
Provided that –
          (a) Where the order is consequential on the appointment of a trustee the land or interest therein shall be vested for such estate as the court may direct in the persons who on the appointment are the trustees; and
          (b) Where the order relates to a trustee entitled or formerly entitled jointly with another person, and such trustee is under disability or out of the jurisdiction of the High Court or cannot be found, or being a corporation has been dissolved, the land interest or right shall be vested in such other person who remains entitled, either alone or with any other person the court may appoint.

45   Orders as to contingent rights of unborn persons

Where any interest in land is subject to a contingent right in an unborn person or class of unborn persons who, on coming into existence, would, in respect thereof, become entitled to or possessed of that interest on any trust, the court may make an order releasing the land or interest therein from the contingent right, or may make an order vesting in any person the estate or interest to or of which the unborn person or class of unborn persons would, on coming into existence, be entitled or possessed in the land.

46   Vesting order in place of conveyance by infant mortgagee

Where any person entitled to or possessed of any interest in land, or entitled to a contingent right in land, by way of security for money, is an infant, the court may make an order vesting or releasing or disposing of the interest in the land or the right in like manner as in the case of a trustee under disability.

47   Vesting order consequential on order for sale or mortgage of land

Where any court gives a judgment or makes an order directing the sale or mortgage of any land, every person who is entitled to or possessed of any interest in the land, or entitled to a contingent right therein, and is a party to the action or proceeding in which the judgment or order is given or made or is otherwise bound by the judgment or order, shall be deemed to be so entitled or possessed, as the case may be, as a trustee for the purposes of this Act, and the court may, if it thinks expedient, make an order vesting the land or any part thereof for such estate or interest as that court thinks fit in the purchaser or mortgagee or in any other person:

Provided that, in the case of a legal mortgage, the estate to be vested in the mortgagee shall be a term of years absolute.

48   Vesting order consequential on judgment for specific performance, etc

Where a judgment is given for the specific performance of a contract concerning any interest in land, or for sale or exchange of an interest in land, or generally where any judgment is given for the conveyance of any interest in land either in cases arising out of the doctrine of election or otherwise, the court may declare –

   (a)   that any of the parties to the action are trustees of any interest in the land or any part thereof within the meaning of this Act; or

   (b)   that the interests of unborn persons who might claim under any party to the action, or under the will or voluntary settlement of any deceased person who was during his lifetime a party to the contract or transaction concerning which the judgment is given, are the interests of persons who, on coming into existence, would be trustees within the meaning of this Act;

and thereupon the court may make a vesting order relating to the rights of those persons, born and unborn, as if they had been trustees.

49   Effect of vesting order

A vesting order under any of the foregoing provisions shall in the case of a vesting order consequential on the appointment of a trustee, have the same effect –

   (a)   as if the persons who before the appointment were the trustees, if any, had duly executed all proper conveyances of the land for such estate or interest as the court directs; or

   (b)   if there is no such person, or no such person of full capacity, as if such person had existed and been of full capacity and had duly executed all proper conveyances of the land for such estate or interest as the court directs;

and shall in every other case have the same effect as if the trustee or other person or description or class of persons to whose rights or supposed rights the said provisions respectively relate had been an ascertained and existing person of full capacity, and had executed a conveyance or release to the effect intended by the order.

50   Power to appoint person to convey
In all cases where a vesting order can be made under any of the foregoing provisions, the court may, if it is more convenient, appoint a person to convey the land or any interest therein or release the contingent right, and a conveyance or release by that person in conformity with the order shall have the same effect as an order under the appropriate provision.

52   Vesting orders of charity property
The powers conferred by this Act as to vesting orders may be exercised for vesting any interest in land, stock, or thing in action in any trustee of a charity or society over which the court would have jurisdiction upon action duly instituted, whether the appointment of the trustee was made by instrument under a power or by the court under its general or statutory jurisdiction.

53   Vesting orders in relation to infant's beneficial interests
Where an infant is beneficially entitled to any property the court may, with a view to the application of the capital or income thereof for the maintenance, education, or benefit of the infant, make an order –
   (a)   appointing a person to convey such property; or
   (b)   in the case of stock, or a thing in action, vesting in any person the right to transfer or call for a transfer of such stock, or to receive the dividends or income thereof, or to sue for and recover such thing in action, upon such terms as the court may think fit.

57   Power of court to authorise dealings with trust property
(1) Where in the management or administration of any property vested in trustees, any sale, lease, mortgage, surrender, release, or other disposition, or any purchase, investment, acquisition, expenditure, or other transaction, is in the opinion of the court expedient, but the same cannot be effected by reason of the absence of any power for that purpose vested in the trustees by the trust instrument, if any, or by law, the court may by order confer upon the trustees, either generally or in any particular instance, the necessary power for the purpose, on such terms, and subject to such provisions and conditions, if any, as the court may think fit and may direct in what manner any money authorised to be expended, and the costs of any transaction, are to be paid or borne as between capital and income.
(2) The court may, from time to time, rescind or vary any order made under this section, or may make any new or further order.
(3) An application to the court under this section may be made by the trustees, or by any of them, or by any person beneficially interested under the trust.
(4) This section does not apply to trustees of a settlement for the purposes of the Settled Land Act 1925.

58   Persons entitled to apply for orders
(1) An order under this Act for the appointment of a new trustee, or concerning any interest in land, stock, or thing in action subject to a trust, may be made on the application of any person beneficially interested in the land, stock, or thing in action, whether under disability or not, or on the application of any person duly appointed trustee thereof.
(2) An order under this Act concerning any interest in land, stock, or thing in action subject to a mortgage may be made on the application of any person beneficially interested in the equity

of redemption, whether under disability or not, or of any person interested in the money secured by the mortgage.

59   Power to give judgment in absence of a trustee

Where in any action the court is satisfied that diligent search has been made for any person who, in the character of trustee, is made a defendant in any action, to serve him with a process of the court, and that he cannot be found, the court may hear and determine the action and give judgment therein against that person in his character of a trustee as if he had been duly served, or had entered an appearance in the action, and had also appeared by his counsel and solicitor at the hearing, but without prejudice to any interest he may have in the matters in question in the action in any other character.

60   Power to charge costs on trust estate

The court may order the costs and expenses of and incident to any application for an order appointing a new trustee, or for a vesting order, or of the incident to any such order, or any conveyance or transfer in pursuance thereof, to be raised and paid out of the property in respect whereof the same is made, or out of the income thereof, or to be borne and paid in such manner and by such persons as to the court may seem just.

61   Power to relieve trustee from personal liability

If it appears to the court that a trustee, whether appointed by the court or otherwise, is or may be personally liable for any breach of trust, whether the transaction alleged to be a breach of trust occurred before or after the commencement of this Act, but has acted honestly and reasonably, and ought fairly to be excused for the breach of trust and for omitting to obtain the directions of the court in the matter in which he committed such breach, then the court may relieve him either wholly or partly from personal liability for the same.

62   Power to make beneficiary indemnify for breach of trust

(1) Where a trustee commits a breach of trust at the instigation or request or with the consent in writing of a beneficiary, the court may, if it thinks fit, make such order as to the court seems just, for impounding all or any part of the interest of the beneficiary in the trust estate by way of indemnity to the trustee or persons claiming through him.

(2) This section applies to breaches of trust committed as well before as after the commencement of this Act.

63   Payment into court by trustees

(1) Trustees, or the majority of trustees, having in their hands or under their control money or securities belonging to a trust, may pay the same into court.

(2) The receipt or certificate of the proper officer shall be a sufficient discharge to trustees for the money or securities so paid into court.

(3) Where money or securities are vested in any persons as trustees, and the majority are desirous of paying the same into court, but the concurrence of the other or others cannot be obtained, the court may order the payment into court to be made by the majority without the concurrence of the other or others.

(4) Where any such money or securities are deposited with any banker, broker or other depositary, the court may order payment or delivery of the money or securities to the majority of the trustees for the purpose of payment into court.

(5) Every transfer payment and delivery made in pursuance of any such order shall be valid and

take effect as if the same had been made on the authority or by the act of all the persons entitled to the money and securities so transferred, paid, or delivered.

PART V

GENERAL PROVISIONS

64 Application of Act to Settled Land Act Trustees

(1) All the powers and provisions contained in this Act with reference to the appointment of new trustees, and the discharge and retirement of trustees, apply to and include trustees for the purposes of the Settled Land Act 1925, and trustees for the purpose of the management of land during a minority, whether such trustees are appointed by the court or by the settlement, or under provisions contained in any instrument.

(2) Where, either before or after the commencement of this Act, trustees of a settlement have been appointed by the court for the purposes of the Settled Land Acts 1882 to 1890, or of the Settled Land Act 1925, then, after the commencement of this Act –

    (a) the person or persons nominated for the purpose of appointing new trustees by the instrument, if any, creating the settlement, though no trustees for the purposes of the said Acts were thereby appointed; or

    (b) if there is no such person, or no such person able and willing to act, the surviving or continuing trustees or trustee for the time being for the purposes of the said Acts or the personal representatives of the last surviving or continuing trustee for those purposes,

shall have the powers conferred by this Act to appoint new or additional trustees of the settlement for the purposes of the said Acts.

(3) Appointments of new trustees for the purposes of the said Acts made or expressed to be made before the commencement of this Act by the trustees or trustee or personal representatives referred to in paragraph (b) of the last preceding sub-section or by the persons referred to in paragraph (a) of that subsection are, without prejudice to any order of the court made before such commencement, hereby confirmed.

67 Jurisdiction of the 'court'

(1) In this Act 'the court' means the High Court or the county court, where those courts respectively have jurisdiction.

(2) The procedure under this Act in county courts shall be in accordance with the Acts and rules regulating the procedure of those courts.

68 Definitions

(1) In this Act, unless the context otherwise requires, the following expressions have the meanings hereby assigned to them respectively, that is to say –

    (1) 'Authorised investments' mean investments authorised by the instrument, if any, creating the trust for the investment of money subject to the trust, or by law; ...

    (6) 'Land' includes land of any tenure, and mines and minerals, where or not severed from the surface, buildings or parts of buildings, whether the division is horizontal, vertical or made in any other way, and other corporeal hereditaments; also a manor, an advowson, and a rent and other incorporeal hereditaments, and an easement, right, privilege, or benefit in, over, or derived from land; and in this definition 'mines and minerals' include any strata or seam of minerals or substances in or under any land, and powers of working and getting

the same; and 'hereditaments' mean real property which under an intestacy occurring before the commencement of this Act might have devolved on an heir;

(7) 'Mortgage' and 'mortgagee' include a charge or chargee by way of legal mortgage, and relate to every estate and interest regarded in equity as merely a security for money, and every person deriving title under the original mortgagee; …

(15) 'Tenant for life', 'statutory owner', 'settled land', 'settlement', 'trust instrument', 'trustees of the settlement' … 'term of years absolute' and 'vesting instrument' have the same meanings as in the Settled Land Act 1925, and 'entailed interest' has the same meaning as in the Law of Property Act 1925; …

(17) 'Trust' does not include the duties incident to an estate conveyed by way of mortgage, but with this exception the expressions 'trust' and 'trustee' extend to implied and constructive trusts, and to cases where the trustee has a beneficial interest in the trust property, and to the duties incident to the office of a personal representative, and 'trustee', where the context admits, includes a personal representative, and 'new trustee' includes an additional trustee;

(18) 'Trust corporation' means the Public Trustee or a corporation either appointed by the court in any particular case to be a trustee, or entitled by rules made under subsection (3) of section four of the Public Trustee Act 1906, to act as custodian trustee;

(19) 'Trust for sale' in relation to land means an immediate trust for sale, whether or not exercisable at the request or with the consent of any person;

(20) 'United Kingdom' means Great Britain and Northern Ireland.

(2) Any reference in this Act to paying money or securities into court shall be construed as referring to paying the money or transferring or depositing the securities into or in the Supreme Court or into or in any other court that has jurisdiction, and any reference in this Act to payment of money or securities into court shall be construed –

(a) with reference to an order of the High Court, as referring to payment of the money or transfer or deposit of the securities into or in the Supreme Court; and

(b) with reference to an order of any other court, as referring to payment of the money or transfer or deposit of the securities into or in that court.

69   Application of Act

(1) This Act, except where otherwise expressly provided, applies to trusts including, so far as this Act applies thereto, executorship and administrationships constituted or created either before or after the commencement of this Act.

(2) The powers conferred by this Act on trustees are in addition to the powers conferred by the instrument, if any, creating the trust, but those powers, unless otherwise stated, apply if and so far only as a contrary intention is not expressed in the instrument, if any, creating the trust, and have effect subject to the terms of that instrument.

As amended by the Law of Property (Amendment) Act 1926, ss7, 8(2), Schedule; Married Women (Restraint upon Anticipation) Act 1949, s1(4), Schedule 2; Mental Health Act 1959, s149(1), (2), Schedules 7, Pt I, and 8, Pt I; Administration of Justice Act 1965, ss17(1), 36(4), Schedules 1, 3; Criminal Law Act 1967, s10, Schedule 3, Pt III; Family Law Reform Act 1969, s1(3), Schedule 1, Pt I; Powers of Attorney Act 1971, s9(1)–(3); Courts Act 1971, s56, Schedule 11, Pt II; Statute Law (Repeals) Act 1978; Mental Health Act 1983, s148, Schedule 4, para 4(a), (b); Family Law Reform Act 1987, s33(1), Schedule 2, para 2; Landlord and Tenant (Covenants) Act 1995, s30(1), Schedule 1, para 1; Trusts of Land and Appointment of Trustees Act 1996, s25(1), (2), Schedule 3, para 3(1)–(14), Schedule 4; Trustee Delegation Act 1999, ss5(1), (2), 8; Trustee Act 2000, ss34(1), (2), 40, Schedule 2, paras 18–25, Schedule 4, Pt II; Civil Partnership Act 2004, s261(1), Schedule 27, paras 5, 6.

LAW OF PROPERTY ACT 1925
(15 Geo 5 c 20)

1   Legal estates and equitable interests

(1) The only estates in land which are capable of subsisting or of being conveyed or created at law are –

(a) An estate in fee simple absolute in possession;

(b) A term of years absolute.

(2) The only interests or charges in or over land which are capable of subsisting or of being conveyed or created at law are –

(a) An easement, right, or privilege in or over land for an interest equivalent to an estate in fee simple absolute in possession or a term of years absolute;

(b) A rentcharge in possession issuing out of or charged on land being either perpetual or for a term of years absolute;

(c) A charge by way of legal mortgage;

(d) Any other similar charge on land which is not created by an instrument;

(e) Rights of entry exercisable over or in respect of a legal term of years absolute, or annexed, for any purpose, to a legal rentcharge.

(3) All other estates, interests, and charges in or over land take effect as equitable interests.

(4) The estates, interests, and charges which under this section are authorised to subsist or to be conveyed or created at law are (when subsisting or conveyed or created at law) in this Act referred to as 'legal estates', and have the same incidents as legal estates subsisting at the commencement of this Act; and the owner of a legal estate is referred to as 'an estate owner' and his legal estate is referred to as his estate.

(5) A legal estate may subsist concurrently with or subject to any other legal estate in the same land in like manner as it could have done before the commencement of this Act.

(6) A legal estate is not capable of subsisting or of being created in an undivided share in land or of being held by an infant.

(7) Every power of appointment over, or power to convey or charge land or any interest therein, whether created by a statute or other instrument or implied by law, and whether created before or after the commencement of this Act (not being a power vested in a legal mortgagee or an estate owner in right of his estate and exercisable by him or by another person in his name and on his behalf), operates only in equity.

(8) Estates, interests, and charges in or over land which are not legal estates are in this Act referred to as 'equitable interests', and powers which by this Act are to operate in equity only are in this Act referred to as 'equitable powers'.

(9) The provisions in any statute or other instrument requiring land to be conveyed to uses shall take effect as directions that the land shall (subject to creating or reserving thereout any legal estate authorised by this Act which may be required) be conveyed to a person of full age upon the requisite trusts.

(10) The repeal of the Statute of Uses (as amended) does not affect the operation thereof in regard to dealings taking effect before the commencement of this Act.

2   Conveyances overreaching certain equitable interests and powers

(1) A conveyance to a purchaser of a legal estate in land shall overreach any equitable interest or power affecting that estate, whether or not he has notice thereof, if –

(i)   the conveyance is made under the powers conferred by the Settled Land Act 1925, or any additional powers conferred by a settlement, and the equitable interest or power is capable of being overreached thereby, and the statutory requirements respecting the payment of capital money arising under the settlement are complied with;

(ii) the conveyance is made by trustees of land and the equitable interest or power is at the date of the conveyance capable of being overreached by such trustees under the provisions of subsection (2) of this section or independently of that subsection, and the requirements of section 27 of this Act respecting the payment of capital money arising on such a conveyance are complied with;

(iii) the conveyance is made by a mortgagee or personal representative in the exercise of his paramount powers, and the equitable interest or power is capable of being overreached by such conveyance, and any capital money arising from the transaction is paid to the mortgagee or personal representative;

(iv) the conveyance is made under an order of the court and the equitable interest or power is bound by such order, and any capital money arising from the transaction is paid into, or in accordance with the order of, the court.

(1A) An equitable interest in land subject to a trust of land which remains in, or is to revert to, the settlor shall (subject to any contrary intention) be overreached by the conveyance if it would be so overreached were it an interest under the trust.

(2) Where the legal estate affected is subject to a trust of land, then if at the date of a conveyance made after the commencement of this Act by the trustees, the trustees (whether original or substituted) are either –

(a) two or more individuals approved or appointed by the court or the successors in office of the individuals so approved or appointed; or

(b) trust corporation,

any equitable interest or power having priority to the trust shall, notwithstanding any stipulation to the contrary, be overreached by the conveyance, and shall, according to its priority, take effect as if created or arising by means of a primary trust affecting the proceeds of sale and the income of the land until sale.

(3) The following equitable interests and powers are excepted from the operation of subsection (2) of this section, namely –

(i) Any equitable interest protected by a deposit of documents relating to the legal estate affected;

(ii) The benefit of any covenant or agreement restrictive of the user of land;

(iii) Any easement, liberty, or privilege over or affecting land and being merely an equitable interest (in this Act referred to as an 'equitable easement');

(iv) The benefit of any contract (in this Act referred to as an 'estate contract') to convey or create a legal estate, including a contract conferring either expressly or by statutory implication a valid option to purchase, a right of pre-emption, or any other like right;

(v) Any equitable interest protected by registration under the Land Charges Act 1925, other than –

(a) an annuity within the meaning of Part II of that Act;

(b) a limited owner's charge or a general equitable charge within the meaning of that Act.

(4) Subject to the protection afforded by this section to the purchaser of a legal estate, nothing contained in this section shall deprive a person entitled to an equitable charge of any of his rights or remedies for enforcing the same.

(5) So far as regards the following interests, created before the commencement of this Act (which accordingly are not within the provisions of the Land Charges Act 1925), namely –

(a) the benefit of any covenant or agreement restrictive of the user of the land;

(b) any equitable easement;

(c) he interest under a puisne mortgage within the meaning of the Land Charges Act 1925, unless and until acquired under a transfer made after the commencement of this Act;

(d) he benefit of an estate contract, unless and until the same is acquired under a conveyance made after the commencement of this Act;

a purchaser of a legal estate shall only take subject thereto if he has notice thereof, and the same are not overreached under the provisions contained or in the manner referred to in this section.

3   Manner of giving effect to equitable interests and powers

(1) All equitable interests and powers in or over land shall be enforceable against the estate owner of the legal estate affected in manner following (that is to say) –

(a) Where the legal estate affected is settled land, the tenant for life or statutory owner shall be bound to give effect to the equitable interests and powers in manner provided by the Settled Land Act 1925;

(c) In any other case, the estate owner shall be bound to give effect to the equitable interests and powers affecting his estate of which he has notice according to their respective priorities. This provision does not affect the priority or powers of a legal mortgagee, or the powers of personal representatives for purposes of administration.

(3) Where, by reason of an equitable right of entry taking effect, or for any other reason, a person becomes entitled to require a legal estate to be vested in him, then and in any such case the estate owner whose estate is affected shall be bound to convey or create such legal estate as the case may require.

(4) If any question arises whether any and what legal estate ought to be transferred or created as aforesaid, any person interested may apply to the court for directions in the manner provided by this Act.

(5) If the estate owners refuse or neglect for one month after demand to transfer or create any such legal estate, or if by reason of their being out of the United Kingdom or being unable to be found, or by reason of the dissolution of a corporation, or for any other reason, the court is satisfied that the transaction cannot otherwise be effected, or cannot be effected without undue delay or expense, the court may, on the application of any person interested, make a vesting order transferring or creating a legal estate in the manner provided by this Act.

(6) This section does not affect a purchaser of a legal estate taking free from an equitable interest or power. …

4   Creation and disposition of equitable interests

(1) Interests in land validly created or arising after the commencement of this Act, which are not capable of subsisting as legal estates, shall take effect as equitable interests, and, save as otherwise expressly provided by statute, interests in land which under the Statute of Uses or otherwise could before the commencement of this Act have been created as legal interests, shall be capable of being created as equitable interests: provided that, after the commencement of this Act (and save as hereinafter expressly enacted), an equitable interest in land shall only be capable of being validly created in any case in which an equivalent equitable interest in property real or personal could have been validly created before such commencement.

(2) All rights and interests in land may be disposed of, including –

(a) a contingent, executory or future equitable interest in any land, or a possibility coupled with an interest in any land, whether or not the object of the gift or limitation of such interest or possibility be ascertained;

(b) a right of entry, into or upon land whether immediate or future, and whether vested or contingent.

(3) All rights of entry affecting a legal estate which are exercisable on condition broken or for any other reason may after the commencement of this Act, be made exercisable by any person and the persons deriving title under him, but, in regard to an estate in fee simple (not being a rentcharge held for a legal estate) only within the period authorised by the rule relating to perpetuities.

20   Infants not to be appointed trustees
The appointment of an infant to be a trustee in relation to any settlement or trust shall be void, but without prejudice to the power to appoint a new trustee to fill the vacancy.

22   Conveyances of behalf of persons suffering from mental disorder and as to land held by them in trust
(1) Where a legal estate in land (whether settled or not) is vested in a person suffering from mental disorder, either solely or jointly with any other person or persons, his receiver or (if no receiver is acting for him) any person authorised in that behalf shall, under an order of the authority having jurisdiction under Part VII of the Mental Health Act 1983, or of the court, or under any statutory power, make or concur in making all requisite dispositions for conveying or creating a legal estate in his name and on his behalf.

(2) If land subject to a trust of land is vested, either solely or jointly with any other person or persons, in a person who is incapable, by reason of mental disorder, of exercising his functions as trustee, a new trustee shall be appointed in the place of that person, or he shall be otherwise discharged from the trust, before the legal estate is dealt with by the trustees.

(3) Subsection (2) of this section does not prevent a legal estate being dealt with without the appointment of a new trustee, or the discharge of the incapable trustee, at a time when the donee of an enduring power (within the meaning of the Enduring Powers of Attorney Act 1985) is entitled to act for the incapable trustee in the dealing.

24   Appointment of trustees of land
(1) The persons having power to appoint new trustees of land shall be bound to appoint the same persons (if any) who are for the time being trustees of any trust of the proceeds of sale of the land.

(2) A purchaser shall not be concerned to see that subsection (1) of this section has been complied with.

(3) This section applies whether the trust of land and the trust of proceeds of sale are created, or arise, before or after the commencement of this Act.

27   Purchaser not to be concerned with the trusts of the proceeds
(1) A purchaser of a legal estate from trustees of land shall not be concerned with the trusts affecting the land, the net income of the land or the proceeds of sale of the land whether or not those trusts are declared by the same instrument as that by which the trust of land is created.

(2) Notwithstanding anything to the contrary in the instrument (if any) creating a trust of land or in any trust affecting the net proceeds of sale of the land if it is sold, the proceeds of sale or other capital money shall not be paid to or applied by direction of fewer than two persons as trustees, except where the trustee is a trust corporation, but this subsection does not affect the right of a sole personal representative as such to give valid receipts for, or direct the application of, proceeds of sales or other capital money, nor, except where capital money arises on the transaction, render it necessary to have more than one trustee.

31   Trust of mortgaged property where right of redemption is barred

(1) Where any property, vested in trustees by way of security, becomes, by virtue of the statutes of limitation, or of an order for foreclosure or otherwise, discharged from the right of redemption, it shall be held by them in trust –

- (a)   to apply the income from the property in the same manner as interest paid on the mortgage debt would have been applicable; and
- (b)   if the property is sold, to apply the net proceeds of sale, after payment of costs and expenses, in the same manner as repayment of the mortgage debt would have been applicable.

(2) Subsection (1) of this section operates without prejudice to any rule of law relating to the apportionment of capital and income between tenant for life and remainderman.

(4) Where –

- (a)   the mortgage money is capital money for the purposes of the Settled Land Act 1925;
- (b)   land other than any forming the whole or part of the property mentioned in subsection (1) of this section is, or is deemed to be, subject to the settlement; and
- (c)   the tenant for life or statutory owner requires the trustees to execute with respect to land forming the whole or part of that property a vesting deed such as would have been required in relation to the land if it had been acquired on a purchase with capital money,

the trustees shall execute such a vesting deed.

(5) This section applies whether the right of redemption was discharged before or after the first day of January, nineteen hundred and twelve, but has effect without prejudice to any dealings or arrangements made before that date.

33   Application of Part I to personal representatives

The provisions of this Part of this Act relating to trustees of land apply to personal representatives holding land in trust, but without prejudice to their rights and powers for purposes of administration.

34   Effect of future dispositions to tenants in common

(1) An undivided share in land shall not be capable of being created except as provided by the Settled Land Act 1925 or as hereinafter mentioned.

(2) Where, after the commencement of this Act, land is expressed to be conveyed to any persons in undivided shares and those persons are of full age, the conveyance shall (notwithstanding anything to the contrary in this Act) operate as if the land had been expressed to be conveyed to the grantees, or, if there are more than four grantees, to the four first named in the conveyance, as joint tenants in trust for the persons interested in the land:

Provided that, where the conveyance is made by way of mortgage, the land shall vest in the grantees or such four of them as aforesaid for a term of years absolute (as provided by this Act) as joint tenants subject to cesser on redemption in like manner as if the mortgage money had belonged to them on a joint account, but without prejudice to the beneficial interests in the mortgage money and interest.

(3) A devise bequest or testamentary appointment, coming into operation after the commencement of this Act, of land to two or more persons in undivided shares shall operate as a devise bequest or appointment of the land to the personal representatives of the testator, and (but without prejudice to the rights and powers of the personal representatives for purposes of administration) in trust for the persons interested in the land.

(3A) In subsections (2) and (3) of this section references to the persons interested in the land include persons interested as trustees or personal representatives (as well as persons beneficially interested).

36   Joint tenancies

(1) Where a legal estate (not being settled land) is beneficially limited to or held in trust for any persons as joint tenants, the same shall be held in trust, in like manner as if the persons beneficially entitled were tenants in common, but not so as to sever their joint tenancy in equity.

(2) No severance of a joint tenancy of a legal estate, so as to create a tenancy in common in land, shall be permissible, whether by operation of law or otherwise, but this subsection does not affect the right of a joint tenant to release his interest to the other joint tenants, or the right to sever a joint tenancy in an equitable interest whether or not the legal estate is vested in the joint tenants: Provided that, where a legal estate (not being settled land) is vested in joint tenants beneficially, and any tenant desires to sever the joint tenancy in equity, he shall give to the other joint tenants a notice in writing of such desire or do such other acts or things as would, in the case of personal estate, have been effectual to sever the tenancy in equity, and thereupon the land shall be held in trust on terms which would have been requisite for giving effect to the beneficial interests if there had been an actual severance.

Nothing in this Act affects the right of a survivor of joint tenants, who is solely and beneficially interested, to deal with his legal estate as if it were not held in trust.

(3) Without prejudice to the right of a joint tenant to release his interest to the other joint tenants, no severance of a mortgage term or trust estate, so as to create a tenancy in common, shall be permissible.

41   Stipulations not of the essence of a contract

Stipulations in a contract, as to time or otherwise, which according to rules of equity are not deemed to be or to have become of the essence of the contract, are also construed and have effect at law in accordance with the same rules.

52   Conveyances to be by deed

(1) All conveyances of land or of any interest therein are void for the purpose of conveying or creating a legal estate unless made by deed. ...

53   Instruments required to be in writing

(1) Subject to the provisions hereinafter contained with respect to the creation of interests in land by parol –

  (a)   no interest in land can be created or disposed of except by writing signed by the person creating or conveying the same, or by an agent thereunto lawfully authorised in writing, or by will, or by operation of law;

  (b)   a declaration of trust respecting any land or any interest therein must be manifested and proved by some writing signed by some person who is able to declare such trust or by his will;

  (c)   a disposition of an equitable interest or trust subsisting at the time of the disposition must be in writing, signed by the person disposing of the same, or by his agent thereunto lawfully authorised in writing or by will.

(2) This section does not affect the creation or operation of resulting, implied or constructive trusts.

54   Creation of interests in land by parol

(1) All interests in land created by parol and not put in writing and signed by the persons so

creating the same, or by their agents thereunto lawfully authorised in writing, have, notwithstanding any consideration having been given for the same, the force and effect of interests at will only.

(2) Nothing in the foregoing provisions of this Part of this Act shall affect the creation by parol of leases taking effect in possession for a term not exceeding three years (whether or not the lessee is given power to extend the term) at the best rent which can be reasonably obtained without taking a fine.

56   Persons taking who are not partial

(1) A person may take an immediate or other interest in land or other property, or the benefit of any condition, right of entry, covenant or agreement over or respecting land or other property, although he may not be named as a party to the conveyance or other instrument. …

60   Abolition of technicalities in regard to conveyances and deeds …

(3) In a voluntary conveyance a resulting trust for the grantor shall not be implied merely by reason that the property is not expressed to be conveyed for the use or benefit of the grantee. …

97   Priorities as between puisne mortgages

Every mortgage affecting a legal estate in land made after the commencement of this Act, whether legal or equitable (not being a mortgage protected by the deposit of documents relating to the legal estate affected), shall rank according to its date of registration as a land charge pursuant to the Land Charges Act 1925.

This section does not apply to mortgages or charges to which the Land Charges Act 1972 does not apply by virtue of section 14(3) of that Act (which excludes certain land charges created by instruments necessitating registration under the Land Registration Act 2002), or to mortgages or charges of registered land or of land …

136   Legal assignments of things in action

(1) Any absolute assignment by writing under the hand of the assignor (not purporting to be by way of charge only) of any debt or other legal thing in action, of which express notice in writing has been given to the debtor, trustee or other person from whom the assignor would have been entitled to claim such debt or thing in action, is effectual in law (subject to equities having priority over the right of the assignee) to pass and transfer from the date of such notice –

    (a) the legal right to such debt or thing in action;
    (b) all legal and other remedies for the same; and
    (c) the power to give a good discharge for the same without the concurrence of the assignor:

Provided that, if the debtor, trustee or other person liable in respect of such debt or thing in action has notice –

    (a) that the assignment is disputed by the assignor or any person claiming under him; or
    (b) of any other opposing or conflicting claims to such debt or thing in action;

he may, if he thinks fit, either call upon the persons making claim thereto to interplead concerning the same, or pay the debts or other thing in action into court under the provisions of the Trustee Act 1925.

(2) This section does not affect the provisions of the Policies of Assurance Act 1867.

(3) The county court has jurisdiction (including power to receive payment of money or securities into court) under the proviso to subsection (1) of this section where the amount or value of the debt or thing in action does not exceed £30,000.

137   Dealings with life interests, reversions and other equitable interests

(1) The law applicable to dealings with equitable things in action which regulates the priority of competing interests therein shall, as respects dealings with equitable interests in land, capital money, and securities representing capital money effected after the commencement of this Act, apply to and regulate the priority of competing interests therein.

This subsection applies whether or not the money or securities are in court.

(2)   (i)   In the case of a dealing with an equitable interest in settled land, capital money or securities representing capital money, the persons to be served with notice of the dealing shall be the trustees of the settlement; and where the equitable interest is created by a derivative or subsidiary settlement, the persons to be served with notice shall be the trustees of that settlement.

(ii)   In the case of a dealing with an equitable interest in land subject to a trust of land, or the proceeds of sale of such land, the persons to be served with notice shall be the trustees.

(iii)   In any other case the person to be served with notice of a dealing with an equitable interest in land shall be the estate owner of the land affected.

The persons on whom notice is served pursuant to this subsection shall be affected thereby in the same manner as if they had been trustees of personal property out of which the equitable interest was created or arose.

This subsection does not apply where the money or securities are in court.

(3) A notice, otherwise than in writing, given to, or received by, a trustee after the commencement of this Act as respects any dealing with an equitable interest in real or personal property, shall not affect the priority of competing claims of purchasers in that equitable interest. ...

162   Restrictions on the perpetuity rule

(1) For removing doubts, it is hereby declared that the rule of law relating to perpetuities does not apply and shall be deemed never to have applied –

(a)   To any power to distrain on or to take possession of land or the income thereof given by way of indemnity against a rent, whether charged upon or payable in respect of any part of that land or not; or

(b)   To any rentcharge created only as an indemnity against another rentcharge, although the indemnity rentcharge may only arise or become payable on breach of a condition or stipulation; or

(c)   To any power, whether exercisable on breach of a condition or stipulation or not, to retain or withhold payment of any instalment of a rentcharge as an indemnity against another rentcharge; or

(d)   To any grant, exception, or reservation of any right of entry on, or user of, the surface of land or of any easements, rights or privileges over or under land for the purpose of –

(i)   winning, working, inspecting, measuring, converting, manufacturing, carrying away, and disposing of mines and minerals;

(ii)   inspecting, grubbing up, felling and carrying away timber and other trees, and the tops and lops thereof;

(iii)   executing repairs, alterations, or additions to any adjoining land, or the buildings and erections thereon;

(iv)   constructing, laying down, altering, repairing, renewing, cleansing, and maintaining sewers, watercourses, cesspools, gutters, drains, water-pipes, gas-pipes, electric wires or cables or other like works.

(2) This section applies to instruments coming into operation before or after the commencement of this Act.

164   General restrictions on accumulation of income

(1) No person may by any instrument or otherwise settle or dispose of any property in such manner that the income thereof shall, save as hereinafter mentioned, be wholly or partially accumulated for any longer period than one of the following, namely –

    (a)   the life of the grantor or settlor; or

    (b)   a term of twenty-one years from the death of the grantor, settlor or testator; or

    (c)   the duration of the minority or respective minorities of any person or persons living or en ventre sa mère at the death of the grantor, settlor or testator; or

    (d)   the duration of the minority or respective minorities only of any person or persons who under the limitations of the instrument directing the accumulations would, for the time being, if of full age, be entitled to the income directed to be accumulated.

In every case where any accumulation is directed otherwise than as aforesaid, the direction shall (save as hereinafter mentioned) be void; and the income of the property directed to be accumulated shall, so long as the same is directed to be accumulated contrary to this section, go to and be received by the person or persons who would have been entitled thereto if such accumulation had not been directed.

(2) This section does not extend to any provision –

    (i)   for payment of the debts of any grantor, settlor, testator or other person;

    (ii)   for raising portions for –

        (a)   any child, children or remoter issue of any grantor, settlor or testator; or

        (b)   any child, children or remoter issue of a person taking any interest under any settlement or other disposition directing the accumulations or to whom any interest is thereby limited;

    (iii) respecting the accumulation of the produce of timber or wood;

and accordingly such provisions may be made as if no statutory restrictions on accumulation of income had been imposed.

(3) The restrictions imposed by this section apply to instruments made on or after the twenty-eighth day of July, eighteen hundred, but in the case of wills only where the testator was living and of testamentary capacity after the end of one year from that date.

165   Qualification of restrictions on accumulation

Where accumulations of surplus income are made during a minority under any statutory power or under the general law, the period for which such accumulations are made is not (whether the trust was created or the accumulations were made before or after the commencement of this Act) to be taken into account in determining the periods for which accumulations are permitted to be made by the last preceding section, and accordingly an express trust for accumulation for any other permitted period shall not be deemed to have been invalidated or become invalid, by reason of accumulations also having been made as aforesaid during such minority.

175   Contingent and future testamentary gifts to carry the intermediate income

(1) A contingent or future specific devise or bequest of property, whether real or personal, and a contingent residuary devise of freehold land, and a specific or residuary devise of freehold land to trustees upon trust for persons whose interests are contingent or executory shall, subject to the statutory provisions relating to accumulations, carry the intermediate income of that property from the death of the testator, except so far as such income, or any part thereof, may be otherwise expressly disposed of.

(2) This section applies only to wills coming into operation after the commencement of this Act.

198 Registration […] to be notice

(1) The registration of any instrument or matter in any register kept under the Land Charges Act 1972 or any local land charges register shall be deemed to constitute actual notice of such instrument or matter, and of the fact of such registration, to all persons and for all purposes connected with the land affected, as from the date of registration or other prescribed date and so long as the registration continues in force.

(2) This section operates without prejudice to the provisions of this Act respecting the making of further advances by a mortgagee, and applies only to instruments and matters required or authorised to be registered in any such register.

199 Restrictions on constructive notice

(1) A purchaser shall not be prejudicially affected by notice of –

(i) any instrument or matter capable of registration under the provisions of the Land Charges Act 1925, or any enactment which it replaces, which is void or not enforceable as against him under that Act or enactment, by reason of the non-registration thereof;

(ii) any other instrument or matter or any fact or thing unless –

(a) it is within his own knowledge, or would have come to his knowledge if such inquiries and inspections had been made as ought reasonably to have been made by him; or

(b) in the same transaction with respect to which a question of notice to the purchaser arises, it has come to the knowledge of his counsel, as such, or of his solicitor or other agent, as such, or would have come to the knowledge of his solicitor or other agent, as such, if such inquiries and inspections had been made as ought reasonably to have been made by the solicitor or other agent.

(2) Paragraph (ii) of the last subsection shall not exempt a purchaser from any liability under, or any obligation to perform or observe, any covenant, condition, provision, or restriction contained in any instrument under which his title is derived, mediately or immediately; and such liability or obligation may be enforced in the same manner and to the same extent as if that paragraph had not been enacted.

(3) A purchaser shall not by reason of anything in this section be affected by notice in any case where he would not have been so affected if this section had not been enacted.

(4) This section applies to purchases made either before or after the commencement of this Act.

205 General definitions

(1) In this Act unless the context otherwise requires, the following expressions have the meanings hereby assigned to them respectively, that is to say – …

(ii) 'Conveyance' includes a mortgage, charge, lease, assent, vesting declaration, vesting instrument, disclaimer, release and every other assurance of property or of an interest therein by any instrument, except a will; 'convey' has a corresponding meaning; and 'disposition' includes a conveyance and also a devise, bequest, or an appointment of property contained in a will; and 'dispose of' has a corresponding meaning; …

(v) 'Estate owner' means the owner of a legal estate, but an infant is not capable of being an estate owner; …

(vii) 'Incumbrance' includes a legal or equitable mortgage and a trust for securing money, and a lien, and a charge of a portion, annuity, or other capital or annual sum; and 'incumbrancer' has a meaning corresponding with that of incumbrance, and includes every person entitled to the benefit of an incumbrance, or to require payment or discharge thereof;

(viii) 'Instrument' does not include a statute, unless the statute creates a settlement;

(ix) 'Land' includes land of any tenure, and mines and minerals, whether or not held apart from the surface, buildings or parts of buildings (whether the division is horizontal, vertical or made in any other way) and other corporeal hereditaments; also a manor, an advowson, and a rent and other incorporeal hereditaments, and an easement, right, privilege, or benefit in, over, or derived from land; and 'mines and minerals' include any strata or seam of minerals or substances in or under any land, and powers of working and getting the same; and 'manor' includes a lordship, and reputed manor or lordship; and 'hereditament' means any real property which on an intestacy occurring before the commencement of this Act might have devolved upon an heir;

(x) 'Legal estates' mean the estate, interests and charges, in or over land (subsisting or created at law) which are by this Act authorised to subsist or to be created as legal estates; 'equitable interests' mean all the other interests and charges in or over land; an equitable interest 'capable of subsisting as a legal estate' means such as could validly subsist or be created as a legal estate under this Act;

(xi) 'Legal powers' include the powers vested in a chargee by way of legal mortgage or in an estate owner under which a legal estate can be transferred or created; and 'equitable powers' mean all the powers in or over land under which equitable interests or powers only can be transferred or created; ...

(xvi) 'Mortgage' includes any charge or lien on any property for securing money or money's worth; 'legal mortgage' means a mortgage by demise or subdemise or a charge by way of legal mortgage and 'legal mortgagee' has a corresponding meaning; 'mortgage money' means money or money's worth secured by a mortgage; 'mortgagor' includes any person from time to time deriving title under the original mortgagor or entitled to redeem a mortgage according to his estate interest or right in the mortgaged property; 'mortgagee' includes a chargee by way of legal mortgage and any person from time to time deriving title under the original mortgagee; and 'mortgagee in possession' is, for the purposes of this Act, a mortgagee who, in right of the mortgage, has entered into and is in possession of the mortgaged property; and 'right of redemption' includes an option to repurchase only if the option in effect creates a right of redemption;

(xvii) 'Notice' includes constructive notice;

(xviii) 'Personal representative' means the executor, original or by representation, or administrator for the time being of a deceased person, and as regards any liability for the payment of death duties includes any person who takes possession of or intermeddles with the property of a deceased person without the authority of the personal representatives or the court;

(xix) 'Possession' includes receipts of rents and profits or the right to receive the same, if any; and 'income' includes rents and profits;

(xx) 'Property' includes any thing in action, and any interest in real or personal property;

(xxi) 'Purchaser' means a purchaser in good faith for valuable consideration and includes a lessee, mortgagee or other person who for valuable consideration acquires an interest in property except that in Part I of this Act and elsewhere where so expressly provided 'purchaser' only means a person who acquires an interest in or charge on property for money or money's worth; and in reference to a legal estate includes a chargee by way of legal mortgage; and where the context so requires 'purchaser' includes an intending purchaser; 'purchase' has a meaning corresponding with that of 'purchaser'; and 'valuable consideration' includes marriage, and formation of a civil partnership, but does not include a nominal consideration in money; ...

(xxiv) 'Sale' includes an extinguishment of manorial incidents, but in other respects means a sale properly so called;

(xxv) 'Securities' include stocks, funds and shares;

(xxvi) 'Tenant for life', 'statutory owner', 'settled land', 'settlement', 'vesting deed', 'subsidiary vesting deed', 'vesting order', 'vesting instrument', 'trust instrument', 'capital money', and 'trustees of the settlement' have the same meaning as in the Settled Land Act 1925; ...

(xxviii) 'Trust Corporation' means the Public Trustee or a corporation either appointed by the court in any particular case to be a trustee or entitled by rules made under subsection (3) of section four of the Public Trustee Act 1906 to act as custodian trustee;

(xxix) 'Trust for sale', in relation to land, means an immediate trust for sale, whether or not exercisable at the request or with the consent of any person; 'trustees for sale' mean the persons (including a personal representative) holding land on trust for sale;

(xxx) 'United Kingdom' means Great Britain and Northern Ireland;

(xxxi) 'Will' includes codicil. ...

(2) Where an equitable interest in or power over property arises by statute or operation of law, references to the creation of an interest or power include references to any interest or power so arising. ...

As amended by the Law of Property (Amendment) Act 1926, s7, Schedule; Mental Health Act 1959, s149(1), Schedule 7, Pt I; Land Charges Act 1972, s18, Schedule 3, para 1; Local Land Charges Act 1975, s17(2), Schedule 1; Mental Health Act 1983, s148, Schedule 4, para 5(a); High Court and County Courts Jurisdiction Order 1991, art 2(8), Schedule; Trusts of Land and Appointment of Trustees Act 1996, ss5(1), 25(1), (2), Schedule 2, paras 1, 3, 4, Schedule 3, para 4(1)–(3), (6)–(9), (15), Schedule 4; Trustee Delegation Act 1999, s9; Land Registration Act 2002, s133, Schedule 11, para 2(1), (10); Civil Partnership Act 2004, s261(1), Schedule 27, para 7.

ADMINISTRATION OF ESTATES ACT 1925
(15 Geo 5 c 23)

33   Trust for sale

(1) On the death of a person intestate as to any real or personal estate, that estate shall be held in trust by his personal representatives with the power to sell it.

(2) The personal representatives shall pay out of –

(a)   the ready money of the deceased (so far as not disposed of by his will, if any); and

(b)   any net money arising from disposing of any other part of his estate (after payment of costs),

all such funeral, testamentary and administration expenses, debts and other liabilities as are properly payable thereout having regard to the rules of administration contained in this Part of this Act, and out of the residue of the said money the personal representatives shall set aside a fund sufficient to provide for any pecuniary legacies bequeathed by the will (if any) of the deceased.

(3) During the minority of any beneficiary or the subsistence of any life interest and pending the distribution of the whole or any part of the estate of the deceased, the personal representatives may invest the residue of the said money, or so much thereof as may not have been distributed, under the Trustee Act 2000.

(4) The residue of the said money and any investments for the time being representing the same, and any part of the estate of the deceased which remains unsold and is not required for the administration purposes aforesaid, is in this Act referred to as 'the residuary estate of the intestate'.

(5) The income (including net rents and profits of real estate and chattels real after payment of rates, taxes, rent, costs of insurance, repairs and other outgoings properly attributable to income) of so much of the real and personal estate of the deceased as may not be disposed of by his will, if any, or may not be required for the administration purposes aforesaid, may, however such estate is invested, as from the death of the deceased, be treated and applied as income, and for that purpose any necessary apportionment may be made between tenant for life and remainderman.

(6) Nothing in this section affects the rights of any creditor of the deceased or the rights of the Crown in respect of death duties.

(7) Where the deceased leaves a will, this section has effect subject to the provisions contained in the will.

42 Power to appoint trustees of infants' property

(1) Where an infant is absolutely entitled under the will or on the intestacy of a person dying before or after the commencement of this Act (in this subsection called 'the deceased') to a devise or legacy, or to the residue of the estate of the deceased, or any share therein, and such devise, legacy, residue or share is not under the will, if any, of the deceased, devised or bequeathed to trustees for the infant, the personal representatives of the deceased may appoint a trust corporation or two or more individuals, not exceeding four (whether or not including the personal representatives or one or more of the personal representatives), to be the trustee or trustees of such devise, legacy, residue or share for the infant, and to be trustees of any land devised or any land being or forming part of such residue or share for the purposes of the Settled Land Act 1925, and of the statutory provisions relating to the management of land during a minority, and may execute or do any assurance or thing requisite for vesting such devise, legacy, residue or share in the trustee or trustees so appointed.

On such appointment the personal representatives, as such, shall be discharged from all further liability in respect of such devise, legacy, residue, or share, and the same may be retained in its existing condition or state of investment, or may be converted into money, and such money may be invested in any authorised investment.

(2) Where a personal representative has before the commencement of this Act retained or sold any such devise, legacy, residue or share, and invested the same or the proceeds thereof in any investments in which he was authorised to invest money subject to the trust, then, subject to any order of the court made before such commencement, he shall not be deemed to have incurred any liability on that account, or by reason of not having paid or transferred the money or property into court.

As amended by the Trusts of Land and Appointment of Trustees Act 1996, s5(1), Schedule 2, para 5; Trustee Act 2000, s40, Schedule 2, Pt II, para 27.

CROWN PROCEEDINGS ACT 1947
(10 & 11 Geo 6 c 44)

21 Nature of relief

(1) In any civil proceedings by or against the Crown the court shall, subject to the provisions of this Act, have power to make all such orders as it has power to make in proceedings between

subjects, and otherwise to give such appropriate relief as the case may require:
Provided that –

    (a) where in any proceedings against the Crown any such relief is sought as might in proceedings between subjects be granted by way of injunction or specific performance, the court shall not grant an injunction or make an order for specific performance, but may in lieu thereof make an order declaratory of the rights of the parties; and

    (b) in any proceedings against the Crown for the recovery of land or other property the court shall not make an order for the recovery of the land or the delivery of the property, but may in lieu thereof make an order declaring that the plaintiff is entitled as against the Crown to the land or property or to the possession thereof.

(2) The court shall not in any civil proceedings grant any injunction or make any order against an officer of the Crown if the effect of granting the injunction or making the order would be to give any relief against the Crown which could not have been obtained in proceedings against the Crown.

CHARITABLE TRUSTS (VALIDATION) ACT 1954
(2 & 3 Eliz 2 c 58)

1   Validation and modification of imperfect trust instruments

(1) In this Act, 'imperfect trust provision' means any provision declaring the objects for which property is to be held or applied, and so describing those objects that, consistently with the terms of the provision, the property could be used exclusively for charitable purposes, but could nevertheless be used for purposes which are not charitable.

(2) Subject to the following provisions of this Act, any imperfect trust provision contained in an instrument taking effect before the sixteenth day of December, nineteen hundred and fifty-two, shall have, and be deemed to have had, effect in relation to any disposition or covenant to which this Act applies –

    (a) as respects the period before the commencement of this Act, as if the whole of the declared objects were charitable; and

    (b as respects the period after that commencement as if the provision had required the property to be held or applied for the declared objects in so far only as they authorise use for charitable purposes.

(3) A document inviting gifts of property to be held or applied for objects declared by the document shall be treated for the purposes of this section as an instrument taking effect when it is first issued.

(4) In this Act 'covenant' includes any agreement, whether under seal or not, and 'covenantor' is to be construed accordingly.

2   Dispositions and covenants to which the Act applies

(1) Subject to the next following subsection, this Act applies to any disposition of property to be held or applied for objects declared by an imperfect trust provision, and to any covenant to make such a disposition, where apart from this Act the disposition or covenant is invalid under the law of England and Wales, but would be valid if the objects were exclusively charitable.

(2) This Act does not apply to a disposition if before the sixteenth day of December, nineteen hundred and fifty-two, property comprised in, or representing that comprised in, the disposition in question, or another disposition made for the objects declared by the same imperfect trust

provision, or income arising from any such property, has been paid or conveyed to, or applied for the benefit of, the persons entitled by reason of the invalidity of the disposition in question or of such other disposition as aforesaid, as the case may be.

(3) A disposition in settlement or other disposition creating more than one interest in the same property shall be treated for the purposes of this Act as a separate disposition in relation to each of the interests created.

RECREATIONAL CHARITIES ACT 1958
(6 & 7 Eliz 2 c 17)

1   General provision as to recreational and similar trusts, etc

(1) Subject to the provisions of this Act, it shall be and be deemed always to have been charitable to provide, or assist in the provision of, facilities for recreation or other leisure-time occupation, if the facilities are provided in the interests of social welfare:

Provided that nothing in this section shall be taken to derogate from the principle that a trust or institution to be charitable must be for the public benefit.

(2) The requirement of the foregoing subsection that the facilities are provided in the interests of social welfare shall not be treated as satisfied unless –

    (a) the facilities are provided with the object of improving the conditions of life for the persons for whom the facilities are primarily intended; and

    (b) either –

        (i) those persons have need of such facilities as aforesaid by reason of their youth, age, infirmity or disablement, poverty or social and economic circumstances; or

        (ii) the facilities are to be available to the members or female members of the public at large.

(3) Subject to the said requirement, subsection (1) of this section applies in particular to the provision of facilities at village halls, community centres and women's institutes, and to the provision and maintenance of grounds and buildings to be used for purposes of recreation or leisure-time occupation, and extends to the provision of facilities for those purposes by the organising of any activity.

[See Appendix, Charities Act 2006, s5(1), (2), Schedule 10, para 2.]

MATRIMONIAL CAUSES (PROPERTY AND MAINTENANCE) ACT 1958
(6 & 7 Eliz 2 c 35)

7   Extension of s17 of Married Women's Property Act 1882

(1) Any right of a wife, under section seventeen of the Married Women's Property Act 1882 to apply to a judge of the High Court or of a county court, in any question between husband and wife as to the title to or possession of property, shall include the right to make such an application where it is claimed by the wife that her husband has had in his possession or under his control –

    (a) money to which, or to a share of which, she was beneficially entitled (whether by reason that it represented the proceeds of property to which, or to an interest in which, she was beneficially entitled, or for any other reason), or

(b) property (other than money) to which, or to an interest in which, she was beneficially entitled,

and that either that money or other property has ceased to be in his possession or under his control or that she does not know whether it is still in his possession or under his control.

(2) Where, on application made to a judge of the High Court or of a county court under the said section seventeen, as extended by the preceding subsection, the judge is satisfied –

(a) that the husband has had in his possession or under his control money or other property as mentioned in paragraph (a) or paragraph (b) of the preceding subsection, and

(b) that he has not made to the wife, in respect of that money or other property, such payment or disposition as would have been appropriate in the circumstances,

the power to make orders under that section shall be extended in accordance with the next following subsection.

(3) Where the last preceding subsection applies, the power to make orders under the said section seventeen shall include power for the judge to order the husband to pay to the wife –

(a) in a case falling within paragraph (a) of subsection (1) of this section, such sum in respect of the money to which the application relates, or the wife's share thereof, as the case may be, or

(b) in a case falling within paragraph (b) of the said subsection (1), such sum in respect of the value of the property to which the application relates, or the wife's interest therein, as the case may be,

as the judge may consider appropriate.

(4) Where on an application under the said section seventeen as extended by this section it appears to the judge that there is any property which –

(a) represents the whole or part of the money or property in question, and

(b) is property in respect of which an order could have been made under that section if an application had been made by the wife thereunder in a question as to the title to or possession of that property,

the judge (either in substitution for or in addition to the making of an order in accordance with the last preceding subsection) may make any order under that section in respect of that property which he could have made on such an application as is mentioned in paragraph (b) of this subsection.

(5) The preceding provisions of this section shall have effect in relation to a husband as they have effect in relation to a wife, as if any reference to the husband were a reference to the wife and any reference to the wife were a reference to the husband.

(6) Any power of a judge which is exercisable on an application under the said section seventeen shall be exercisable in relation to an application made under that section as extended by this section.

(7) For the avoidance of doubt it is hereby declared that any power conferred by the said section seventeen to make orders with respect to any property includes power to order a sale of the property.

As amended by the Matrimonial and Family Proceedings Act 1984, s46(1), Schedule 1, para 3.

VARIATION OF TRUSTS ACT 1958
(6 & 7 Eliz 2 c 53)

1   Jurisdiction of courts to vary trusts

(1) Where property, whether real or personal, is held on trusts arising, whether before or after the passing of this Act, under any will, settlement or other disposition, the court may if it thinks fit by order approve on behalf of –

 (a) any person having, directly or indirectly, an interest, whether vested or contingent, under the trusts who by reason of infancy or other incapacity is incapable or assenting, or

 (b) any person (whether ascertained or not) who may become entitled, directly or indirectly, to an interest under the trusts as being at a future date or on the happening of a future event a person of any specified description or a member of any specified class of persons, so however that this paragraph shall not include any person who would be of that description, or a member of that class, as the case may be, if the said date had fallen or the said event had happened at the date of the application to the court, or

 (c) any person unborn, or

 (d) any person in respect of any discretionary interest of his under protective trusts where the interest of the principal beneficiary has not failed or determined,

any arrangement (by whomsoever proposed, and whether or not there is any other person beneficially interested who is capable of assenting thereto) varying or revoking all or any of the trusts, or enlarging the powers of the trustees of managing or administering any of the property subject to the trusts:

Provided that except by virtue of paragraph (d) of this subsection the court shall not approve an arrangement on behalf of any person unless the carrying out thereof would be for the benefit of that person.

(2) In the foregoing subsection 'protective trusts' means the trusts specified in paragraphs (i) and (ii) of subsection (1) of section thirty-three of the Trustee Act 1925, or any like trusts, 'the principal beneficiary' has the same meaning as in the said subsection (1) and 'discretionary interest' means an interest arising under the trust specified in paragraph (ii) of the said subsection (1) or any like trust.

(3) The jurisdiction conferred by subsection (1) of this section shall be exercisable by the High Court, except that the question whether the carrying out of any arrangement would be for the benefit of a person falling within paragraph (a) of the said subsection (1) shall be determined by order of the authority having jurisdiction under Part VII of the Mental Health Act 1983, if that person is a patient within the meaning of the said Part VII.

(5) Nothing in the foregoing provisions of this section shall apply to trusts affecting property settled by Act of Parliament.

(6) Nothing in this section shall be taken to limit the powers conferred by section sixty-four of the Settled Land Act 1925, section fifty-seven of the Trustee Act 1925, or the powers of the authority having jurisdiction under Part VII of the Mental Health Act 1983.

As amended by the County Courts Act 1959, s204, Schedule 3, and the Mental Health Act 1983, s148, Schedule 4, para 14.

PERPETUITIES AND ACCUMULATIONS ACT 1964
(1964 c 55)

1   Power to specify perpetuity period

(1) Subject to section 9(2) of this Act and subsection (2) below, where the instrument by which any disposition is made so provides, the perpetuity period applicable to the disposition under the rule against perpetuities, instead of being of any other duration, shall be of a duration equal to such number of years not exceeding eighty as is specified in that behalf in the instrument.

(2) Subsection (1) above shall not have effect where the disposition is made in exercise of a special power of appointment, but where a period is specified under that subsection in the instrument creating such a power the period shall apply in relation to any disposition under the power as it applies in relation to the power itself.

2   Presumptions and evidence as to future parenthood

(1) Where in any proceedings there arises on the rule against perpetuities a question which turns on the ability of a person to have a child at some future time, then –

    (a)   subject to paragraph (b) below, it shall be presumed that a male can have a child at the age of fourteen years or over, but not under that age, and that a female can have a child at the age of twelve years or over, but not under that age or over the age of fifty-five years; but

    (b)   in the case of a living person evidence may be given to show that he or she will or will not be able to have a child at the time in question.

(2) Where any such question is decided by treating a person as unable to have a child at a particular time, and he or she does so, the High Court may make such order as it thinks fit for placing the persons interested in the property comprised in the disposition, so far as may be just, in the position they would have held if the question had not been so decided.

(3) Subject to subsection (2) above, where any such question is decided in relation to a disposition by treating a person as able or unable to have a child at a particular time, then he or she shall be so treated for the purpose of any question which may arise on the rule against perpetuities in relation to the same disposition in any subsequent proceedings.

(4) In the foregoing provisions of this section references to having a child are references to begetting or giving birth to a child, but those provisions (except subsection (1)(b)) shall apply in relation to the possibility that a person will at any time have a child by adoption, legitimation or other means as they apply to his or her ability at that time to beget or give birth to a child.

3   Uncertainty as to remoteness

(1), Where, apart from the provisions of this section and sections 4 and 5 of this Act, a disposition would be void on the ground that the interest disposed of might not become vested until too remote a time, the disposition shall be treated, until such time (if any) as it becomes established that the vesting must occur, if at all, after the end of the perpetuity period, as if the disposition were not subject to the rule against perpetuities; and its becoming so established shall not affect the validity of anything previously done in relation to the interest disposed of by way of advancement, application of intermediate income or otherwise.

(2) Where, apart from the said provisions, a disposition consisting of the conferring of a general power of appointment would be void on the ground that the power might not become exercisable until too remote a time, the disposition shall be treated, until such time (if any) as it becomes established that the power will not be exercisable within the perpetuity period, as if the disposition were not subject to the rule against perpetuities.

(3) Where, apart from the said provisions, a disposition consisting of the conferring of any power, option or other right would be void on the ground that the right might be exercised at too remote a time, the disposition shall be treated as regards any exercise of the right within the perpetuity period as if it were not subject to the rule against perpetuities and, subject to the said provisions, shall be treated as void for remoteness only if, and so far as, the right is not fully exercised within that period.

(4) Where this section applies to a disposition and the duration of the perpetuity period is not determined by virtue of section 1 or 9(2) of this Act, it shall be determined as follows –

    (a) where any persons falling within subsection (5) below are individuals in being and ascertainable at the commencement of the perpetuity period the duration of the period shall be determined by reference to their lives and no others, but so that the lives of any description of persons falling within paragraph (b) or (c) of that subsection shall be disregarded if the number of persons of that description is such as to render it impracticable to ascertain the date of death of the survivor;

    (b) where there are no lives under paragraph (a) above the period shall be twenty-one years.

(5) The said persons are as follows –

    (a) the person by whom the disposition was made;

    (b) a person to whom or in whose favour the disposition was made, that is to say –

        (i) in the case of a disposition to a class of persons, any member or potential member of the class;

        (ii) in the case of an individual disposition to a person taking only on certain conditions being satisfied, any person as to whom some of the conditions are satisfied and the remainder may in time be satisfied;

        (iii) in the case of a special power of appointment exercisable in favour of members of a class, any member or potential member of the class;

        (iv) in the case of a special power of appointment exercisable in favour of one person only, that person or, where the object of the power is ascertainable only on certain conditions being satisfied, any person as to whom some of the conditions are satisfied and the remainder may in time be satisfied;

        (v) in the case of any power, option or other right, the person on whom the right is conferred;

    (c) a person having a child or grandchild within sub-paragraphs (i) to (iv) of paragraph (b) above, or any of whose children or grandchildren, if subsequently born, would by virtue of his or her descent fall within those sub-paragraphs;

    (d) any person on the failure or determination of whose prior interest the disposition is limited to take effect.

4   Reduction of age and exclusion of class members to avoid remoteness

(1) Where a disposition is limited by reference to the attainment by any person or persons of a specified age exceeding twenty-one years, and it is apparent at the time the disposition is made or becomes apparent at a subsequent time –

    (a) that the disposition would, apart from this section, be void for remoteness, but

    (b) hat it would not be so void if the specified age had been twenty-one years,

the disposition shall be treated for all purposes as if, instead of being limited by reference to the age in fact specified, it had been limited by reference to the age nearest to that age which would, if specified instead, have prevented the disposition from being so void.

(2) Where in the case of any disposition different ages exceeding twenty-one years are specified in relation to different persons –

    (a) the reference in paragraph (b) of subsection (1) above to the specified age shall be construed as a reference to all the specified ages, and

    (b) that subsection shall operate to reduce each such age so far as is necessary to save the disposition from being void for remoteness.

(3) Where the inclusion of any persons, being potential members of a class or unborn persons who at birth would become members or potential members of the class, prevents the foregoing provisions of this section from operating to save a disposition from being void for remoteness, those persons shall thenceforth be deemed for all the purposes of the disposition to be excluded from the class, and the said provisions shall thereupon have effect accordingly.

(4) Where, in the case of a disposition to which subsection (3) above does not apply, it is apparent at the time the disposition is made or becomes apparent at a subsequent time that, apart from this subsection, the inclusion of any persons, being potential members of a class or unborn persons who at birth would become members or potential members of the class, would cause the disposition to be treated as void for remoteness, those persons shall, unless their exclusion would exhaust the class, thenceforth be deemed for all the purposes of the disposition to be excluded from the class.

(5) Where this section has effect in relation to a disposition to which section 3 above applies, the operation of this section shall not affect the validity of anything previously done in relation to the interest disposed of by way of advancement, application of intermediate income or otherwise. ...

(7) For the avoidance of doubt it is hereby declared that a question arising under section 3 of this Act or subsection (1)(a) above of whether a disposition would be void apart from this section is to be determined as if subsection (6) above had been a separate section of this Act.

5   Condition relating to death of surviving spouse

Where a disposition is limited by reference to the time of death of the survivor of a person in being at the commencement of the perpetuity period and any spouse of that person, and that time has not arrived at the end of the perpetuity period, the disposition shall be treated for all purposes, where to do so would save it from being void for remoteness, as if it had instead been limited by reference to the time immediately before the end of that period.

6   Saving and acceleration of expectant interests

A disposition shall not be treated as void for remoteness by reason only that the interest disposed of is ulterior to and dependent upon an interest under a disposition which is so void, and the vesting of an interest shall not be prevented from being accelerated on the failure of a prior interest by reason only that the failure arises because of remoteness.

7   Powers of appointment

For the purposes of the rule against perpetuities, a power of appointment shall be treated as a special power unless –

    (a) in the instrument creating the power it is expressed to be exercisable by one person only, and

    (b) it could, at all times during its currency when that person is of full age and capacity, be exercised by him so as immediately to transfer to himself the whole of the interest governed by the power without the consent of any other person or compliance with any other condition, not being a formal condition relating only to the mode of exercise of the power:

Provided that for the purpose of determining whether a disposition made under a power of appointment exercisable by will only is void for remoteness, the power shall be treated as a general power where it would have fallen to be so treated if exercisable by deed.

8 Administrative powers of trustees

(1) The rule against perpetuities shall not operate to invalidate a power conferred on trustees or other persons to sell, lease, exchange or otherwise dispose of any property for full consideration, or to do any other act in the administration (as opposed to the distribution) of any property, and shall not prevent the payment to trustees or other persons of reasonable remuneration for their services.

(2) Subsection (1) above shall apply for the purpose of enabling a power to be exercised at any time after the commencement of this Act notwithstanding that the power is conferred by an instrument which took effect before that commencement.

9 Options relating to land

(1) The rule against perpetuities shall not apply to a disposition consisting of the conferring of an option to acquire for valuable consideration an interest reversionary (whether directly or indirectly) on the term of a lease if –

    (a) the option is exercisable only by the lessee or his successors in title, and

    (b) it ceases to be exercisable at or before the expiration of one year following the determination of the lease.

This subsection shall apply in relation to an agreement for a lease as it applies in relation to a lease, and 'lessee' shall be construed accordingly.

(2) In the case of a disposition consisting of the conferring of an option to acquire for valuable consideration any interest in land, the perpetuity period under the rule against perpetuities shall be twenty-one years, and section 1 of this Act shall not apply:

Provided that this subsection shall not apply to a right of pre-emption conferred on a public or local authority in respect of land used or to be used for religious purposes where the right becomes exercisable only if the land ceases to be used for such purposes.

10 Avoidance of contractual and other rights in cases of remoteness

Where a disposition inter vivos would fall to be treated as void for remoteness if the rights and duties thereunder were capable of transmission to persons other than the original parties and had been so transmitted, it shall be treated as void as between the person by whom it was made and the person to whom or in whose favour it was made or any successor of his, and no remedy shall lie in contract or otherwise for giving effect to it or making restitution for its lack of effect.

12 Possibilities of reverter, conditions subsequent, exceptions and reservations

(1) In the case of –

    (a) a possibility of reverter on the determination of a determinable fee simple, or

    (b) a possibility of a resulting trust on the determination of any other determinable interest in property,

the rule against perpetuities shall apply in relation to the provision causing the interest to be determinable as it would apply if that provision were expressed in the form of a condition subsequent giving rise, on breach thereof, to a right of re-entry or an equivalent right in the case of property other than land, and where the provision falls to be treated as void for remoteness the determinable interest shall become an absolute interest.

(2) Where a disposition is subject to any such provision, or to any such condition subsequent, or to any exception or reservation, the disposition shall be treated for the purposes of this Act as

including a separate disposition of any rights arising by virtue of the provision, condition subsequent, exception or reservation.

13 Amendment of s164 of Law of Property Act 1925

(1) The periods for which accumulations of income under a settlement or other disposition are permitted by section 164 of the Law of Property Act 1925 shall include –

(a) a term of twenty-one years from the date of the making of the disposition, and

(b) the duration of the minority or respective minorities of any person or persons in being at that date.

(2) It is hereby declared that the restrictions imposed by the said section 164 apply in relation to a power to accumulate income whether or not there is a duty to exercise that power, and that they apply whether or not the power to accumulate extends to income produced by the investment of income previously accumulated.

14 Right to stop accumulation

Section 2 above shall apply to any question as to the right of beneficiaries to put an end to accumulations of income under any disposition as it applies to questions arising on the rule against perpetuities.

15 Short title, interpretation and extent

(1) This Act may be cited as the Perpetuities and Accumulations Act 1964.

(2) In this Act –

'disposition' includes the conferring of a power of appointment and any other disposition of an interest in or right over property, and references to the interest disposed of shall be construed accordingly;

'in being' means living or en ventre sa mere;

'power of appointment' includes the discretionary power to transfer a beneficial interest in property without the furnishing of valuable consideration;

'will' includes a codicil;

and for the purposes of this Act a disposition contained in a will shall be deemed to be made at the death of the testator.

(3) For the purposes of this Act a person shall be treated as a member of a class if in his case all the conditions identifying a member of the class are satisfied, and shall be treated as a potential member if in his case some only of those conditions are satisfied but there is a possibility that the remainder will in time be satisfied.

(4) Nothing in this Act shall affect the operation of the rule of law rendering void for remoteness certain dispositions under which property is limited to be applied for purposes other than the benefit of any person or class of persons in cases where the property may be so applied after the end of the perpetuity period.

(5) The foregoing sections of this Act shall apply (except as provided in section 8(2) above) only in relation to instruments taking effect after the commencement of this Act, and in the case of an instrument made in the exercise of a special power of appointment shall apply only where the instrument creating the power takes effect after that commencement;

Provided that section 7 above shall apply in all cases for construing the foregoing reference to a special power of appointment.

(6) This Act shall apply in relation to a disposition made otherwise than by an instrument as if the disposition had been contained in an instrument taking effect when the disposition was made.

(7) This Act binds the Crown. ...

As amended by the Children Act 1975, s108(1)(a), Schedule 3, para 43.

WILLS ACT 1968
(1968 c 28)

1   Restriction of operation of Wills Act 1837, s15
(1) For the purposes of section 15 of the Wills Act 1837 (avoidance of gifts to attesting witnesses and their spouses) the attestation of a will by a person to whom or to whose spouse there is given or made any such disposition as is described in that section shall be disregarded if the will is duly executed without his attestation and without that of any other such person.
(2) This section applies to the will of any person dying after the passing of this Act, whether executed before or after the passing of this Act.

PARISH COUNCILS AND BURIAL AUTHORITIES (MISCELLANEOUS PROVISIONS) ACT 1970
(1970 c 29)

1   Maintenance of private graves
(1) A burial authority or a local authority may agree with any person in consideration of the payment of a sum by him, to maintain –
> (b) a monument or other memorial to any person situated in any place within the area of the authority to which the authority have a right of access;

so, however, that no agreement or, as the case may be, none of the agreements made under this subsection by any authority with respect to a particular monument or other memorial may impose on the authority an obligation with respect to maintenance for a period exceeding 99 years from the date of that agreement. ...

As amended by the Local Authorities' Cemeteries Order 1974, art 17, Schedule 3.

MATRIMONIAL PROCEEDINGS AND PROPERTY ACT 1970
(1970 c 45)

37   Contributions by spouse in money or money's worth to the improvement of property
It is hereby declared that where a husband or wife contributes in money or money's worth to the improvement of real or personal property in which or in the proceeds of sale of which either or both of them has or have a beneficial interest, the husband or wife so contributing shall, if the contribution is of a substantial nature and subject to any agreement between them to the contrary express or implied, be treated as having then acquired by virtue of his or her contribution a share or an enlarged share, as the case may be, in that beneficial interest of such an extent as may have

been then agreed or, in default of such agreement, as may seem in all the circumstances just to any court before which the question of the existence or extent of the beneficial interest of the husband or wife arises (whether in proceedings between them or in any other proceedings).

39 Extension of s17 of Married Women's Property Act 1882

An application may be made to the High Court or a county court under section 17 of the Married Women's Property Act 1882 (powers of the court in disputes between husband and wife about property) (including that section as extended by section 7 of the Matrimonial Causes (Property and Maintenance) Act 1958) by either of the parties to a marriage notwithstanding that their marriage has been dissolved or annulled so long as the application is made within the period of three years beginning with the date on which the marriage was dissolved or annulled; and references in the said section 17 and the said section 7 to a husband or a wife shall be construed accordingly.

SEX DISCRIMINATION ACT 1975
(1975 c 65)

43 Charities

(1) Nothing in Parts II to IV shall –
    (a) be construed as affecting a provision to which this subsection applies, or
    (b) render unlawful an act which is done in order to give effect to such a provision.

(2) Subsection (1) applies to a provision for conferring benefits on persons of one sex only (disregarding any benefits to persons of the opposite sex which are exceptional or are relatively insignificant), being a provision which is contained in a charitable instrument.

(3) In this section 'charitable instrument' means an enactment or other instrument so far as it relates to charitable purposes …

In the application of this section to England and Wales, 'charitable purpose' means purposes which are exclusively charitable according to the law of England and Wales.

78 Educational charities in England and Wales

(1) This section applies to any trust deed or other instrument –
    (a) which concerns property applicable for or in connection with the provision of education in any establishment in paragraphs 1 to 5 of the Table in section 22, and
    (b) which in any way restricts the benefits available under the instrument to persons of one sex.

(2) If on the application of the trustees, or of the responsible body (as defined in section 22), the Secretary of State is satisfied that the removal or modification of the restriction would conduce to the advancement of education without sex discrimination, he may by order make such modifications of the instrument as appear to him expedient for removing or modifying the restriction, and for any supplemental or incidental purposes.

(3) If the trust was created by gift or bequest, no order shall be made until 25 years after the date on which the gift or bequest took effect, unless the donor or his personal representatives, or the personal representatives of the testator, have consented in writing to the making of the application for the order.

As amended by the Sex Discrimination Act 1975 (Amendment of section 43) Order 1977, art 2.

RACE RELATIONS ACT 1976
(1976 c 74)

34   Charities

(1) A provision which is contained in a charitable instrument (whenever that instrument took or takes effect) and which provides for conferring benefits on persons of a class defined by reference to colour shall have effect for all purposes as if it provided for conferring the like benefits –

   (a) on persons of the class which results if the restriction by reference to colour is disregarded; or

   (b) where the original class is defined by reference to colour only, on persons generally;

but nothing in this subsection shall be taken to alter the effect of any provision as regards any time before the coming into operation of this subsection.

(2) Nothing in Parts II to IV shall –

   (a) be construed as affecting a provision to which this subsection applies; or

   (b) render unlawful an act which is done in order to give effect to such a provision.

(3) Subsection (2) applies to any provision which is contained in a charitable instrument (whenever that instrument took or takes effect) and which provides for conferring benefits on persons of a class defined otherwise than by reference to colour (including a class resulting from the operation of subsection (1)).

(3A) Subsection (2)(b) does not apply to an act which is unlawful, on grounds of race or national origins, by virtue of section 4 or 7.

(4) In this section 'charitable instrument' means an enactment or other instrument passed or made for charitable purposes, or an enactment or other instrument so far as it relates to charitable purposes ...

In the application of this section to England and Wales, 'charitable purposes' means purposes which are exclusively charitable according to the law of England and Wales.

As amended by the Race Relations Act 1976 (Amendment) Regulations 2003, reg 33.

SALE OF GOODS ACT 1979
(1979 c 54)

48E   Powers of the court

(1) In any proceedings in which a remedy is sought by virtue of this Part [Additional Rights of Buyer in Consumer Cases] the court, in addition to any other power it has, may act under this section.

(2) On the application of the buyer the court may make an order requiring specific performance ... by the seller of any obligation imposed on him by virtue of section 48B [repair of replacement of the goods] above.

(3) Subsection (4) applies if –

   (a) the buyer requires the seller to give effect to a remedy under section 48B or 48C [reduction of purchase price or rescission of contract] above or has claims to rescind under section 48C, but

   (b) the court decides that another remedy under section 48B or 48C is appropriate.

(4) The court may proceed –

(a) as if the buyer had required the seller to give effect to the other remedy, or if the other remedy is rescission under section 48C;

(b) as if the buyer had claimed to rescind the contract under that section.

(5) If the buyer has claimed to rescind the contract the court may order that any reimbursement to the buyer is reduced to take account of the use he has had of the goods since they were delivered to him.

(6) The court may make an order under this section unconditionally or on such terms and conditions as to damages, payment of the price and otherwise as it thinks just.

52   Specific performance

(1) In any action for breach of contract to deliver specific or ascertained goods the court may, if it thinks fit, on the plaintiff's application, by its judgment or decree direct that the contract shall be performed specifically, without giving the defendant the option of retaining the goods on payment of damages.

(2) The plaintiff's application may be made at any time before judgment or decree.

(3) The judgment or decree may be unconditional, or on such terms and conditions as to damages, payment of the price and otherwise as seem just to the court. ...

61   Interpretation

(1) In this Act, unless the context or subject matter otherwise requires –

'action' includes counterclaim and set-off ...; ...

'goods' includes all personal chattels other than things in action and money ...; and in particular 'goods' includes emblements, industrial growing crops, and things attached to or forming part of the land which are agreed to be severed before sale or under the contract of sale and includes an undivided share in goods; ...

'specific goods' means goods identified and agreed on at the time a contract of sale is made and includes an undivided share, specified as a fraction or percentage, of goods identified and agreed on as aforesaid; ...

As amended by the Sale of Goods (Amendment) Act 1995, s2; Sale and Supply of Goods to Consumers Regulations 2002, reg 5.

LIMITATION ACT 1980

(1980 c 58)

PART I

ORDINARY TIME LIMITS FOR DIFFERENT CLASSES OF ACTION

1   Time limits under Part I subject to extension or exclusion under Part II

(1) This Part of this Act gives the ordinary time limits for bringing actions of the various classes mentioned in the following provisions of this Part.

(2) The ordinary time limits given in this Part of this Act are subject to extension or exclusion in accordance with the provisions of Part II of this Act.

10   Special time limits for claiming contribution

(1) Where under section 1 of the Civil Liability (Contribution) Act 1978 any person becomes entitled to a right to recover contribution in respect of any damage from any other person, no

action to recover contribution by virtue of that right shall be brought after the expiration of two years from the date on which that right accrued.

(2) For the purposes of this section the date on which a right to recover contribution in respect of any damage accrues to any person (referred to below in this section as 'the relevant date') shall be ascertained as provided in subsections (3) and (4) below.

(3) If the person in question is held liable in respect of that damage –

    (a) by a judgment given in any civil proceedings; or

    (b) by an award made on any arbitration;

the relevant date shall be the date on which the judgment is given, or the date of the award (as the case may be).

For the purposes of this subsection no account shall be taken of any judgment or award given or made on appeal in so far as it varies the amount of damages awarded against the person in question.

(4) If, in any case not within subsection (3) above, the person in question makes or agrees to make any payment to one or more persons in compensation for that damage (whether he admits any liability in respect of the damage or not), the relevant date shall be the earliest date on which the amount to be paid by him is agreed between him (or his representative) and the person (or each of the persons, as the case may be) to whom the payment is to be made.

(5) An action to recover contribution shall be one to which sections 28, 32 and 35 of this Act apply, but otherwise Parts II and III of this Act (except sections 34, 37 and 38) shall not apply for the purposes of this section.

21   Time limit for actions in respect of trust property

(1) No period of limitation prescribed by this Act shall apply to an action by the beneficiary under a trust, being an action –

    (a) in respect of any fraud or fraudulent breach of trust to which the trustee was a party or privy; or

    (b) to recover from the trustee trust property or the proceeds of trust property in the possession of the trustee, or previously received by the trustee and converted to his use.

(2) Where a trustee who is also a beneficiary under the trust receives or retains trust property or its proceeds as his share on a distribution of trust property under the trust, his liability in any action brought by virtue of subsection (1)(b) above to recover that property or its proceeds after the expiration of the period of limitation prescribed by this Act for bringing an action to recover trust property shall be limited to the excess over his proper share.

This subsection only applies if the trustee acted honestly and reasonably in making the distribution.

(3) Subject to the preceding provisions of this section, an action by a beneficiary to recover trust property or in respect of any breach of trust, not being an action for which a period of limitation is prescribed by any other provisions of this Act, shall not be brought after the expiration of six years from the date on which the right of action accrued.

For the purposes of this subsection, the right of action shall not be treated as having accrued to any beneficiary entitled to a future interest in the trust property until the interest fell into possession.

(4) No beneficiary as against whom there would be a good defence under this Act shall derive any greater or other benefit from a judgment or order obtained by any other beneficiary than he could have obtained if he had brought the action and this Act had been pleaded in defence.

22   Time limit for actions claiming personal estate of a deceased person
Subject to section 21(1) and (2) of this Act –

(a) no action in respect of any claim to the personal estate of a deceased person or to any share or interest in any such estate (whether under a will or on intestacy) shall be brought after the expiration of twelve years from the date on which the right to receive the share or interest accrued; and

(b) no action to recover arrears of interest in respect of any legacy, or damages in respect of such arrears, shall be brought after the expiration of six years from the date on which the interest became due.

23   Time limit in respect of actions for an account
An action for an account shall not be brought after the expiration of any time limit under this Act which is applicable to the claim which is the basis of the duty to account.

PART II
EXTENSION OR EXCLUSION OF ORDINARY TIME LIMITS

28   Extension of limitation period in case of disability
(1) Subject to the following provisions of this section, if on the date when any right of action accrued for which a period of limitation is prescribed by this Act, the person to whom it accrued was under a disability, the action may be brought at any time before the expiration of six years from the date when he ceased to be under a disability or died (whichever first occurred) notwithstanding that the period of limitation has expired.
(2) This section shall not affect any case where the right of action first accrued to some person (not under a disability) through whom the person under a disability claims.
(3) When a right of action which has accrued to a person under a disability accrues, on the death of that person while still under a disability, to another person under a disability, no further extension of time shall be allowed by reason of the disability of the second person.
(4) No action to recover land or money charged on land shall be brought by virtue of this section by any person after the expiration of thirty years from the date on which the right of action accrued to that person or some person through whom he claims. ...
(5) If the action is one to which section 10 of this Act applies, subsection (1) above shall have effect as if for the words 'six years' there were substituted the words 'two years'. ...

32   Postponement of limitation period in case of fraud, concealment or mistake
(1) Subject to subsection (3) ... below, where in the case of any action for which a period of limitation is prescribed by this Act, either –

(a) the action is based upon the fraud of the defendant; or

(b) any fact relevant to the plaintiff's right of action has been deliberately concealed from him by the defendant; or

(c) the action is for relief from the consequences of a mistake;

the period of limitation shall not begin to run until the plaintiff has discovered the fraud, concealment or mistake (as the case may be) or could with reasonable diligence have discovered it. Reference in this subsection to the defendant include references to the defendant's agent and to any person through whom the defendant claims and his agent.
(2) For the purposes of subsection (1) above, deliberate commission of a breach of duty in circumstances in which it is unlikely to be discovered for some time amounts to deliberate concealment of the facts involved in that breach of duty.

(3) Nothing in this section shall enable any action –

    (a) to recover, or recover the value of, any property; or

    (b) to enforce any charge against, or set aside any transaction affecting, any property;

to be brought against the purchaser of the property or any person claiming through him in any case where the property has been purchased for valuable consideration by an innocent third party since the fraud or concealment or (as the case may be) the transaction in which the mistake was made took place.

(4) A purchaser is an innocent third party for the purposes of this section –

    (a) in the case of fraud or concealment of any fact relevant to the plaintiff's right of action, if he was not a party to the fraud or (as the case may be) to the concealment of that fact and did not at the time of the purchase know or have reason to believe that the fraud or concealment had taken place; and

    (b) in the case of mistake, if he did not at the time of the purchase know or have reason to believe that the mistake had been made. …

PART III

MISCELLANEOUS AND GENERAL

36   Equitable jurisdiction and remedies

(1) The following time limits under this Act, that is to say –

    (a) the time limit under section 2 for actions founded on tort;

    (aa) the time limit under section 4A for actions for libel or slander, or for slander of title, slander of goods or other malicious falsehood;

    (b) the time limit under section 5 for actions founded on simple contract;

    (c) the time limit under section 7 for actions to enforce awards where the submission is not by an instrument under seal;

    (d) the time limit under section 8 for actions on a specialty;

    (e) the time limit under section 9 for actions to recover a sum recoverable by virtue of any enactment; and

    (f) the time limit under section 24 for actions to enforce a judgment;

shall not apply to any claim for specific performance of a contract or for an injunction or for other equitable relief, except in so far as any such time limit may be applied by the court by analogy in like manner as the corresponding time limit under any enactment repealed by the Limitation Act 1939 was applied before 1 July 1940.

(2) Nothing in this Act shall affect any equitable jurisdiction to refuse relief on the ground of acquiescence or otherwise.

38   Interpretation

(1) In this Act, unless the context otherwise requires –

    'action' includes any proceeding in a court of law, including an ecclesiastical court; …

    'personal estate' and 'personal property' do not include chattels real; …

    'trust' and 'trustee' have the same meanings respectively as in the Trustee Act 1925; …

(2) For the purposes of this Act a person shall be treated as under a disability while he is an infant, or of unsound mind.

(3) For the purposes of subsection (2) above a person is of unsound mind if he is a person who, by reason of mental disorder is incapable of managing and administering his property and affairs; and in this section 'mental disorder' has the same meaning as in the Mental Health Act 1983.

(4) Without prejudice to the generality of subsection (3) above, a person shall be conclusively presumed for the purposes of subsection (2) above to be of unsound mind –

    (a) while he is liable to be detained or subject to guardianship under the Mental Health Act 1983 (otherwise than by virtue of section 35 or 89); and

    (b) while he is receiving treatment for mental disorder as an in-patient in any hospital within the meaning of the Mental Health Act 1983 or independent hospital or care home within the meaning of the Care Standards Act 2000 without being liable to be detained under the said Act of 1983 (otherwise than by virtue of section 35 or 89), being treatment which follows without any interval a period during which he was liable to be detained or subject to guardianship under the Mental Health Act 1959, or the said Act of 1983 (otherwise than by virtue of section 35 or 89) or by virtue of any enactment repealed or excluded by the Mental Health Act 1959.

(5) Subject to subsection (6) below, a person shall be treated as claiming through another person if he became entitled by, through, under, or by the act of that other person to the right claimed, and any person whose estate or interest might have been barred by a person entitled to an entailed interest in possession shall be treated as claiming through the person so entitled.

(6) A person becoming entitled to any estate or interest by virtue of a special power of appointment shall not be treated as claiming through the appointor. ...

(9) References in Part II of this Act to a right of action shall include references to –

    (a) a cause of action;

    (b) a right to receive money secured by a mortgage or charge on any property;

    (c) a right to recover proceeds of the sale of land; and

    (d) a right to receive a share or interest in the personal estate of a deceased person.

(10) References in Part II to the date of the accrual of a right of action shall be construed –

    (a) in the case of an action upon a judgment, as references to the date on which the judgment became enforceable; and

    (b) in the case of an action to recover arrears of rent or interest, or damages in respect of arrears of rent or interest, as references to the date on which the rent or interest became due.

As amended by the Mental Health Act 1983, s148, Schedule 4, para 55; Administration of Justice Act 1985, s57(5); Defamation Act 1996, s5(1), (5); Care Standards Act 2000, s116, Schedule 4, para 8.

SUPREME COURT ACT 1981

(1981 c 54)

37   Powers of High Court with respect to injunctions and receivers

(1) The High Court may by order (whether interlocutory or final) grant an injunction or appoint a receiver in all cases in which it appears to the court to be just and convenient to do so.

(2) Any such order may be made either unconditionally or on such terms and conditions as the court thinks just.

(3) The power of the High Court under subsection (1) to grant an interlocutory injunction restraining a party to any proceedings from removing from the jurisdiction of the High Court, or otherwise dealing with, assets located within that jurisdiction shall be exercisable in cases where the party is, as well as in cases where he is not, domiciled, resident or present within that jurisdiction.

(4) The power of the High Court to appoint a receiver by way of equitable execution shall operate in relation to all legal estates and interests in land; and that power –

    (a) may be exercised in relation to an estate or interest in land whether or not a charge has been imposed on that land under section 1 of the Charging Orders Act 1979 for the purpose of enforcing the judgment, order or award in question; and

    (b) shall be in addition to, and not in derogation of, any power of any court to appoint a receiver in proceedings for enforcing such a charge.

(5) Where an order under the said section 1 imposing a charge for the purpose of enforcing a judgment, order or award has been, or has effect as if, registered under section 6 of the Land Charges Act 1972, subsection (4) of the said section 6 (effect of non-registration of writs and orders registrable under that section) shall not apply to an order appointing a receiver made either –

    (a) in proceedings for enforcing the charge; or

    (b) by way of equitable execution of the judgment, order or award or, as the case may be, of so much of it as requires payment of moneys secured by the charge.

49   Concurrent administration of law and equity

(1) Subject to the provisions of this or any other Act, every court exercising jurisdiction in England or Wales in any civil cause or matter shall continue to administer law and equity on the basis that, wherever there is any conflict or variance between the rules of equity and the rules of the common law with reference to the same matter, the rules of equity shall prevail.

(2) Every such court shall give the same effect as hitherto –

    (a) to all equitable estates, titles, rights, reliefs, defences and counterclaims, and to all equitable duties and liabilities; and

    (b) subject thereto, to all legal claims and demands and all estates, titles, rights, duties, obligations and liabilities existing by the common law or by any custom or created by any statute,

and, subject to the provisions of this or any other Act, shall so exercise its jurisdiction in every cause or matter before it as to secure that, as far as possible, all matters in dispute between the parties are completely and finally determined, and all multiplicity of legal proceedings with respect to any of those matters is avoided.

(3) Nothing in this Act shall affect the power of the Court of Appeal or the High Court to stay any proceedings before it, where it thinks fit to do so, either of its own motion or on the application of any person, whether or not a party to the proceedings.

50   Power to award damages as well as, or in substitution for, injunction or specific performance

Where the Court of Appeal or the High Court has jurisdiction to entertain an application for an injunction or specific performance, it may award damages in addition to, or in substitution for, an injunction or specific performance.

ADMINISTRATION OF JUSTICE ACT 1985
(1985 c 61)

48   Power of High Court to authorise action to be taken in reliance on counsel's opinion

(1) Where –

    (a) any question of construction has arisen out of the terms of a will or a trust; and

(b) an opinion in writing given by a person who has a ten year High Court qualification, within the meaning of section 71 of the Courts and Legal Services Act 1990, has been obtained on that question by the personal representatives or trustees under the will or trust,

the High Court may, on the application of the personal representatives or trustees and without hearing argument, make an order authorising those persons to take such steps in reliance on the said opinion as are specified in the order.

(2) The High Court shall not make an order under subsection (1) if it appears to the court that a dispute exists which would make it inappropriate for the court to make the order without hearing argument.

50   Power of High Court to appoint substitute for, or to remove, personal representative

(1) Where an application relating to the estate of a deceased person is made to the High Court under this subsection by or on behalf of a personal representative of the deceased or a beneficiary of the estate, the court may in its discretion –

(a) appoint a person (in this section called a substituted personal representative) to act as personal representative of the deceased in place of the existing personal representative or representatives of the deceased or any of them; or

(b) if there are two or more existing personal representatives of the deceased, terminate the appointment of one or more, but not all, of those persons.

(3) The court may authorise a person appointed as a substituted personal representative to charge remuneration for his services as such, on such terms (whether or not involving the submission of bills of charges for taxation by the court) as the court may think fit. …

As amended by the Courts and Legal Services Act 1990, s71(2), Schedule 10, para 63.

LANDLORD AND TENANT ACT 1985
(1985 c 70)

17   Specific performance of landlord's repairing obligations

(1) In proceedings in which a tenant of a dwelling alleges a breach on the part of his landlord of a repairing covenant relating to any part of the premises in which the dwelling is comprised, the court may order specific performance of the covenant whether or not the breach relates to a part of the premises let to the tenant and notwithstanding any equitable rule restricting the scope of the remedy, whether on the basis of a lack of mutuality or otherwise.

(2) In this section –

(a) 'tenant' includes a statutory tenant,

(b) in relation to a statutory tenant the reference to the premises let to him is to the premises of which he is a statutory tenant,

(c) 'landlord', in relation to a tenant, includes any person against whom the tenant has a right to enforce a repairing covenant, and

(d) 'repairing covenant' means a covenant to repair, maintain, renew, construct or replace any property.

INSOLVENCY ACT 1986
(1986 c 45)

339 Transactions at an undervalue

(1) Subject as follows in this section and sections 341 and 342, where an individual is adjudged bankrupt and he has at a relevant time (defined in section 341) entered into a transaction with any person at an undervalue, the trustee of the bankrupt's estate may apply to the court for an order under this section.

(2) The court shall, on such an application, make such order as it thinks fit for restoring the position to what it would have been if that individual had not entered into that transaction.

(3) For the purposes of this section and sections 341 and 342, an individual enters into a transaction with a person at an undervalue if –

(a) he makes a gift to that person or he otherwise enters into a transaction with that person on terms that provide for him to receive no consideration,

(b) he enters into a transaction with that person in consideration of marriage or the formation of a civil partnership, or

(c) he enters into a transaction with that person for a consideration the value of which, in money or money's worth, is significantly less than the value, in money or money's worth, of the consideration provided by the individual.

340 Preferences

(1) Subject as follows in this and the next two sections, where an individual is adjudged bankrupt and he has at a relevant time (defined in section 341) given a preference to any person, the trustee of the bankrupt's estate may apply to the court for an order under this section.

(2) The court shall, on such an application, make such order as it thinks fit for restoring the position to what it would have been if that individual had not given that preference.

(3) For the purposes of this and the next two sections, an individual gives a preference to a person if –

(a) that person is one of the individual's creditors or a surety or guarantee for any of his debts or other liabilities, and

(b) the individual does anything or suffers anything to be done which (in either case) has the effect of putting that person into a position which, in the event of the individual's bankruptcy, will be better than the position he would have been in if that thing had not been done.

(4) The court shall not make an order under this section in respect of a preference given to any person unless the individual who gave the preference was influenced in deciding to give it by a desire to produce in relation to that person the effect mentioned in subsection (3)(b) above.

(5) An individual who has given a preference to a person who, at the time the preference was given, was an associate of his (otherwise than by reason only of being his employee) is presumed, unless the contrary is shown, to have been influenced in deciding to give it by such a desire as is mentioned in subsection (4).

(6) The fact that something has been done in pursuance of the order of a court does not, without more, prevent the doing or suffering of that thing from constituting the giving of a preference.

341 'Relevant time' under ss339, 340

(1) Subject as follows, the time at which an individual enters into a transaction at an undervalue or gives a preference is a relevant time if the transaction is entered into or the preference given –

(a) in the case of a transaction at an undervalue, at a time in the period of 5 years ending with the day of the presentation of the bankruptcy petition on which the individual is adjudged bankrupt,

(b) in the case of a preference which is not a transaction at an undervalue and is given to a person who is an associate of the individual (otherwise than by reason only of being his employee), at a time in the period of 2 years ending with that day, and

(c) in any other case of a preference which is not a transaction at an undervalue, at a time in the period of 6 months ending with that day.

(2) Where an individual enters into a transaction at an undervalue or gives a preference at a time mentioned in paragraph (a), (b) or (c) of subsection (1) (not being, in the case of a transaction at an undervalue, a time less than 2 years before the end of the period mentioned in paragraph (a)), that time is not a relevant time for the purposes of sections 339 and 340 unless the individual –

(a) is insolvent at that time, or

(b) becomes insolvent in consequence of the transaction or preference;

but the requirements of this subsection are presumed to be satisfied, unless the contrary is shown, in relation to any transaction at any undervalue which is entered into by an individual with a person who is an associate of his (otherwise than by reason only of being his employee).

(3) For the purposes of subsection (2), an individual is insolvent if –

(a) he is unable to pay his debts as they fall due, or

(b) the value of his assets is less than the amount of his liabilities, taking into account his contingent and prospective liabilities. …

342   Orders under ss339, 340

(1) Without prejudice to the generality of section 339(2) or 340(2), an order under either of those sections with respect to a transaction or preference entered into or given by an individual who is subsequently adjudged bankrupt may (subject as follows) –

(a) require any property transferred as part of the transaction, or in connection with the giving of the preference, to be vested in the trustee of the bankrupt's estate as part of that estate;

(b) require any property to be so vested if it represents in any person's hands the application either of the proceeds of sale of property so transferred or of money so transferred;

(c) release or discharge (in whole or in part) any security given by the individual;

(d) require any person to pay, in respect of benefits received by him from the individual, such sums to the trustee of his estate as the court may direct;

(e) provide for any surety or guarantor whose obligations to any person were released or discharged (in whole or in part) under the transaction or by the giving of the preference to be under such new or revived obligations to that person as the court thinks appropriate;

(f) provide for security to be provided for the discharge of any obligation imposed by or arising under the order, for such an obligation to be charged on any property and for the security or charge to have the same priority as a security or charge released or discharged (in whole or in part) under the transaction or by the giving of the preference; and

(g) provide for the extent to which any person whose property is vested by the order in the trustee of the bankrupt's estate, or on whom obligations are imposed by the order, is to be able to prove in the bankruptcy for debts or other liabilities which arose from, or were released or discharged (in whole or in part) under or by, the transaction or the giving of the preference.

(2) An order under section 339 or 340 may affect the property of, or impose any obligation on, any person whether or not he is the person with whom the individual in question entered into the transaction or, as the case may be, the person to whom the preference was given; but such an order –

    (a) shall not prejudice any interest in property which was acquired from a person other than that individual and was acquired in good faith and for value, or prejudice any interest deriving from such an interest, and

    (b) shall not require a person who received a benefit from the transaction or preference in good faith and for value, to pay a sum to the trustee of the bankrupt's estate, except where he was a party to the transaction or the payment is to be in respect of a preference given to that person at a time when he was a creditor of that individual.

(2A) Where a person has acquired an interest in property from a person other than the individual in question, or has received a benefit from the transaction or preference, and at the time of that acquisition or receipt –

    (a) he had notice of the relevant surrounding circumstances and of the relevant proceedings, or

    (b) he was an associate of, or was connected with, either the individual in question or the person with whom that individual entered into the transaction or to whom that individual gave the preference,

then, unless the contrary is shown, it shall be presumed for the purposes of paragraph (a) or (as the case may be) paragraph (b) of subsection (2) that the interest was acquired or the benefit was received otherwise than in good faith.

(3) Any sums required to be paid to the trustee in accordance with an order under section 339 or 340 shall be comprised in the bankrupt's estate.

(4) For the purposes of subsection (2A)(a), the relevant surrounding circumstances are (as the case may require) –

    (a) the fact that the individual in question entered into the transaction at an undervalue; or

    (b) the circumstances which amounted to the giving of the preference by the individual in question.

(5) For the purposes of subsection (2A)(a), a person has notice of the relevant proceedings if he has notice –

    (a) of the fact that the petition on which the individual in question is adjudged bankrupt has been presented; or

    (b) of the fact that the individual in question has been adjudged bankrupt.

(6) Section 249 ['connected' with a company] in Part VII of this Act shall apply for the purposes of subsection (2A)(b) as it applies for the purposes of the first Group of Parts.

423 Transactions defrauding creditors

(1) This section relates to transactions entered into at an undervalue; and a person enters into such a transaction with another person if –

    (a) he makes a gift to the other person or he otherwise enters into a transaction with the other on terms that provide for him to receive no consideration;

    (b) he enters into a transaction with the other in consideration of marriage or the formation of a civil partnership; or

    (c) he enters into a transaction with the other for a consideration the value of which, in money or money's worth, is significantly less than the value, in money or money's worth, of the consideration provided by himself.

(2) Where a person has entered into such a transaction, the court may, if satisfied under the next subsection, make such order as it thinks fit for –

    (a) restoring the position to what it would have been if the transaction had not been entered into, and

    (b) protecting the interests of persons who are victims of the transaction.

(3) In the case of a person entering into such a transaction, an order shall only be made if the court is satisfied that it was entered into by him for the purpose –

    (a) of putting assets beyond the reach of a person who is making, or may at some time make, a claim against him, or

    (b) of otherwise prejudicing the interests of such a person in relation to the claim which he is making or may make.

(4) In this section 'the court' means the High Court or –

    (a) if the person entering into the transaction is an individual, any other court which would have jurisdiction in relation to a bankruptcy petition relating to him;

    (b) if that person is a body capable of being wound up under Part IV or V of this Act, any other court having jurisdiction to wind it up.

(5) In relation to a transaction at an undervalue, references here and below to a victim of the transaction are to a person who is, or is capable of being, prejudiced by it; and in the following two sections the person entering into the transaction is referred to as 'the debtor'.

424 Those who may apply for an order under s423

(1) An application for an order under section 423 shall not be made in relation to a transcript except –

    (a) in a case where the debtor has been adjudged bankrupt or is a body corporate which is being wound up or is in administration, by the official receiver, by the trustee of the bankrupt's estate or the liquidator or administrator of the body corporate or (with the leave of the court) by a victim of the transaction;

    (b) in a case where a victim of the transaction is bound by a voluntary arrangement approved under Part I or Part VIII of this Act, by the supervisor of the voluntary arrangement or by any person who (whether or not so bound) is such a victim; or

    (c) in any other case, by a victim of the transaction.

(2) An application made under any of the paragraphs of subsection (1) is to be treated as made on behalf of every victim of the transaction.

425 Provision which may be made by order under s423

(1) Without prejudice to the generality of section 423, an order made under that section with respect to a transaction may (subject as follows) –

    (a) require any property transferred as part of the transaction to be vested in any person, either absolutely or for the benefit of all persons on whose behalf the application for the order is treated as made;

    (b) require any property to be so vested if it represents, in any person's hands, the application either of the proceeds of sale of property so transferred or of money so transferred;

    (c) release or discharge (in whole or in part) any security given by the debtor;

    (d) require any person to pay to any other person in respect of benefits received from the debtor such sums as the court may direct;

    (e) provide for any surety or guarantor whose obligations to any person were released or discharged (in whole or in part) under the transaction to be under such new or revived obligations as the court thinks appropriate;

(f) provide for security to be provided for the discharge of any obligation imposed by or arising under the order, for such an obligation to be charged on any property and for such security or charge to have the same priority as a security or charge released or discharged (in whole or in part) under the transaction.

(2) An order under section 423 may affect the property of, or impose any obligation on, any person whether or not he is the person with whom the debtor entered into the transaction; but such an order –

(a) shall not prejudice any interest in property which was acquired from a person other than the debtor and was acquired in good faith, for value and without notice of the relevant circumstances, or prejudice any interest deriving from such an interest, and

(b) shall not require a person who received a benefit from the transaction in good faith, for value and without notice of the relevant circumstances to pay any sum unless he was a party to the transaction.

(3) For the purposes of this section the relevant circumstances in relation to a transaction are the circumstances by virtue of which an order under section 423 may be made in respect of the transaction.

(4) In this section 'security' means any mortgage, charge, lien or other security.

As amended by the Insolvency (No 2) Act 1994, s2; Enterprise Act 2002, s248(3), Schedule 17, paras 9, 36; Civil Partnership Act 2004, s261(1), Schedule 27, paras 119, 121.

RECOGNITION OF TRUSTS ACT 1987
(1987 c 14)

1 Applicable law and recognition of trusts

(1) The provisions of the Convention set out in the Schedule to this Act shall have the force of law in the United Kingdom.

(2) Those provisions shall, so far as applicable, have effect not only in relation to the trusts described in Articles 2 and 3 of the Convention but also in relation to any other trusts of property arising under the law of any part of the United Kingdom or by virtue of a judicial decision whether in the United Kingdom or elsewhere.

(3) In accordance with Articles 15 and 16 such provisions of the law as are there mentioned shall, to the extent there specified, apply to the exclusion of the other provisions of the Convention.

(4) In Article 17 the reference to a State includes a reference to any country or territory (whether or not a party to the Convention and whether or not forming part of the United Kingdom) which has its own system of law.

(5) Article 22 shall not be construed as affecting the law to be applied in relation to anything done or omitted before the coming into force of this Act.

SCHEDULE

CONVENTION ON THE LAW APPLICABLE TO TRUSTS AND ON THEIR RECOGNITION

CHAPTER I – SCOPE

Article 1
This Convention specifies the law applicable to trusts and governs their recognition.

Article 2
For the purposes of this Convention, the term 'trust' refers to the legal relationship created – inter vivos or on death – by a person, the settlor, when assets have been placed under the control of a trustee for the benefit of a beneficiary or for a specified purpose. A trust has the following characteristics –

(a) the assets constitute a separate fund and are not a part of the trustee's own estate;

(b) title to the trust assets stands in the name of the trustee or in the name of another person on behalf of the trustee;

(c) the trustee has the power and the duty, in respect of which he is accountable, to manage, employ or dispose of the assets in accordance with the terms of the trust and the special duties imposed upon him by law.

The reservation by the settlor of certain rights and powers, and the fact that the trustee may himself have rights as a beneficiary, are not necessarily inconsistent with the existence of a trust.

Article 3
The Convention applies only to trusts created voluntarily and evidenced in writing.

Article 4
The Convention does not apply to preliminary issues relating to the validity of wills or of other acts by virtue of which assets are transferred to the trustee.

Article 5
The Convention does not apply to the extent that the law specified by Chapter II does not provide for trusts or the category of trusts involved

CHAPTER II – APPLICABLE LAW

Article 6
A trust shall be governed by the law chosen by the settlor. The choice must be express or be implied in the terms of the instrument creating or the writing evidencing the trust, interpreted, if necessary, in the light of the circumstances of the case.

Where the law chosen under the previous paragraph does not provide for trusts or the category of trusts involved, the choice shall not be effective and the law specified in Article 7 shall apply.

Article 7
Where no applicable law has been chosen, a trust shall be governed by the law with which it is most closely connected. In ascertaining the law with which a trust is most closely connected reference shall be made in particular to –

(a) the place of administration of the trust designated by the settlor;

(b) the situs of the assets of the trust;

    (c) the place of residence or business of the trustee;

    (d) the objects of the trust and the places where they are to be fulfilled.

Article 8

The law specified by Article 6 or 7 shall govern the validity of the trust, its construction, its effects and the administration of the trust. In particular that law shall govern –

    (a) the appointment, resignation and removal of trustees, the capacity to act as a trustee, and the devolution of the office of trustee;

    (b) the rights and duties of trustees among themselves;

    (c) the right of trustees to delegate in whole or in part the discharge of their duties or the exercise of their powers;

    (d) the power of trustees to administer or to dispose of trust assets, to create security interests in the trust assets, or to acquire new assets;

    (e) the powers of investment of trustees;

    (f) restrictions upon the duration of the trust, and upon the power to accumulate the income of the trust;

    (g) the relationships between the trustees and the beneficiaries including the personal liability of the trustees to the beneficiaries;

    (h) the variation of termination of the trust;

    (i) the distribution of the trust assets;

    (j) the duty of trustees to account for their administration.

Article 9

In applying this Chapter a severable aspect of the trust, particularly matters of administration, may be governed by a different law.

Article 10

The law applicable to the validity of the trust shall determine whether that law or the law governing a severable aspect of the trust may be replaced by another law.

CHAPTER III – RECOGNITION

Article 11

A trust created in accordance with the law specified by the preceding Chapter shall be recognised as a trust. Such recognition shall imply, as a minimum, that the trust property constitutes a separate fund, that the trustee may sue and be sued in his capacity as trustee, and that he may appear or act in this capacity before a notary or any person acting in an official capacity. In so far as the law applicable to the trust requires or provides, such recognition shall imply in particular –

    (a) that personal creditors of the trustee shall have no recourse against the trust assets;

    (b) that the trust assets shall not form part of the trustee's estate upon his insolvency or bankruptcy;

    (c) that the trust assets shall not form part of the matrimonial property of the trustee or his spouse nor part of the trustee's estate upon his death;

    (d) that the trust assets may be recovered when the trustee, in breach of trust, has mingled trust assets with his own property or his alienated trust assets. However, the rights and obligations of any third party holder of the assets shall remain subject to the law determined by the choice of law rules of the forum.

Article 12

Where the trustee desires to register assets, movable or immovable, or documents of title to them, he shall be entitled, in so far as this is not prohibited by or inconsistent with the law of the State where registration is sought, to do so in his capacity as trustee or in such other way that the existence of the trust is disclosed.

Article 14

The Convention shall not prevent the application of rules of law more favourable to the recognition of trusts.

CHAPTER IV – GENERAL CLAUSES

Article 15

The Convention does not prevent the application of provisions of the law designated by the conflicts rules of the forum, in so far as those provisions cannot be derogated from by voluntary act, relating in particular to the following matters –

   (a) the protection of minors and incapable parties;
   (b) the personal and proprietary effects of marriage;
   (c) succession rights, testate and intestate, especially the indefeasible shares of spouses and relatives;
   (d) the transfer of title to property and security interests in property;
   (e) the protection of creditors in matters of insolvency;
   (f) the protection, in other respects, of third parties acting in good faith.

If recognition of a trust is prevented by application of the preceding paragraph, the court shall try to give effect to the objects of the trust by other means.

Article 16

The Convention does not prevent the application of those provisions of the law of the forum which must be applied even to international situations, irrespective of rules of conflict of laws.

Article 17

In the Convention the word 'law' means the rules of law in force in a State other than its rules of conflict of laws.

Article 18

The provisions of the Convention may be disregarded when their application would be manifestly incompatible with public policy.

Article 22

The Convention applies to trusts regardless of the date on which they were created.

FAMILY LAW REFORM ACT 1987
(1987 c 42)

1   General principle

(1) In this Act and enactments passed and instruments made after the coming into force of this section, references (however expressed) to any relationship between two persons shall, unless the contrary intention appears, be construed without regard to whether or not the father and mother

of either of them, or the father and mother of any person through whom the relationship is deduced, have or had been married to each other at any time.

(2) In this Act and enactments passed after the coming into force of this section, unless the contrary intention appears –

(a)   references to a person whose father and mother were married to each other at the time of his birth include, and

(b)   references to a person whose father and mother were not married to each other at the time of his birth do not include,

references to any person to whom subsection (3) below applies, and cognate references shall be construed accordingly.

(3) This subsection applies to any person who –

(a)   is treated as legitimate by virtue of section 1 of the Legitimacy Act 1976;

(b)   is a legitimated person within the meaning of section 10 of that Act;

(c)   is an adopted person within the meaning of Chapter 4 of Part 1 of the Adoption and Children Act 2002; or

(d)   is otherwise treated in law as legitimate.

(4) For the purpose of construing references falling within subsection (2) above, the time of a person's birth shall be taken to include any time during the period beginning with –

(a)   the insemination resulting in his birth; or

(b)   where there was no such insemination, his conception,

and (in either case) ending with his birth.

19   Dispositions of property

(1) In the following dispositions, namely –

(a)   dispositions inter vivos made on or after the date on which this section comes into force; and

(b)   dispositions by will or codicil where the will or codicil is made on or after that date,

references (whether express or implied) to any relationship between two persons shall be construed in accordance with section 1 above.

(2) It is hereby declared that the use, without more, of the word 'heir' or 'heirs' or any expression purporting to create an entailed interest in real or personal property does not show a contrary intention for the purposes of section 1 as applied by subsection (1) above.

(3) In relation to the dispositions mentioned in subsection (1) above, section 33 of the Trustee Act 1925 (which specifies the trust implied by a direction that income is to be held on protective trusts for the benefit of any person) shall have effect as if any reference (however expressed) to any relationship between two persons were construed in accordance with section 1 above. ...

(6) In this section 'disposition' means a disposition, including an oral disposition, of real or personal property whether inter vivos or by will or codicil.

(7) Notwithstanding any rule of law, a disposition made by will or codicil executed before the date on which this section comes into force shall not be treated for the purposes of this section as made on or after that date by reason only that the will or codicil is confirmed by a codicil executed on or after that date.

As amended by the Trusts of Land and Appointment of Trustees Act 1996, s25(1), Schedule 3, para 25; Adoption and Children Act 2002, s139(1), Schedule 3, paras 50, 51.

LAW OF PROPERTY (MISCELLANEOUS PROVISIONS) ACT 1989

(1989 c 34)

2 Contracts for sale, etc of land to be made by signed writing

(1) A contract for the sale or other disposition of an interest in land can only be made in writing and only by incorporating all the terms which the parties have expressly agreed in one document or, where contracts are exchanged, in each.

(2) The terms may be incorporated in a document either by being set out in it or by reference to some other document.

(3) The document incorporating the terms or, where contracts are exchanged, one of the documents incorporating them (but not necessarily the same one) must be signed by or on behalf of each party to the contract.

(4) Where a contract for the sale or other disposition of an interest in land satisfied the conditions of this section by reason only of the rectification of one or more documents in pursuance of an order of a court, the contract shall come into being, or be deemed to have come into being, at such time as may be specified in the order.

(5) This section does not apply in relation to –

    (a)   a contract to grant such a lease as is mentioned in section 54(2) of the Law of Property Act 1925 (short leases);

    (b)   a contract made in the course of a public auction; or

    (c)   a contract regulated under the Financial Services and Markets Act 2000, other than a regulated mortgage contract, a regulated home reversion plan or a regulated home purchase plan;

and nothing in this section affects the creation or operation of resulting, implied or constructive trusts.

(6) In this section –

'disposition' has the same meaning as in the Law of Property Act 1925;

'interest in land' means any estate, interest or charge in or over land;

'regulated mortgage contract', 'regulated home reversion plan' and 'regulated home purchase plan' must be read with –

    (a)   section 22 of the Financial Services and Markets Act 2000,

    (b)   any relevant order under that section, and

    (c)   Schedule 22 to that Act.

(7) Nothing in this section shall apply in relation to contracts made before this section comes into force.

(8) Section 40 of the Law of Property Act 1925 (which is superseded by this section) shall cease to have effect.

As amended by the Trusts of Land and Appointment of Trustees Act 1996, s25(2), Schedule 4; Financial Services and Markets Act 2000 (Consequential Amendments and Repeals) Order 2001, art 317; Financial Services and Markets Act 2000 (Regulated Activities) (Amendment) (No 2) Order 2006, art 27(a), (b).

CHARITIES ACT 1993

(1993 c 10)

PART I

THE CHARITY COMMISSION AND THE OFFICIAL CUSTODIAN FOR CHARITIES

1A   The Charity Commission

(1) There shall be a body corporate to be known as the Charity Commission for England and Wales (in this Act referred to as 'the Commission').

(2) In Welsh the Commission shall be known as 'Comisiwn Elusennau Cymru a Lloegr'.

(3) The functions of the Commission shall be performed on behalf of the Crown.

(4) In the exercise of its functions the Commission shall not be subject to the direction or control of any Minister of the Crown or other government department.

(5) But subsection (4) above does not affect –

  (a) any provision made by or under any enactment;

  (b) any administrative controls exercised over the Commission's expenditure by the Treasury.

(6) The provisions of Schedule 1A to this Act shall have effect with respect to the Commission.

[See Appendix, Charities Act 2006, s7.]

2   The official custodian for charities

(1) There shall continue to be an officer known as the official custodian for charities (in this Act referred to as 'the official custodian') whose function it shall be to act as trustee for charities in the cases provided for by this Act; and the official custodian shall be by that name a corporation sole having perpetual succession and using an official seal which shall be officially and judicially noticed.

(2) Such individual as the Commission may from time to time designate shall be the official custodian.

(3) The official custodian shall perform his duties in accordance with such general or special directions as may be given him by the Commission, and his expenses (except those re-imbursed to him or recovered by him as trustee for any charity) shall be defrayed by the Commission.

(4) Anything which is required to or may be done by, to or before the official custodian may be done by, to or before any member of the staff of the Commission generally or specially authorised by it to act for him during a vacancy in his office or otherwise.

(5) The official custodian shall not be liable as trustee for any charity in respect of any loss or of the mis-application of any property unless it is occasioned by or through the wilful neglect or default of the custodian or of any person acting for him; but the Consolidated Fund shall be liable to make good to a charity any sums for which the custodian may be liable by reason of any such neglect or default. ...

PART II

REGISTRATION AND NAMES OF CHARITIES:

3   The register of charities

(1) The Commissioners shall continue to keep a register of charities, which shall be kept by them in such manner as they think fit.

(2) There shall be entered in the register every charity not excepted by subsection (5) below; and a charity so excepted (other than one excepted by paragraph (a) of that subsection) may be entered in the register at the request of the charity, but (whether or not it was excepted at the time of registration) may at any time, and shall at the request of the charity, be removed from the register.

(3) The register shall contain –

(a) the name of every registered charity; and

(b) such other particulars of, and such other information relating to, every such charity as the Commissioners think fit.

(4) Any institution which no longer appears to the Commissioners to be a charity shall be removed from the register, with effect, where the removal is due to any change in its purposes or trusts, from the date of that change; and there shall also be removed from the register any charity which ceases to exist or does not operate.

(5) The following charities are not required to be registered –

(a) any charity comprised in Schedule 2 to this Act (in this Act referred to as an 'exempt charity');

(b) any charity which is excepted by order or regulations;

(c) any charity whose gross income does not exceed £5,000;

and no charity is required to be registered in respect of any registered place of worship.

(5A) In subsection (5) above, paragraph (a) shall be read as referring also to –

(a) any higher education corporation within the meaning of the Education Reform Act 1988, and

(b) any further education corporation within the meaning of the Further and Higher Education Act 1992.

(5B) In addition, in subsection (5) above –

(a) paragraph (a) shall be read as referring also to –

(i) any body to which section 23(1)(a) or (b) of the School Standards and Framework Act 1998 applies, and

(ii) any Education Action Forum established by virtue of section 10(1) of that Act; and

(b) paragraph (b) shall be read as referring also to any foundation to which section 2(3) of that Act applies;

but an order of the Commissioners, or regulations made by the Secretary of State, may provide that section 23(3) of that Act shall cease to apply to any such foundation as is mentioned in that provision or to any such foundation of a description specified in the order or regulations.

(6) With any application for a charity to be registered there shall be supplied to the Commissioners copies of its trusts (or, if they are not set out in any extant document, particulars of them), and such other documents or information as may be prescribed by regulations made by the Minister or as the Commissioners may require for the purpose of the application.

(7) It shall be the duty –

(a) of the charity trustees of any charity which is not registered nor excepted from registration to apply for it to be registered, and to supply the documents and information required by subsection (6) above; and

(b) of the charity trustees (or last charity trustees) of any institution which is for the time being registered to notify the Commissioners if it ceases to exist, or if there is any change in its trusts or in the particulars of it entered in the register, and to supply to the Commissioners particulars of any such change and copies of any new trusts or alterations of the trusts.

(8) The register (including the entries cancelled when institutions are removed from the register) shall be open to public inspection at all reasonable times; and copies (or particulars) of the trusts of any registered charity as supplied to the Commissioners under this section shall, so long as it

remains on the register, be kept by them and be open to public inspection at all reasonable times, except in so far as regulations made by the Minister otherwise provide.

(9) Where any information contained in the register is not in documentary form, subsection (8) above shall be construed as requiring the information to be available for public inspection in legible form at all reasonable times.

(10) If the Commissioners so determine, subsection (8) above shall not apply to any particular information contained in the register and specified in their determination.

(11) Nothing in the foregoing subsections shall require any person to supply the Commissioners with copies of schemes for the administration of a charity made otherwise than by the court, or to notify the Commissioners of any change made with respect to a registered charity by such a scheme, or require a person, if he refers the Commissioners to a document or copy already in the possession of the Commissioners, to supply a further copy of the document; but where by virtue of this subsection a copy of any document need not be supplied to the Commissioners, a copy of it, if it relates to a registered charity, shall be open to inspection under subsection (8) above as if supplied to the Commissioners under this section.

(12) If the Minister thinks it expedient to do so –

    (a) in consequence of changes in the value of money, or

    (b) with a view to extending the scope of the exception provided for by subsection (5)(c) above,

he may by order amend subsection (5)(c) by substituting a different sum for the sum for the time being specified there.

(13) The reference in subsection (5)(b) above to a charity which is excepted by order or regulations is to a charity which –

    (a) is for the time being permanently or temporarily excepted by order of the Commissioners; or

    (b) is of a description permanently or temporarily excepted by regulations made by the Minister,

and which complies with any conditions of the exception.

(13A) In this section any reference to a charity's 'gross income' shall be construed, in relation to a particular time –

    (a) as a reference to the charity's gross income in its financial year immediately preceding that time, or

    (b) if the Commission so determines, as a reference to the amount which the Commission estimates to be the likely amount of the charity's gross income in such financial year of the charity as is specified in the determination.

(14) In this section 'registered place of worship' means any land or building falling within section 9 of the Places of Worship Registration Act 1855 (that is to say, the land and buildings which if the Charities Act 1960 had not been passed, would by virtue of that section as amended by subsequent enactments be partially exempted from the operation of the Charitable Trusts Act 1853), and for the purposes of this subsection 'building' includes part of a building.

[See Appendix, Charities Act 2006, s9.]

4   Effect of, and claims and objections to, registration

(1) An institution shall for all purposes other than rectification of the register be conclusively presumed to be or to have been a charity at any time when it is or was on the register of charities.

(2) Any person who is or may be affected by the registration of an institution as a charity may, on the ground that it is not a charity, object to its being entered by the Commission in the register, or apply to the Commission for it to be removed from the register; and provision may

be made by regulations made by the Minister as to the manner in which any such objection or application is to be made, prosecuted or dealt with.

(3) An appeal against any decision of the Commission to enter or not to enter an institution in the register of charities, or to remove or not to remove an institution from the register, may be brought in the High Court by the Attorney General, or by the persons who are or claim to be the charity trustees of the institution, or by any person whose objection or application under subsection (2) above is disallowed by the decision.

(4) If there is an appeal to the High Court against any decision of the Commission to enter an institution in the register, or not to remove an institution from the register, then until the Commission is satisfied whether the decision of the Commission is or is not to stand, the entry in the register shall be maintained, but shall be in suspense and marked to indicate that it is in suspense; and for the purposes of subsection (1) above an institution shall be deemed not to be on the register during any period when the entry relating to it is in suspense under this subsection.

(5) Any question affecting the registration or removal from the register of an institution may, notwithstanding that it has been determined by a decision on appeal under subsection (3) above, be considered afresh by the Commission and shall not be concluded by that decision, if it appears to the Commission that there has been a change of circumstances or that the decision is inconsistent with a later judicial decision, whether given on such an appeal or not.

[See Appendix, Charities Act 2006, Schedule 8, paras 96, 99(3), (4)(a), (5)(a), (c).]

6   Power of Commission to require charity's name to be changed

(1) Where this subsection applies to a charity, the Commission may give a direction requiring the name of the charity to be changed, within such period as is specified in the direction, to such other name as the charity trustees may determine with the approval of the Commission.

(2) Subsection (1) above applies to a charity if –

(a) it is a registered charity and its name ('the registered name') –
  (i)   is the same as, or
  (ii) is in the opinion of the Commission too like,
  the name, at the time when the registered name was entered in the register in respect of the charity, of any other charity (whether registered or not);

(b) the name of the charity is in the opinion of the Commission likely to mislead the public as to the true nature –
  (i)   of the purposes of the charity as set out in its trusts, or
  (ii) of the activities which the charity carries on under its trusts in pursuit of those purposes;

(c) the name of the charity includes any word or expression for the time being specified in regulations made by the Minister and the inclusion in its name of that word or expression is in the opinion of the Commission likely to mislead the public in any respect as to the status of the charity;

(d) the name of the charity is in the opinion of the Commission likely to give the impression that the charity is connected in some way with Her Majesty's Government or any local authority, or with any other body of persons or any individual, when it is not so connected; or

(e) the name of the charity is in the opinion of the Commission offensive;

and in this subsection any reference to the name of a charity is, in relation to a registered charity, a reference to the name by which it is registered.

(3) Any direction given by virtue of subsection (2)(a) above must be given within twelve months of the time when the registered name was entered in the register in respect of the charity.

(4) Any direction given under this section with respect to a charity shall be given to the charity trustees; and on receiving any such direction the charity trustees shall give effect to it notwithstanding anything in the trusts of the charity.

(5) Where the name of any charity is changed under this section, then (without prejudice to section 3(7)(b) above) it shall be the duty of the charity trustees forthwith to notify the Commission of the charity's new name and of the date on which the change occurred.

(6) A change of name by a charity under this section does not affect any rights or obligations of the charity; and any legal proceedings that might have been continued or commenced by or against it in its former name may be continued or commenced by or against it in its new name.

(7) Section 26(3) of the Companies Act 1985 (minor variations in names to be disregarded) shall apply for the purposes of this section as if the reference to section 26(1)(c) of that Act were a reference to subsection (2)(a) above.

(8) Any reference in this section to the charity trustees of a charity shall, in relation to a charity which is a company, be read as a reference to the directors of the company.

(9) Nothing in this section applies to an exempt charity.

[See Appendix, Charities Act 2006, Schedule 8, para 100(1), (3).]

7   Effect of direction under s6 where charity is a company

(1) Where any direction is given under section 6 above with respect to a charity which is a company, the direction shall be taken to require the name of the charity to be changed by resolution of the directors of the company.

(2) Section 380 of the Companies Act 1985 (registration etc of resolutions and agreements) shall apply to any resolution passed by the directors in compliance with any such direction.

(3) Where the name of such a charity is changed in compliance with any such direction, the registrar of companies –

>   (a) shall, subject to section 26 of the Companies Act 1985 (prohibition on registration of certain names), enter the new name on the register of companies in place of the former name, and
>
>   (b) shall issue a certificate of incorporation altered to meet the circumstances of the case;

and the change of name has effect from the date on which the altered certificate is issued.

PART III

INFORMATION POWERS

8   General power to institute inquiries

(1) The Commission may from time to time institute inquiries with regard to charities or a particular charity or class of charities, either generally or for particular purposes, but no such inquiry shall extend to any exempt charity.

(2) The Commission may either conduct such an inquiry itself or appoint a person to conduct it and make a report to the Commission.

(3) For the purposes of any such inquiry the Commission, or a person appointed by the Commission to conduct it, may direct any person (subject to the provisions of this section) –

>   (a) to furnish accounts and statements in writing with respect to any matter in question at the inquiry, being a matter on which he has or can reasonably obtain information, or to return answers in writing to any questions or inquiries addressed to him on any such matter, and to verify any such accounts, statements or answers by statutory declaration;

    (b)   to furnish copies of documents in his custody or under his control which relate to any matter in question at the inquiry, and to verify any such copies by statutory declaration;

    (c)   to attend at a specified time and place and give evidence or produce any such documents.

(4) For the purposes of any such inquiry evidence may be taken on oath, and the person conducting the inquiry may for that purpose administer oaths, or may instead of administering an oath require the person examined to make and subscribe a declaration of the truth of the matters about which he is examined.

(5) The Commission may pay to any person the necessary expenses of his attendance to give evidence or produce documents for the purpose of an inquiry under this section, and a person shall not be required in obedience to a direction under paragraph (c) of subsection (3) above to go more than ten miles from his place of residence unless those expenses are paid or tendered to him.

(6) Where an inquiry has been held under this section, the Commission may either –

    (a)   cause the report of the person conducting the inquiry, or such other statement of the results of the inquiry as the Commission thinks fit, to be printed and published, or

    (b)   publish any such report or statement in some other way which is calculated in the Commission's opinion to bring it to the attention of persons who may wish to make representations to the Commission about the action to be taken.

(7) The council of a county or district, the Common Council of the City of London and the council of a London borough may contribute to the expenses of the Commission in connection with inquiries under this section into local charities in the council's area.

[See Appendix, Charities Act 2006, Schedule 5, para 2.]

9   Power to call for documents and search records

(1) The Commission may by order –

    (a)   require any person to furnish the Commission with any information in his possession which relates to any charity and is relevant to the discharge of the Commission's functions or of the functions of the official custodian;

    (b)   require any person who has in his custody or under his control any document which relates to any charity and is relevant to the discharge of the Commission's functions or of the functions of the official custodian –

        (i)   to furnish the Commission with a copy of or extract from the document, or

        (ii)   (unless the document forms part of the records or other documents of a court or of a public or local authority) to transmit the document itself to the Commission for its inspection.

(2) Any member of the staff of the Commission, if so authorised by it, shall be entitled without payment to inspect and take copies of or extracts from the records or other documents of any court, or of any public registry or office of records, for any purpose connected with the discharge of the functions of the Commission or of the official custodian.

(3) The Commission shall be entitled without payment to keep any copy or extract furnished to it under subsection (1) above; and where a document transmitted to the Commission under that subsection for it to inspect relates only to one or more charities and is not held by any person entitled as trustee or otherwise to the custody of it, the Commission may keep it or may deliver it to the charity trustees or to any other person who may be so entitled.

(4) No person properly having the custody of documents relating only to an exempt charity shall be required under subsection (1) above to transmit to the Commissioners any of those documents, or to furnish any copy of or extract from any of them.

(5) The rights conferred by subsection (2) above shall, in relation to information recorded otherwise than in legible form, include the right to require the information to be made available in legible form for inspection or for a copy or extract to be made of or from it.

(6) In subsection (2) the reference to a member of the staff of the Commission includes the official custodian even if he is not a member of the staff of the Commission.

[See Appendix, Charities Act 2006, Schedule 5, para 3, Schedule 9.]

PART IV

APPLICATION OF PROPERTY CY-PRÈS AND ASSISTANCE AND SUPERVISION OF CHARITIES BY COURT AND COMMISSION

13   Occasions for applying property cy-près

(1) Subject to subsection (2) below, the circumstances in which the original purposes of a charitable gift can be altered to allow the property given or part of it to be applied cy-près shall be as follows –

  (a) where the original purposes, in whole or in part –
    (i)   have been as far as may be fulfilled; or
    (ii) cannot be carried out, or not according to the directions given and to the spirit of the gift; or
  (b) where the original purposes provide a use for part only of the property available by virtue of the gift; or
  (c) where the property available by virtue of the gift and other property applicable for similar purposes can be more effectively used in conjunction, and to that end can suitably, regard being had to the spirit of the gift, be made applicable to common purposes; or
  (d) where the original purposes were laid down by reference to an area which then was but has since ceased to be a unit for some other purpose, or by reference to a class of persons or to an area which has for any reason since ceased to be suitable, regard being had to the spirit of the gift, or to be practical in administering the gift; or
  (e) where the original purposes, in whole or in part, have, since they were laid down, –
    (i)   been adequately provided for by other means; or
    (ii) ceased, as being useless or harmful to the community or for other reasons, to be in law charitable; or
    (iii) ceased in any other way to provide a suitable and effective method of using the property available by virtue of the gift, regard being had to the spirit of the gift.

(2) Subsection (1) above shall not affect the conditions which must be satisfied in order that property given for charitable purposes may be applied cy-près except in so far as those conditions require a failure of the original purposes.

(3) References in the foregoing subsections to the original purposes of a gift shall be construed, where the application of the property given has been altered or regulated by a scheme or otherwise, as referring to the purposes for which the property is for the time being applicable.

(4) Without prejudice to the power to make schemes in circumstances falling within subsection (1) above, the court may by scheme made under the court's jurisdiction with respect to charities, in any case where the purposes for which the property is held are laid down by reference to any such area as is mentioned in the first column in Schedule 3 to this Act, provide for enlarging the area to any such area as is mentioned in the second column in the same entry in that Schedule.

(5) It is hereby declared that a trust for charitable purposes places a trustee under a duty, where

the case permits and requires the property or some part of it to be applied cy-près, to secure its effective use for charity by taking steps to enable it to be so applied.

[See Appendix, Charities Act 2006, ss15–18.]

14   Application cy-près of gifts of donors unknown or disclaiming

(1) Property given for specific charitable purposes which fail shall be applicable cy-près as if given for charitable purposes generally, where it belongs –

  (a) to a donor who after –

     (i)   the prescribed advertisements and inquiries have been published and made, and

     (ii) the prescribed period beginning with the publication of those advertisements has expired,

  cannot be identified or cannot be found; or

  (b) to a donor who has executed a disclaimer in the prescribed form of his right to have the property returned.

(2) Where the prescribed advertisements and inquiries have been published and made by or on behalf of trustees with respect to any such property, the trustees shall not be liable to any person in respect of the property if no claim by him to be interested in it is received by them before the expiry of the period mentioned in subsection (1)(a)(ii) above.

(3) For the purposes of this section property shall be conclusively presumed (without any advertisement or inquiry) to belong to donors who cannot be identified, in so far as it consists –

  (a) of the proceeds of cash collections made by means of collecting boxes or by other means not adapted for distinguishing one gift from another; or

  (b) of the proceeds of any lottery, competition, entertainment, sale or similar money-raising activity, after allowing for property given to provide prizes or articles for sale or otherwise to enable the activity to be undertaken.

(4) The court may by order direct that property not falling within subsection (3) above shall for the purposes of this section be treated (without any advertisement or inquiry) as belonging to donors who cannot be identified where it appears to the court either –

  (a) that it would be unreasonable, having regard to the amounts likely to be returned to the donors, to incur expense with a view to returning the property; or

  (b) that it would be unreasonable, having regard to the nature, circumstances and amounts of the gifts, and to the lapse of time since the gifts were made, for the donors to expect the property to be returned.

(5) Where property is applied cy-près by virtue of this section, the donor shall be deemed to have parted with all his interest at the time when the gift was made; but where property is so applied as belonging to donors who cannot be identified or cannot be found, and is not so applied by virtue of subsection (3) or (4) above –

  (a) the scheme shall specify the total amount of that property; and

  (b) the donor of any part of that amount shall be entitled, if he makes a claim not later than six months after the date on which the scheme is made, to recover from the charity for which the property is applied a sum equal to that part, less any expenses properly incurred by the charity trustees after that date in connection with claims relating to his gift; and

  (c) the scheme may include directions as to the provision to be made for meeting any such claim.

(6) Where –

  (a) any sum is, in accordance with any such directions, set aside for meeting any such claims, but

(b) the aggregate amount of any such claims actually made exceeds the relevant amount, then, if the Commission so directs, each of the donors in question shall be entitled only to such proportion of the relevant amount as the amount of his claim bears to the aggregate amount referred to in paragraph (b) above; and for this purpose 'the relevant amount' means the amount of the sum so set aside after deduction of any expenses properly incurred by the charity trustees in connection with claims relating to the donors' gifts.

(7) For the purposes of this section, charitable purposes shall be deemed to 'fail' where any difficulty in applying property to those purposes makes that property or the part not applicable cy-près available to be returned to the donors.

(8) In this section 'prescribed' means prescribed by regulations made by the Commission; and such regulations may, as respects the advertisements which are to be published for the purposes of subsection (1)(a) above, make provision as to the form and content of such advertisements as well as the manner in which they are to be published.

(9) Any regulations made by the Commission under this section shall be published by the Commission in such manner as it thinks fit.

(10) In this section, except in so far as the context otherwise requires, references to a donor include persons claiming through or under the original donor, and references to property given include the property for the time being representing the property originally given or property derived from it.

(11) This section shall apply to property given for charitable purposes, notwithstanding that it was so given before the commencement of this Act.

[See Appendix, Charities Act 2006, s16.]

15   Charities governed by charter, or by or under statute

(1) Where a Royal charter establishing or regulating a body corporate is amendable by the grant and acceptance of a further charter, a scheme relating to the body corporate or to the administration of property held by the body (including a scheme for the cy-près application of any such property) may be made by the court under the court's jurisdiction with respect to charities notwithstanding that the scheme cannot take effect without the alteration of the charter, but shall be so framed that the scheme, or such part of it as cannot take effect without the alteration of the charter, does not purport to come into operation unless or until Her Majesty thinks fit to amend the charter in such manner as will permit the scheme or that part of it to have effect.

(2) Where under the court's jurisdiction with respect to charities or the corresponding jurisdiction of a court in Northern Ireland, or under powers conferred by this Act or by any Northern Ireland legislation relating to charities, a scheme is made with respect to a body corporate, and it appears to Her Majesty expedient, having regard to the scheme, to amend any Royal charter relating to that body, Her Majesty may, on the application of that body, amend the charter accordingly by Order in Council in any way in which the charter could be amended by the grant and acceptance of a further charter; and any such Order in Council may be revoked or varied in like manner as the charter it amends.

(3) The jurisdiction of the court with respect to charities shall not be excluded or restricted in the case of a charity of any description mentioned in Schedule 4 to this Act by the operation of the enactments or instruments there mentioned in relation to that description, and a scheme established for any such charity may modify or supersede in relation to it the provision made by any such enactment or instrument as if made by a scheme of the court, and may also make any such provision as is authorised by that Schedule.

16 Concurrent jurisdiction with High Court for certain purposes

(1) Subject to the provisions of this Act, the Commission may by order exercise the same jurisdiction and powers as are exercisable by the High Court in charity proceedings for the following purposes –

(a) establishing a scheme for the administration of a charity;

(b) appointing, discharging or removing a charity trustee or trustee for a charity, or removing an officer or employee;

(c) vesting or transferring property, or requiring or entitling any person to call for or make any transfer of property or any payment.

(2) Where the court directs a scheme for the administration of a charity to be established, the court may by order refer the matter to the Commission for it to prepare or settle a scheme in accordance with such directions (if any) as the court sees fit to give, and any such order may provide for the scheme to be put into effect by order of the Commission as if prepared under subsection (1) above and without any further order of the court.

(3) The Commission shall not have jurisdiction under this section to try or determine the title at law or in equity to any property as between a charity or trustee for a charity and a person holding or claiming the property or an interest in it adversely to the charity, or to try or determine any question as to the existence or extent of any charge or trust.

(4) Subject to the following subsections, the Commission shall not exercise its jurisdiction under this section as respects any charity, except –

(a) on the application of the charity; or

(b) on an order of the court under subsection (2) above; or

(c) in the case of a charity other than an exempt charity, on the application of the Attorney General.

(5) In the case of a charity which is not an exempt charity and whose gross income does not exceed £500 a year, the Commission may exercise its jurisdiction under this section on the application –

(a) of any one or more of the charity trustees; or

(b) of any person interested in the charity; or

(c) of any two or more inhabitants of the area of the charity if it is a local charity.

(6) Where in the case of a charity, other than an exempt charity, the Commission is satisfied that the charity trustees ought in the interests of the charity to apply for a scheme, but have unreasonably refused or neglected to do so and the Commission has given the charity trustees an opportunity to make representations to them, the Commission may proceed as if an application for a scheme had been made by the charity but the Commission shall not have power in a case where it acts by virtue of this subsection to alter the purposes of a charity, unless forty years have elapsed from the date of its foundation.

(7) Where –

(a) a charity cannot apply to the Commission for a scheme by reason of any vacancy among the charity trustees or the absence or incapacity of any of them, but

(b) such an application is made by such number of the charity trustees as the Commission considers appropriate in the circumstances of the case,

the Commission may nevertheless proceed as if the application were an application made by the charity.

(8) The Commission may on the application of any charity trustee or trustee for a charity exercise its jurisdiction under this section for the purpose of discharging him from his trusteeship.

(9) Before exercising any jurisdiction under this section otherwise than on an order of the court, the Commission shall give notice of its intention to do so to each of the charity trustees, except

any that cannot be found or has no known address in the United Kingdom or who is party or privy to an application for the exercise of the jurisdiction; and any such notice may be given by post, and, if given by post, may be addressed to the recipient's last known address in the United Kingdom.

(10) The Commission shall not exercise its jurisdiction under this section in any case (not referred to them by order of the court) which, by reason of its contentious character, or of any special question of law or of fact which it may involve, or for other reasons, the Commission may consider more fit to be adjudicated on by the court.

(11) An appeal against any order of the Commissioners under this section may be brought in the High Court by the Attorney General.

(12) An appeal against any order of the Commissioners under this section may also, at any time within the three months beginning with the day following that on which the order is published, be brought in the High Court by the charity or any of the charity trustees, or by any person removed from any office or employment by the order (unless he is removed with the concurrence of the charity trustees or with the approval of the special visitor, if any, of the charity).

(13) No appeal shall be brought under subsection (12) above except with a certificate of the Commissioners that it is a proper case for an appeal or with the leave of one of the judges of the High Court attached to the Chancery Division.

(14) Where an order of the Commissioners under this section establishes a scheme for the administration of a charity, any person interested in the charity shall have the like right of appeal under subsection (12) above as a charity trustee, and so also, in the case of a charity which is a local charity in any area, shall any two or more inhabitants of the area and the council of any parish or (in Wales) any community comprising the area or any part of it.

(15) If the Minister thinks it expedient to do so –

    (a) in consequence of changes in the value of money, or

    (b) with a view to increasing the number of charities in respect of which the Commission may exercise its jurisdiction under this section in accordance with subsection (5) above,

he may by order amend that subsection by substituting a different sum for the sum for the time being specified there.

[See Appendix, Charities Act 2006, Schedule 5, paras 1, 4, Schedule 8, paras 96, 109(1), (12), Schedule 9.]

17   Further powers to make schemes or alter application of charitable property

(1) Where it appears to the Commission that a scheme should be established for the administration of a charity, but also that it is necessary or desirable for the scheme to alter the provision made by an Act of Parliament establishing or regulating the charity or to make any other provision which goes or might go beyond the powers exercisable by the Commission apart from this section, or that it is for any reason proper for the scheme to be subject to parliamentary review, then (subject to subsection (6) below) the Commission may settle a scheme accordingly with a view to its being given effect under this section.

(2) A scheme settled by the Commission under this section may be given effect by order of the Minister, and a draft of the order shall be laid before Parliament. ...

18   Power to act for protection of charities

(1) Where, at any time after it has instituted an inquiry under section 8 above with respect to any charity, the Commission is satisfied –

    (a) that there is or has been any misconduct or mismanagement in the administration of the charity; or

    (b) that it is necessary or desirable to act for the purpose of protecting the property of the charity or securing a proper application for the purposes of the charity of that property or of property coming to the charity,

the Commission may of its own motion do one or more of the following things –

    (i)   by order suspend any trustee, charity trustee, officer, agent or employee of the charity from the exercise of his office or employment pending consideration being given to his removal (whether under this section or otherwise);

    (ii) by order appoint such number of additional charity trustees as it considers necessary for the proper administration of the charity;

    (iii) by order vest any property held by or in trust for the charity in the official custodian, or require the persons in whom any such property is vested to transfer it to him, or appoint any person to transfer any such property to him;

    (iv) order any person who holds any property on behalf of the charity, or of any trustee for it, not to part with the property without the approval of the Commission;

    (v) order any debtor of the charity not to make any payment in or towards the discharge of his liability to the charity without the approval of the Commission;

    (vi) by order restrict (notwithstanding anything in the trusts of the charity) the transactions which may be entered into, or the nature or amount of the payments which may be made, in the administration of the charity without the approval of the Commission;

    (vii) by order appoint (in accordance with section 19 below) an interim manager, who shall act as receiver and manager in respect of the property and affairs of the charity.

(2) Where, at any time after it has instituted an inquiry under section 8 above with respect to any charity, the Commission is satisfied –

    (a) that there is or has been any misconduct or mismanagement in the administration of the charity; and

    (b) that it is necessary or desirable to act for the purpose of protecting the property of the charity or securing a proper application for the purposes of the charity of that property or of property coming to the charity,

the Commission may of its own motion do either or both of the following things –

    (i)   by order remove any trustee, charity trustee, officer, agent or employee of the charity who has been responsible for or privy to the misconduct or mismanagement or has by his conduct contributed to it or facilitated it;

    (ii) by order establish a scheme for the administration of the charity.

(3) The references in subsection (1) or (2) above to misconduct or mismanagement shall (notwithstanding anything in the trusts of the charity) extend to the employment for the remuneration or reward of persons acting in the affairs of the charity, or for other administrative purposes, of sums which are excessive in relation to the property which is or is likely to be applied or applicable for the purposes of the charity.

(4) The Commission may also remove a charity trustee by order made of its own motion –

    (a) where, within the last five years, the trustee –

        (i) having previously been adjudged bankrupt or had his estate sequestrated, has been discharged, or

        (ii) having previously made a composition or arrangement with, or granted a trust deed for, his creditors, has been discharged in respect of it;

    (b) where the trustee is a corporation in liquidation;

    (c) where the trustee is incapable of acting by reason of mental disorder within the meaning of the Mental Health Act 1983;

    (d) where the trustee has not acted, and will not declare his willingness or unwillingness to act;

    (e) where the trustee is outside England and Wales or cannot be found or does not act, and his absence or failure to act impedes the proper administration of the charity.

(5) The Commission may by order made of its own motion appoint a person to be a charity trustee –

    (a) in place of a charity trustee removed by the Commission under this section or otherwise;

    (b) where there are no charity trustees, or where by reason of vacancies in their number or the absence or incapacity of any of their number the charity cannot apply for the appointment;

    (c) where there is a single charity trustee, not being a corporation aggregate, and the Commission is of opinion that it is necessary to increase the number for the proper administration of the charity;

    (d) where the Commission is of opinion that it is necessary for the proper administration of the charity to have an additional charity trustee because one of the existing charity trustees who ought nevertheless to remain a charity trustee either cannot be found or does not act or is outside England and Wales.

(6) The powers of the Commission under this section to remove or appoint charity trustees of its own motion shall include power to make any such order with respect to the vesting in or transfer to the charity trustees of any property as the Commission could make on the removal or appointment of a charity trustee by it under section 16 above.

(7) Any order under this section for the removal or appointment of a charity trustee or trustee for a charity, or for the vesting or transfer of any property, shall be of the like effect as an order made under section 16 above.

(8) Subject to subsection (9) below, subsections (11) to (13) of section 16 above shall apply to orders under this section as they apply to orders under that section.

(9) The requirement to obtain any such certificate or leave as is mentioned in section 16(13) above shall not apply to –

    (a) an appeal by a charity or any of the charity trustees of a charity against an order under subsection (1)(vii) above appointing a receiver and manager in respect of the charity's property and affairs, or

    (b) an appeal by a person against an order under subsection (2)(i) or (4)(a) above removing him from his office or employment.

(10) Subsection (14) of section 16 above shall apply to an order under this section which establishes a scheme for the administration of a charity as it applies to such an order under that section.

(11) The power of the Commission to make an order under subsection (1)(i) above shall not be exercisable so as to suspend any person from the exercise of his office or employment for a period of more than twelve months; but (without prejudice to the generality of section 89(1) below), any such order made in the case of any person may make provision as respects the period of his suspension for matters arising out of it, and in particular for enabling any person to execute any instrument in his name or otherwise act for him and, in the case of a charity trustee, for adjusting any rules governing the proceedings of the charity trustees to take account of the reduction in the number capable of acting.

(12) Before exercising any jurisdiction under this section otherwise than by virtue of subsection (1) above, the Commission shall give notice of its intention to do so to each of the charity trustees, except any that cannot be found or has no known address in the United Kingdom; and any such

notice may be given by post and, if given by post, may be addressed to the recipient's last known address in the United Kingdom.

(13) The Commission shall, at such intervals as it thinks fit, review any order made by it under paragraph (i), or any of paragraphs (iii) to (vii), of subsection (1) above; and, if on any such review it appears to the Commission that it would be appropriate to discharge the order in whole or in part, the Commission shall so discharge it (whether subject to any savings or other transitional provisions or not).

(14) If any person contravenes an order under subsection (1)(iv), (v) or (vi) above, he shall be guilty of an offence and liable on summary conviction to a fine not exceeding level 5 on the standard scale.

(15) Subsection (14) above shall not be taken to preclude the bringing of proceedings for breach of trust against any charity trustee or trustee for a charity in respect of a contravention of an order under subsection (1)(iv) or (vi) above (whether proceedings in respect of the contravention are brought against him under subsection (14) above or not).

(16) This section shall not apply to an exempt charity.

[See Appendix, Charities Act 2006, Schedule 5, para 6, Schedule 8, paras 96, 111(1), (7).]

19   Supplementary provisions relating to interim manager appointed for a charity

(1) The Commission may under section 18(1)(vii) above appoint to be interim manager in respect of a charity such person (other than a member of its staff) as it thinks fit.

(2) Without prejudice to the generality of section 89(1) below, any order made by the Commission under section 18(1)(vii) above may make provision with respect to the functions to be discharged by the interim manager appointed by the order; and those functions shall be discharged by him under the supervision of the Commission.

(3) In connection with the discharge of those functions any such order may provide –

   (a) for the interim manager appointed by the order to have such powers and duties of the charity trustees of the charity concerned (whether arising under this Act or otherwise) as are specified in the order;

   (b) for any powers or duties exercisable or falling to be performed by the interim manager by virtue of paragraph (a) above to be exercisable or performed by him to the exclusion of those trustees.

(4) Where a person has been appointed interim manager by any such order –

   (a) section 29 below shall apply to him and to his functions as a person so appointed as it applies to a charity trustee of the charity concerned and to his duties as such; and

   (b) the Commission may apply to the High Court for directions in relation to any particular matter arising in connection with the discharge of those functions.

(5) The High Court may on an application under subsection (4)(b) above –

   (a) give such directions, or

   (b) make such orders declaring the rights of any persons (whether before the court or not),

as it thinks just; and the costs of any such application shall be paid by the charity concerned. …

20   Publicity relating to schemes

(1) The Commission may not –

   (a) make any order under this Act to establish a scheme for the administration of a charity, or

   (b) submit such a scheme to the court or the Minister for an order giving it effect,

unless, before doing so, the Commission has complied with the publicity requirements in subsection (2) below.

This is subject to any disapplication of those requirements under subsection (4) below.

(2) The publicity requirements are –

(a) that the Commission must give public notice of its proposals, inviting representations to be made to it within a period specified in the notice; and

(b) that, in the case of a scheme relating to a local charity (other than an ecclesiastical charity) in a parish or in a community in Wales, the Commission must communicate a draft of the scheme to the parish or community council (or, where a parish has no council, to the chairman of the parish meeting).

(3) The time when any such notice is given or any such communication takes place is to be decided by the Commission.

(4) The Commission may determine that either or both of the publicity requirements is or are not to apply in relation to a particular scheme if it is satisfied that –

(a) by reason of the nature of the scheme, or

(b) for any other reason,

compliance with the requirement or requirements is unnecessary.

(5) Where the Commission gives public notice of any proposals under this section, the Commission –

(a) must take into account any representations made to it within the period specified in the notice, and

(b) may (without further notice) proceed with the proposals either without modifications or with such modifications as it thinks desirable.

(6) Where the Commission makes an order under this Act to establish a scheme for the administration of a charity, a copy of the order must be available, for at least a month after the order is published, for public inspection at all reasonable times –

(a) at the Commission's office, and

(b) if the charity is a local charity, at some convenient place in the area of the charity.

Paragraph (b) does not apply if the Commission is satisfied that for any reason it is unnecessary for a copy of the scheme to be available locally.

(7) Any public notice of any proposals which is to be given under this section –

(a) is to contain such particulars of the proposals, or such directions for obtaining information about them, as the Commission thinks sufficient and appropriate, and

(b) is to be given in such manner as the Commission thinks sufficient and appropriate.

20A Publicity for orders relating to trustees or other individuals

(1) The Commission may not make any order under this Act to appoint, discharge or remove a charity trustee or trustee for a charity, other than –

(a) an order relating to the official custodian, or

(b) an order under section 18(1)(ii) above,

unless, before doing so, the Commission has complied with the publicity requirement in subsection (2) below.

This is subject to any disapplication of that requirement under subsection (4) below.

(2) The publicity requirement is that the Commission must give public notice of its proposals, inviting representations to be made to it within a period specified in the notice.

(3) The time when any such notice is given is to be decided by the Commission.

(4) The Commission may determine that the publicity requirement is not to apply in relation to a particular order if it is satisfied that for any reason compliance with the requirement is unnecessary.

(5) Before the Commission makes an order under this Act to remove without his consent –

(a) a charity trustee or trustee for a charity, or

(b) an officer, agent or employee of a charity,

the Commission must give him not less than one month's notice of its proposals, inviting representations to be made to it within a period specified in the notice.

This does not apply if the person cannot be found or has no known address in the United Kingdom.

(6) Where the Commission gives notice of any proposals under this section, the Commission –

(a) must take into account any representations made to it within the period specified in the notice, and

(b) may (without further notice) proceed with the proposals either without modifications or with such modifications as it thinks desirable.

(7) Any notice of any proposals which is to be given under this section –

(a) is to contain such particulars of the proposals, or such directions for obtaining information about them, as the Commission thinks sufficient and appropriate, and

(b) (in the case of a public notice) is to be given in such manner as the Commission thinks sufficient and appropriate.

(8) Any notice to be given under subsection (5) –

(a) may be given by post, and

(b) if given by post, may be addressed to the recipient's last known address in the United Kingdom.

21   Entrusting charity property to official custodian, and termination of trust

(1) The court may by order –

(a) vest in the official custodian any land held by or in trust for a charity;

(b) authorise or require the persons in whom any such land is vested to transfer it to him; or

(c) appoint any person to transfer any such land to him;

but this subsection does not apply to any interest in land by way of mortgage or other security.

(2) Where property is vested in the official custodian in trust for a charity, the court may make an order discharging him from the trusteeship as respects all or any of that property.

(3) Where the official custodian is discharged from his trusteeship of any property, or the trusts on which he holds any property come to an end, the court may make such vesting orders and give such directions as may seem to the court to be necessary or expedient in consequence.

(4) No person shall be liable for any loss occasioned by his acting in conformity with an order under this section or by his giving effect to anything done in pursuance of such an order, or be excused from so doing by reason of the order having been in any respect improperly obtained.

24   Schemes to establish common investment funds

(1) The court or the Commission may by order make and bring into effect schemes (in this section referred to as 'common investment schemes') for the establishment of common investment funds under trusts which provide –

(a) for property transferred to the fund by or on behalf of a charity participating in the scheme to be invested under the control of trustees appointed to manage the fund; and

(b) for the participating charities to be entitled (subject to the provisions of the scheme) to the capital and income of the fund in shares determined by reference to the amount or value of the property transferred to it by or on behalf of each of them and to the value of the fund at the time of the transfers.

(2) The court or the Commission may make a common investment scheme on the application of any two or more charities.

(3) A common investment scheme may be made in terms admitting any charity to participate, or the scheme may restrict the right to participate in any manner.

(3A) A common investment scheme may provide for appropriate bodies to be admitted to participate in the scheme (in addition to the participating charities) to such extent as the trustees appointed to manage the fund may determine.

(3B) In this section 'appropriate body' means –

    (a) a Scottish recognised body, or

    (b) a Northern Ireland charity [as defined in section 25A],

and, in the application of the relevant provisions in relation to a scheme which contains provisions authorised by subsection (3A) above, 'charity' includes an appropriate body.

'The relevant provisions' are subsections (1) and (4) to (6) and (in relation only to a charity within paragraph (b)) subsection (7).

(4) A common investment scheme may make provision for, and for all matters connected with, the establishment, investment, management and winding up of the common investment fund, and may in particular include provision –

    (a) for remunerating persons appointed trustees to hold or manage the fund or any part of it, with or without provision authorising a person to receive the remuneration notwithstanding that he is also a charity trustee of or trustee for a participating charity;

    (b) for restricting the size of the fund, and for regulating as to time, amount or otherwise the right to transfer property to to withdraw it from the fund, and for enabling sums to be advanced out of the fund by way of loan to a participating charity pending the withdrawal of property from the fund by the charity;

    (c) for enabling income to be withheld from distribution with a view to avoiding fluctuations in the amounts distributed, and generally for regulating distributions of income;

    (d) for enabling money to be borrowed temporarily for the purpose of meeting payments to be made out of the funds;

    (e) for enabling questions arising under the scheme as to the right of a charity to participate, or as to the rights of participating charities, or as to any other matter, to be conclusively determined by the decision of the trustees managing the fund or in any other manner;

    (f) for regulating the accounts and information to be supplied to participating charities.

    …

(6) Except in so far as a common investment scheme provides to the contrary, the rights under it of a participating charity shall not be capable of being assigned or charged, nor shall any trustee or other person concerned in the management of the common investment fund be required or entitled to take account of any trust or other equity affecting a participating charity or its property or rights.

(7) The powers of investment of every charity shall include power to participate in common investment schemes unless the power is excluded by a provision specifically referring to common investment schemes in the trusts of the charity.

(8) A common investment fund shall be deemed for all purposes to be a charity; and if the scheme admits only exempt charities, the fund shall be an exempt charity for the purposes of this Act.

(9) Subsection (8) above shall apply not only to common investment funds established under the

powers of this section, but also to any similar fund established for the exclusive benefit of charities by or under any enactment relating to any particular charities or class of charity.

[See Appendix, Charities Act 2006, s11(10), Schedule 9.]

25 Schemes to establish common deposit funds

(1) The court or the Commission may by order make and bring into effect schemes (in this section referred to as 'common deposit schemes') for the establishment of common deposit funds under trusts which provide –

(a) for sums to be deposited by or on behalf of a charity participating in the scheme and invested under the control of trustees appointed to manage the fund; and

(b) for any such charity to be entitled (subject to the provisions of the scheme) to repayment of any sums so deposited and to interest thereon at a rate determined under the scheme.

(2) Subject to subsection (3) below, the following provisions of section 24 above, namely –

(a) subsections (2), (3) and (4), and

(b) subsections (6) to (9),

shall have effect in relation to common deposit schemes and common deposit funds as they have effect in relation to common investment schemes and common investment funds.

(3) In its application in accordance with subsection (2) above, subsection (4) of that section shall have effect with the substitution for paragraphs (b) and (c) of the following paragraphs –

(b) for regulating as to time, amount or otherwise the right to repayment of sums deposited in the fund;

(c) for authorising a part of the income for any year to be credited to a reserve account maintained for the purpose of counteracting any losses accruing to the fund, and generally for regulating the manner in which the rate of interest on deposits is to be determined from time to time;'.

(4) A common deposit scheme may provide for appropriate bodies to be admitted to participate in the scheme (in addition to the participating charities) to such extent as the trustees appointed to manage the fund may determine.

(5) In this section 'appropriate body' means –

(a) a Scottish recognised body, or

(b) a Northern Ireland charity [as defined in section 25A],

and, in the application of the relevant provisions in relation to a scheme which contains provisions authorised by subsection (4) above, 'charity' includes an appropriate body.

(6) 'The relevant provisions' are –

(a) subsection (1) above, and

(b) subsections (4) and (6) of section 24 above, as they apply in accordance with subsections (2) and (3) above, and

(c) (in relation only to a charity within subsection (5)(b) above) subsection (7) of that section, as it so applies.

26 Power to authorise dealings with charity property, etc

(1) Subject to the provisions of this section, where it appears to the Commission that any action proposed or contemplated in the administration of a charity is expedient in the interests of the charity, the Commission may by order sanction that action, whether or not it would otherwise be within the powers exercisable by the charity trustees in the administration of the charity; and anything done under the authority of such an order shall be deemed to be properly done in the exercise of those powers.

(2) An order under this section may be made so as to authorise a particular transaction, compromise or the like, or a particular application of property, or so as to give a more general authority, and (without prejudice to the generality of subsection (1) above) may authorise a charity to use common premises, or employ a common staff, or otherwise combine for any purpose of administration, with any other charity.

(3) An order under this section may give directions as to the manner in which any expenditure is to be borne and as to other matters connected with or arising out of the action thereby authorised; and where anything is done in pursuance of an authority given by any such order, any directions given in connection therewith shall be binding on the charity trustees for the time being as if contained in the trusts of the charity; but any such directions may on the application of the charity be modified or superseded by a further order.

(4) Without prejudice to the generality of subsection (3) above, the directions which may be given by an order under this section shall in particular include directions for meeting any expenditure out of a specified fund, for charging any expenditure to capital or to income, for requiring expenditure charged to capital to be recouped out of income within a specified period, for restricting the costs to be incurred at the expense of the charity, or for the investment of moneys arising from any transaction. ...

27 Power to authorise ex gratia payments, etc

(1) Subject to subsection (3) below, the Commission may by order exercise the same power as is exercisable by the Attorney General to authorise the charity trustees of a charity –

> (a) to make any application of property of the charity, or
> (b) to waive to any extent, on behalf of the charity, its entitlement to receive any property,

in a case where the charity trustees –

>> (i) (apart from this section) have no power to do so, but
>> (ii) in all the circumstances regard themselves as being under a moral obligation to do so.

(2) The power conferred on the Commission by subsection (1) above shall be exercisable by the Commission under the supervision of, and in accordance with such directions as may be given by, the Attorney General; and any such directions may in particular require the Commission, in such circumstances as are specified in the directions –

> (a) to refrain from exercising that power; or
> (b) to consult the Attorney General before exercising it.

(3) Where –

> (a) an application is made to the Commission for it to exercise that power in a case where it is not precluded from doing so by any such directions, but
> (b) the Commission considers that it would nevertheless be desirable for the application to be entertained by the Attorney General rather than by the Commission,

the Commission shall refer the application to the Attorney General.

(4) It is hereby declared that where, in the case of any application made to the Commission as mentioned in subsection (3)(a) above, the Commission determines the application by refusing to authorise charity trustees to take any action falling within subsection (1)(a) or (b) above, that refusal shall not preclude the Attorney General, on an application subsequently made to him by the trustees, from authorising the trustees to take that action.

28 Power to give directions about dormant bank accounts of charities

(1) Where the Commission –

> (a) is informed by a relevant institution –

(i)   that it holds one or more accounts in the name of or on behalf of a particular charity ('the relevant charity'), and

(ii) that the account, or (if it so holds two or more accounts) each of the accounts, is dormant, and

(b) is unable, after making reasonable inquiries, to locate that charity or any of its trustees,

it may give a direction under subsection (2) below.

(2) A direction under this subsection is a direction which –

(a) requires the institution concerned to transfer the amount, or (as the case may be) the aggregate amount, standing to the credit of the relevant charity in the account or accounts in question to such other charity as is specified in the direction in accordance with subsection (3) below; or

(b) requires the institution concerned to transfer to each of two or more other charities so specified in the direction such part of that amount or aggregate amount as is there specified in relation to that charity.

(3) The Commission may specify in a direction under subsection (2) above such other charity or charities as it considers appropriate, having regard, in a case where the purposes of the relevant charity are known to the Commission, to those purposes and to the purposes of the other charity or charities; but the Commission shall not so specify any charity unless it has received from the charity trustees written confirmation that those trustees are willing to accept the amount proposed to be transferred to the charity.

(4) Any amount received by a charity by virtue of this section shall be received by the charity on terms that –

(a) it shall be held and applied by the charity for the purposes of the charity, but

(b) it shall, as property of the charity, nevertheless be subject to any restrictions on expenditure to which it was subject as property of the relevant charity.

(5) Where –

(a) the Commission has been informed as mentioned in subsection (1)(a) above by any relevant institution, and

(b) before any transfer is made by the institution in pursuance of a direction under subsection (2) above, the institution has, by reason of any circumstances, cause to believe that the account, or (as the case may be) any of the accounts, held by it in the name of or on behalf of the relevant charity is no longer dormant,

the institution shall forthwith notify those circumstances in writing to the Commission; and, if it appears to the Commission that the account or accounts in question is or are no longer dormant, it shall revoke any direction under subsection (2) above which has previously been given by it to the institution with respect to the relevant charity.

(6) The receipt of any charity trustees or trustee for a charity in respect of any amount received from a relevant institution by virtue of this section shall be a complete discharge of the institution in respect of that amount.

(7) No obligation as to secrecy or other restriction on disclosure (however imposed) shall preclude a relevant institution from disclosing any information to the Commission for the purpose of enabling the Commission to discharge its functions under this section.

(8) For the purposes of this section –

(a) an account is dormant if no transaction, other than –

(i)   a transaction consisting in a payment into the account, or

(ii) a transaction which the institution holding the account has itself caused to be effected,

has been effected in relation to the account within the period of five years immediately preceding the date when the Commission is informed as mentioned in paragraph (a) of subsection (1) above; ...

(10) Subsection (1) above shall not apply to any account held in the name of or on behalf of an exempt charity.

[See Appendix, Charities Act 2006, Schedule 5, para 7, Schedule 9.]

29   Power to give advice and guidance

(1) The Commission may, on the written application of any charity trustee or trustee for a charity, give that person its opinion or advice in relation to any matter –
  (a) relating to the performance of any duties of his, as such a trustee, in relation to the charity concerned, or
  (b) otherwise relating to the proper administration of the charity.

(2) A charity trustee or trustee for a charity who acts in accordance with any opinion or advice given by the Commission under subsection (1) above (whether to him or to another trustee) is to be taken, as regards his responsibility for so acting, to have acted in accordance with his trust.

(3) But subsection (2) above does not apply to a person if, when so acting, either –
  (a) he knows or has reasonable cause to suspect that the opinion or advice was given in ignorance of material facts, or
  (b) a decision of the court or the Tribunal has been obtained on the matter or proceedings are pending to obtain one.

(4) The Commission may, in connection with its second general function mentioned in section 1C(2) above, give such advice or guidance with respect to the administration of charities as it considers appropriate.

(5) Any advice or guidance so given may relate to –
  (a) charities generally,
  (b) any class of charities, or
  (c) any particular charity,
and may take such form, and be given in such manner, as the Commission considers appropriate.

29A   Power to determine membership of charity

(1) The Commission may –
  (a) on the application of a charity, or
  (b) at any time after the institution of an inquiry under section 8 above with respect to a charity,
determine who are the members of the charity.

(2) The Commission's power under subsection (1) may also be exercised by a person appointed by the Commission for the purpose.

(3) In a case within subsection (1)(b) the Commission may, if it thinks fit, so appoint the person appointed to conduct the inquiry.

30   Powers for preservation of charity documents

(1) The Commission may provide books in which any deed, will or other document relating to a charity may be enrolled.

(2) The Commission may accept for safe keeping any document of or relating to a charity, and the charity trustees or other persons having the custody of documents of or relating to a charity (including a charity which has ceased to exist) may with the consent of the Commission deposit them with the Commission for safe keeping, except in the case of documents required by some other enactment to be kept elsewhere. ...

31   Power to order taxation of solicitor's bill

(1) The Commission may order that a solicitor's bill of costs for business done for a charity, or for charity trustees or trustees for a charity, shall be taxed, together with the costs of the taxation, by a taxing officer in such division of the High Court as may be specified in the order, or by the taxing officer of any other court having jurisdiction to order the taxation of the bill.

(2) On any order under this section for the taxation of a solicitor's bill the taxation shall proceed, and the taxing officer shall have the same powers and duties, and the costs of the taxation shall be borne, as if the order had been made, on the application of the person chargeable with the bill, by the court in which the costs are taxed.

(3) No order under this section for the taxation of a solicitor's bill shall be made after payment of the bill unless the Commission is of opinion that it contains exorbitant charges; and no such order shall in any case be made where the solicitor's costs are not subject to taxation on an order of the High Court by reason either of an agreement as to his remuneration or the lapse of time since payment of the bill.

32   Proceedings by Commission

(1) Subject to subsection (2) below, the Commission may exercise the same powers with respect to –

    (a) the taking of legal proceedings with reference to charities or the property or affairs of charities, or

    (b) the compromise of claims with a view to avoiding or ending such proceedings,

as are exercisable by the Attorney General acting ex officio.

(2) Subsection (1) above does not apply to the power of the Attorney General under section 63(1) below to present a petition for the winding up of a charity.

(3) The practice and procedure to be followed in relation to any proceedings taken by the Commission under subsection (1) above shall be the same in all respects (and in particular as regards costs) as if they were proceedings taken by the Attorney General acting ex officio.

(4) No rule of law or practice shall be taken to require the Attorney General to be a party to any such proceedings.

(5) The powers exercisable by the Commission by virtue of this section shall be exercisable by the Commission of its own motion, but shall be exercisable only with the agreement of the Attorney General on each occasion.

33   Proceedings by other persons

(1) Charity proceedings may be taken with reference to a charity either by the charity, or by any of the charity trustees, or by any person interested in the charity, or by any two or more inhabitants of the area of the charity if it is a local charity, but not by any other person.

(2) Subject to the following provisions of this section, no charity proceedings relating to a charity (other than an exempt charity) shall be entertained or proceeded with in any court unless the taking of the proceedings is authorised by order of the Commission.

(3) The Commission shall not, without special reasons, authorise the taking of charity proceedings where in its opinion the case can be dealt with by the Commission under the powers of this Act other than those conferred by section 32 above.

(4) This section shall not require any order for the taking of proceedings in a pending cause or matter or for the bringing of any appeal.

(5) Where the foregoing provisions of this section require the taking of charity proceedings to be authorised by an order of the Commission, the proceedings may nevertheless be entertained or proceeded with if, after the order had been applied for and refused, leave to take the proceedings

was obtained from one of the judges of the High Court attached to the Chancery Division.

(6) Nothing in the foregoing subsections shall apply to the taking of proceedings by the Attorney General, with or without a relator, or to the taking of proceedings by the Commission in accordance with section 32 above.

(7) Where it appears to the Commission, on an application for an order under this section or otherwise, that it is desirable for legal proceedings to be taken with reference to any charity (other than an exempt charity) or its property or affairs, and for the proceedings to be taken by the Attorney General, the Commission shall so inform the Attorney General, and send him such statements and particulars as the Commission thinks necessary to explain the matter.

(8) In this section 'charity proceedings' means proceedings in any court in England or Wales brought under the court's jurisdiction with respect to charities, or brought under the court's jurisdiction with respect to trusts in relation to the administration of a trust for charitable purposes.

[See Appendix, Charities Act 2006, Schedule 5, para 8, Schedule 9.]

34   Report of s8 inquiry to be evidence in certain proceedings

(1) A copy of the report of the person conducting an inquiry under section 8 above shall, if certified by the Commission to be a true copy, be admissible in any proceedings to which this section applies –

   (a)   as evidence of any fact stated in the report; and

   (b)   as evidence of the opinion of that person as to any matter referred to in it.

(2) This section applies to –

   (a)   any legal proceedings instituted by the Commission under this Part of this Act; and

   (b)   any legal proceedings instituted by the Attorney General in respect of a charity.

(3) A document purporting to be a certificate issued for the purposes of subsection (1) above shall be received in evidence and be deemed to be such a certificate, unless the contrary is proved.

PART V

CHARITY LAND

36   Restrictions on dispositions

(1) Subject to the following provisions of this section and section 40 below, no land held by or in trust for a charity shall be conveyed, transferred, leased or otherwise disposed of without an order of the court or of the Commission.

(2) Subsection (1) above shall not apply to a disposition of such land if –

   (a)   the disposition is made to a person who is not –

      (i)   a connected person (as defined in Schedule 5 to this Act), or

      (ii)   a trustee for, or nominee of, a connected person; and

   (b)   the requirements of subsection (3) or (5) below have been complied with in relation to it.

(3) Except where the proposed disposition is the granting of such a lease as is mentioned in subsection (5) below, the requirements mentioned in subsection (2)(b) above are that the charity trustees must, before entering into an agreement for the sale, or (as the case may be) for a lease or other disposition, of the land –

   (a)   obtain and consider a written report on the proposed disposition from a qualified surveyor instructed by the trustees and acting exclusively for the charity;

   (b)   advertise the proposed disposition for such period and in such manner as the surveyor has advised in his report (unless he has there advised that it would not be in the best interests of the charity to advertise the proposed disposition); and

(c) decide that they are satisfied, having considered the surveyor's report, that the terms on which the disposition is proposed to be made are the best that can reasonably be obtained for the charity.

(4) For the purposes of subsection (3) above a person is a qualified surveyor if –

(a) he is a fellow or professional associate of the Royal Institution of Chartered Surveyors or of the Incorporated Society of Valuers and Auctioneers or satisfies such other requirement or requirements as may be prescribed by regulations made by the Minister; and

(b) he is reasonably believed by the charity trustees to have ability in, and experience of, the valuation of land of the particular kind, and in the particular area, in question;

and any report prepared for the purposes of that subsection shall contain such information, and deal with such matters, as may be prescribed by regulations so made.

(5) Where the proposed disposition is the granting of a lease for a term ending not more than seven years after it is granted (other than one granted wholly or partly in consideration of a fine), the requirements mentioned in subsection (2)(b) above are that the charity trustees must, before entering into an agreement for the lease –

(a) obtain and consider the advice on the proposed disposition of a person who is reasonably believed by the trustees to have the requisite ability and practical experience to provide them with competent advice on the proposed disposition; and

(b) decide that they are satisfied, having considered that person's advice, that the terms on which the disposition is proposed to be made are the best that can reasonably be obtained for the charity.

(6) Where –

(a) any land is held by or in trust for a charity, and

(b) the trusts on which it is so held stipulate that it is to be used for the purposes, or any particular purposes, of the charity,

then (subject to subsections (7) and (8) below and without prejudice to the operation of the preceding provisions of this section) the land shall not be conveyed, transferred, leased or otherwise disposed of unless the charity trustees have before the relevant time –

(i) given public notice of the proposed disposition, inviting representations to be made to them within a time specified in the notice, being not less than one month from the date of the notice; and

(ii) taken into consideration any representations made to them within that time about the proposed disposition.

(6A) In subsection (6) above 'the relevant time' means –

(a) where the charity trustees enter into an agreement for the sale, or (as the case may be) for the lease or other disposition, the time when they enter into that agreement, and

(b) in any other case, the time of the disposition.

(7) Subsection (6) above shall not apply to any such disposition of land as is there mentioned if –

(a) the disposition is to be effected with a view to acquiring by way of replacement other property which is to be held on the trusts referred to in paragraph (b) of that subsection; or

(b) the disposition is the granting of a lease for a term ending not more than two years after it is granted (other than one granted wholly or partly in consideration of a fine).

(8) The Commission may direct –

(a) that subsection (6) above shall not apply to dispositions of land held by or in trust for a charity or class of charities (whether generally or only in the case of a specified class of dispositions or land, or otherwise as may be provided in the direction), or

(b) that that subsection shall not apply to a particular disposition of land held by or in trust for a charity,

if, on an application made to them in writing by or on behalf of the charity or charities in question, the Commission is satisfied that it would be in the interests of the charity or charities for the Commission to give the direction.

(9) The restrictions on disposition imposed by this section apply notwithstanding anything in the trusts of a charity; but nothing in this section applies –

(a) to any disposition for which general or special authority is expressly given (without the authority being made subject to the sanction of an order of the court) by any statutory provision contained in or having effect under an Act of Parliament or by any scheme legally established; or

(b) to any disposition of land held by or in trust for a charity which –

(i)   is made to another charity otherwise than for the best price that can reasonably be obtained, and

(ii) is authorised to be so made by the trusts of the first-mentioned charity; or

(c) to the granting, by or on behalf of a charity and in accordance with its trusts, of a lease to any beneficiary under those trusts where the lease –

(i)   is granted otherwise than for the best rent that can reasonably be obtained; and

(ii) is intended to enable the demised premises to be occupied for the purposes, or any particular purposes, of the charity.

(10) Nothing in this section applies –

(a) to any disposition of land held by or in trust for an exempt charity;

(b) to any disposition of land by way of mortgage or other security; or

(c) to any disposition of an advowson.

(11) In this section 'land' means land in England or Wales.

38   Restrictions on mortgaging

(1) Subject to subsection (2) below, no mortgage of land held by or in trust for a charity shall be granted without an order of the court or of the Commission

(2) Subsection (1) above shall not apply to a mortgage of any such land if the charity trustees have, before executing the mortgage, obtained and considered proper advice, given to them in writing, on the relevant matters or matter mentioned in subsection (3) or (3A) below (as the case may be).

(3) In the case of a mortgage to secure the repayment of a proposed loan or grant, the relevant matters are –

(a) whether the loan or grant is necessary in order for the charity trustees to be able to pursue the particular course of action in connection with which they are seeking the loan or grant;

(b) whether the terms of the loan or grant are reasonable having regard to the status of the charity as the prospective recipient of the loan or grant; and

(c) the ability of the charity to repay on those terms the sum proposed to be paid by way of loan or grant.

(3A) In the case of a mortgage to secure the discharge of any other proposed obligation, the relevant matter is whether it is reasonable for the charity trustees to undertake to discharge the obligation, having regard to the charity's purposes.

(3B) Subsection (3) or (as the case may be) subsection (3A) above applies in relation to such a mortgage as is mentioned in that subsection whether the mortgage –

    (a) would only have effect to secure the repayment of the proposed loan or grant or the discharge of the proposed obligation, or

    (b) would also have effect to secure the repayment of sums paid by way of loan or grant, or the discharge of other obligations undertaken, after the date of its execution.

(3C) Subsection (3D) below applies where –

    (a) the charity trustees of a charity have executed a mortgage of land held by or in trust for a charity in accordance with subsection (2) above, and

    (b) the mortgage has effect to secure the repayment of sums paid by way of loan or grant, or the discharge of other obligations undertaken, after the date of its execution.

(3D) In such a case, the charity trustees must not after that date enter into any transaction involving –

    (a) the payment of any such sums, or

    (b) the undertaking of any such obligations,

unless they have, before entering into the transaction, obtained and considered proper advice, given to them in writing, on the matters or matter mentioned in subsection (3)(a) to (c) or (3A) above (as the case may be).

(4) For the purposes of this section above proper advice is the advice of a person –

    (a) who is reasonably believed by the charity trustees to be qualified by his ability in and practical experience of financial matters; and

    (b) who has no financial interest in relation to the loan, grant or other transaction in connection with which his advice is given;

and such advice may constitute proper advice for those purposes notwithstanding that the person giving it does so in the course of his employment as an officer or employee of the charity or of the charity trustees.

(5) This section applies notwithstanding anything in the trusts of a charity; but nothing in this section applies to any mortgage for which general or special authority is given as mentioned in section 36(9)(a) above.

(6) In this section –

    'land' means land in England or Wales;

    'mortgage' includes a charge.

(7) Nothing in this section applies to an exempt charity.

PART VI

CHARITY ACCOUNTS, REPORTS AND RETURNS

41   Duty to keep accounting records

(1) The charity trustees of a charity shall ensure that accounting records are kept in respect of the charity which are sufficient to show and explain all the charity's transactions, and which are such as to –

    (a) disclose at any time, with reasonable accuracy, the financial position of the charity at that time, and

    (b) enable the trustees to ensure that, where any statements of accounts are prepared by them under section 42(1) below, those statements of accounts comply with the requirements of regulations under that provision.

(2) The accounting records shall in particular contain –

    (a) entries showing from day to day all sums of money received and expended by the charity, and the matters in respect of which the receipt and expenditure takes place; and

    (b) a record of the assets and liabilities of the charity.

(3) The charity trustees of a charity shall preserve any accounting records made for the purposes of this section in respect of the charity for at least six years from the end of the financial year of the charity in which they are made.

(4) Where a charity ceases to exist within the period of six years mentioned in subsection (3) above as it applies to any accounting records, the obligation to preserve those records in accordance with that subsection shall continue to be discharged by the last charity trustees of the charity, unless the Commission consents in writing to the records being destroyed or otherwise disposed of.

(5) Nothing in this section applies to a charity which is a company.

42   Annual statements of accounts

(1) The charity trustees of a charity shall (subject to subsection (3) below) prepare in respect of each financial year of the charity a statement of accounts complying with such requirements as to its form and contents as may be prescribed by regulations made by the Minister.

(2) Without prejudice to the generality of subsection (1) above, regulations under that subsection may make provision –

    (a) for any such statement to be prepared in accordance with such methods and principles as are specified or referred to in the regulations;

    (b) as to any information to be provided by way of notes to the accounts;

and regulations under that subsection may also make provision for determining the financial years of a charity for the purposes of this Act and any regulations made under it.

(3) Where a charity's gross income in any financial year does not exceed £100,000, the charity trustees may, in respect of that year, elect to prepare the following, namely –

    (a) a receipts and payments account, and

    (b) a statement of assets and liabilities,

instead of a statement of accounts under subsection (1) above.

(4) The charity trustees of a charity shall preserve –

    (a) any statement of accounts prepared by them under subsection (1) above, or

    (b) any account and statement prepared by them under subsection (3) above,

for at least six years from the end of the financial year to which any such statement relates or (as the case may be) to which any such account and statement relate.

(5) Subsection (4) of section 41 above shall apply in relation to the preservation of any such statement or account and statement as it applies in relation to the preservation of any accounting records (the references to subsection (3) of that section being read as references to subsection (4) above).

(6) The Minister may by order amend subsection (3) above by substituting a different sum for the sum for the time being specified there.

(7) Nothing in this section applies to a charity which is a company.

[See Appendix, Charities Act 2006, Schedule 8, paras 96, 133.]

43   Annual audit or examination of charity accounts

(1) Subsection (2) below applies to a financial year of a charity if –

    (a) the charity's gross income in that year exceeds £500,000; or

    (b) the charity's gross income in that year exceeds the accounts threshold and at the end of the year the aggregate value of its assets (before deduction of liabilities) exceeds £2.8 million.

'The accounts threshold' means £100,000 or such other sum as is for the time being specified in section 42(3) above.

(2) If this subsection applies to a financial year of a charity, the accounts of the charity for that year shall be audited by a person who –

    (a) would be eligible for appointment as auditor of the charity under Part 2 of the Companies Act 1989 if the charity were a company, or

    (b) is a member of a body for the time being specified in regulations under section 44 below and is under the rules of that body eligible for appointment as auditor of the charity.

(3) If subsection (2) above does not apply to a financial year of a charity and its gross income in that year exceeds £10,000, the accounts of the charity for that year shall, at the election of the charity trustees, either –

    (a) be examined by an independent examiner, that is to say an independent person who is reasonably believed by the trustees to have the requisite ability and practical experience to carry out a competent examination of the accounts, or

    (b) be audited by such a person as is mentioned in subsection (2) above.

This is subject to the requirements of subsection (3A) below where the gross income exceeds £250,000, and to any order under subsection (4) below.

(3A) If subsection (3) above applies to the accounts of a charity for a year and the charity's gross income in that year exceeds £250,000, a person qualifies as an independent examiner for the purposes of paragraph (a) of that subsection if (and only if) he is an independent person who is –

    (a) a member of a body for the time being specified in section 249D(3) of the Companies Act 1985 (reporting accountants);

    (b) a member of the Chartered Institute of Public Finance and Accountancy; or

    (c) a Fellow of the Association of Charity Independent Examiners.

(4) Where it appears to the Commission –

    (a) that subsection (2), or (as the case may be) subsection (3) above, has not been complied with in relation to a financial year of a charity within ten months from the end of that year, or

    (b) that, although subsection (2) above does not apply to a financial year of a charity, it would nevertheless be desirable for the accounts of the charity for that year to be audited by such a person as is mentioned in that subsection,

the Commission may by order require the accounts of the charity for that year to be audited by such a person as is mentioned in that subsection. …

(9) Nothing in this section applies to a charity which is a company. …

45   Annual reports

(1) The charity trustees of a charity shall prepare in respect of each financial year of the charity an annual report containing –

    (a) such a report by the trustees on the activities of the charity during that year, and

    (b) such other information relating to the charity or to its trustees or officers,

as may be prescribed by regulations made by the Minister.

(2) Without prejudice to the generality of subsection (1) above, regulations under that subsection may make provision –

(a) for any such report as is mentioned in paragraph (a) of that subsection to be prepared in accordance with such principles as are specified or referred to in the regulations;

(b) enabling the Commission to dispense with any requirement prescribed by virtue of subsection (1)(b) above in the case of a particular charity or a particular class of charities, or in the case of a particular financial year of a charity or of any class of charities.

(3) Where a charity's gross income in any financial year exceeds £10,000, a copy of the annual report required to be prepared under this section in respect of that year shall be transmitted to the Commission by the charity trustees –

(a) within ten months from the end of that year, or

(b) within such longer period as the Commission may for any special reason allow in the case of that report.

(3A) Where a charity's gross income in any financial year does not exceed £10,000, a copy of the the annual report required to be prepared under this section in respect of that year shall, if the Commission so requests, be transmitted to it by the charity trustees –

(a) in the case of a request made before the end of seven months from the end of the financial year to which the report relates, within ten months from the end of that year, and

(b) in the case of a request not so made, within three months from the date of the request, or, in either case, within such longer period as the Commission may for any special reason allow in the case of that report.

(4) Subject to subsection (5) below, any copy of an annual report transmitted to the Commission under this section shall have attached to it a copy of the statement of accounts prepared for the financial year in question under section 42(1) above or (as the case may be) a copy of the account and statement so prepared under section 42(3) above, together with –

(a) where the accounts of the charity for that year have been audited under section 43 … above, a copy of the report made by the auditor on that statement of accounts or (as the case may be) on that account and statement;

(b) where the accounts of the charity for that year have been examined under section 43 … above, a copy of the report made by the independent examiner in respect of the examination carried out by him under that section.

(5) Subsection (4) above does not apply to a charity which is a company, and any copy of an annual report transmitted by the charity trustees of such a charity under this section shall instead have attached to it a copy of the charity's annual accounts prepared for the financial year in question under Part VII of the Companies Act 1985, together with a copy of any auditors' report or report made for the purposes of section 249A(2) of that Act on those accounts. …

[See Appendix, Charities Act 2006, Schedule 7, Part 2, paras 3, 4.]

46 Special provision as respects accounts and annual reports of exempt and other excepted charities

(1) Nothing in sections 41 to 45 above applies to any exempt charity; but the charity trustees of an exempt charity shall keep proper books of account with respect to the affairs of the charity, and if not required by or under the authority of any other Act to prepare periodical statements of account shall prepare consecutive statements of account consisting on each occasion of an income and expenditure account relating to a period of not more than fifteen months and a balance sheet relating to the end of that period.

(2) The books of accounts and statements of account relating to an exempt charity shall be

preserved for a period of six years at least unless the charity ceases to exist and the Commission consents in writing to their being destroyed or otherwise disposed of.

(3) Nothing in sections 43 ... or 45 above applies to any charity which –

    (a) falls within section 3(5)(c) above, and

    (b) is not registered.

(4) Except in accordance with subsection (7) below, nothing in section 45 above applies to any charity (other than an exempt charity or a charity which falls within section 3(5)(c) above) which –

    (a) is excepted by section 3(5) above, and

    (b) is not registered.

(5) If requested to do so by the Commission, the charity trustees of any such charity as is mentioned in subsection (4) above shall prepare an annual report in respect of such financial year of the charity as is specified in the Commission's request.

(6) Any report prepared under subsection (5) above shall contain –

    (a) such a report by the charity trustees on the activities of the charity during the year in question, and

    (b) such other information relating to the charity or to its trustees or officers,

as may be prescribed by regulations made under section 45(1) above in relation to annual reports prepared under that provision. ...

[See Appendix, Charities Act 2006, s29(2), Schedule 8, paras 96, 139(1), (3), (4).]

47   Public inspection of annual reports, etc

(1) Any annual report or other document kept by the Commissioners in pursuance of section 45(6) above shall be open to public inspection at all reasonable times –

    (a) during the period for which it is so kept; or

    (b) if the Commissioners so determine, during such lesser period as they may specify.

(2) Where any person –

    (a) requests the charity trustees of a charity in writing to provide him with a copy of the charity's most recent accounts, and

    (b) pays them such reasonable fee (if any) as they may require in respect of the costs of complying with the request,

those trustees shall comply with the request within the period of two months beginning with the date on which it is made. ...

[See Appendix, Charities Act 2006, Schedule 8, paras 96, 140(1)–(3).]

48   Annual returns by registered charities

(1) Subject to subsection (1A) below, every registered charity shall prepare in respect of each of its financial years an annual return in such form, and containing such information, as may be prescribed by regulations made by the Commission.

(1A) Subsection (1) above shall not apply in relation to any financial year of a charity in which neither the gross income nor the total expenditure of the charity exceeds £10,000.

(2) Any such return shall be transmitted to the Commission by the date by which the charity trustees are, by virtue of section 45(3) above, required to transmit to the Commission the annual report required to be prepared in respect of the financial year in question. ...

[See Appendix, Charities Act 2006, Schedule 7, Part 2, paras 3, 5, Schedule 8, paras 96, 141(1), (3), (4).]

49   Offences

(1) If any requirement imposed –

    (a) by section 45(3) or (3A) above (taken with section 45(3B), (4) and (5), as applicable), or

    (b) by section 47(2) or 48(2) above,

is not complied with, each person who immediately before the date for compliance specified in the section in question was a charity trustee of the charity shall be guilty of an offence and liable on summary conviction to the penalty mentioned in subsection (2).

(2) The penalty is –

    (a) a fine not exceeding level 4 on the standard scale, and

    (b) for continued contravention, a daily default fine not exceeding 10% of level 4 on the standard scale for so long as the person in question remains a charity trustee of the charity.

(3) It is a defence for a person charged with an offence under subsection (1) to prove that he took all reasonable steps for securing that the requirement in question would be complied with in time.

PART VII

INCORPORATION OF CHARITY TRUSTEES

50   Incorporation of trustees of a charity

(1) Where –

    (a) the trustees of a charity, in accordance with section 52 below, apply to the Commission for a certificate of incorporation of the trustees as a body corporate, and

    (b) the Commission considers that the incorporation of the trustees would be in the interests of the charity,

the Commission may grant such a certificate, subject to such conditions or directions as the Commission thinks fit to insert in it.

(2) The Commissioners shall not, however, grant such a certificate in a case where the charity appears to them to be required to be registered under section 3 above but is not so registered.

(3) On the grant of such a certificate –

    (a) the trustees of the charity shall become a body corporate by such name as is specified in the certificate; and

    (b) (without prejudice to the operation of section 54 below) any relevant rights or liabilities of those trustees shall become rights or liabilities of that body.

(4) After their incorporation the trustees –

    (a) may sue and be sued in their corporate name; and

    (b) shall have the same powers, and be subject to the same restrictions and limitations, as respects the holding, acquisition and disposal of property for or in connection with the purposes of the charity as they had or were subject to while unincorporated;

and any relevant legal proceedings that might have been continued or commenced by or against the trustees may be continued or commenced by or against them in their corporate name.

(5) A body incorporated under this section need not have a common seal.

(6) In this section –

    'relevant rights or liabilities' means rights or liabilities in connection with any property vesting in the body in question under section 51 below; and

    'relevant legal proceedings' means legal proceedings in connection with any such property.

[See Appendix, Charities Act 2006, Schedule 8, para 143(1), (3).]

51   Estate to vest in body corporate

The certificate of incorporation shall vest in the body corporate all real and personal estate, of whatever nature or tenure, belonging to or held by any person or persons in trust for the charity, and thereupon any person or persons in whose name or names any stocks, funds or securities are standing in trust for the charity, shall transfer them into the name of the body corporate, except that the foregoing provisions shall not apply to property vested in the official custodian.

61   Power of Commission to dissolve incorporated body

(1) Where the Commission is satisfied –

    (a) that an incorporated body has no assets or does not operate, or

    (b) that the relevant charity in the case of an incorporated body has ceased to exist, or

    (c) that the institution previously constituting, or treated by the Commission as constituting, any such charity has ceased to be, or (as the case may be) was not at the time of the body's incorporation, a charity, or

    (d) that the purposes of the relevant charity in the case of an incorporated body have been achieved so far as is possible or are in practice incapable of being achieved,

the Commission may of its own motion make an order dissolving the body as from such date as is specified in the order.

(2) Where the Commission is satisfied, on the application of the trustees of the relevant charity in the case of an incorporated body, that it would be in the interests of the charity for that body to be dissolved, the Commission may make an order dissolving the body as from such date as is specified in the order.

(3) Subject to subsection (4) below, an order made under this section with respect to an incorporated body shall have the effect of vesting in the trustees of the relevant charity, in trust for that charity, all property for the time being vested –

    (a) in the body, or

    (b) in any other person (apart from the official custodian),

in trust for that charity.

(4) If the Commission so directs in the order –

    (a) all or any specified part of that property shall, instead of vesting in the trustees of the relevant charity, vest –

        (i) in a specified person as trustee for, or nominee of, that charity, or

        (ii) in such persons (other than the trustees of the relevant charity) as may be specified;

    (b) any specified investments, or any specified class or description of investments, held by any person in trust for the relevant charity shall be transferred –

        (i) to the trustees of that charity, or

        (ii) to any such person or persons as is or are mentioned in paragraph (a)(i) or (ii) above;

and for this purpose 'specified' means specified by the Commission in the order.

(5) Where an order to which this subsection applies is made with respect to an incorporated body –

    (a) any rights or liabilities of the body shall become rights or liabilities of the trustees of the relevant charity; and

    (b) any legal proceedings that might have been continued or commenced by or against the body may be continued or commenced by or against those trustees.

(6) Subsection (5) above applies to any order under this section by virtue of which –

    (a) any property vested as mentioned in subsection (3) above is vested –

        (i) in the trustees of the relevant charity, or

    (ii) in any person as trustee for, or nominee of, that charity; or
- (b) any investments held by any person in trust for the relevant charity are required to be transferred –
  - (i) to the trustees of that charity, or
  - (ii) to any person as trustee for, or nominee of, that charity.

62   Interpretation of Part VII

In this Part of this Act –

    'incorporated body' means a body incorporated under section 50 above;

    'the relevant charity', in relation to an incorporated body, means the charity the trustees of which have been incorporated as that body;

    'the trustees', in relation to a charity, means the charity trustees.

PART VIII

CHARITABLE COMPANIES

63   Winding up

(1) Where a charity may be wound up by the High Court under the Insolvency Act 1986, a petition for it to be wound up under that Act by any court in England or Wales having jurisdiction may be presented by the Attorney General, as well as by any person authorised by that Act.

(2) Where a charity may be so wound up by the High Court, such a petition may also be presented by the Commission if, at any time after it has instituted an inquiry under section 8 above with respect to the charity, it is satisfied as mentioned in section 18(1)(a) or (b) above.

(3) Where a charitable company is dissolved, the Commission may make an application under section 651 of the Companies Act 1985 (power of court to declare dissolution of company void) for an order to be made under that section with respect to the company; and for this purpose subsection (1) of that section shall have effect in relation to a charitable company as if the reference to the liquidator of the company included a reference to the Commission.

(4) Where a charitable company's name has been struck off the register of companies under section 652 of the Companies Act 1985 (power of registrar to strike defunct company off register), the Commission may make an application under section 653(2) of that Act (objection to striking off by person aggrieved) for an order restoring the company's name to that register; and for this purpose section 653(2) shall have effect in relation to a charitable company as if the reference to any such person aggrieved as is there mentioned included a reference to the Commission.

(5) The powers exercisable by the Commission by virtue of this section shall be exercisable by the Commission of its own motion, but shall be exercisable only with the agreement of the Attorney General on each occasion.

(6) In this section 'charitable company' means a company which is a charity.

64   Alteration of objects clause

(1) Where a charity is a company or other body corporate having power to alter the instruments establishing or regulating it as a body corporate, no exercise of that power which has the effect of the body ceasing to be a charity shall be valid so as to affect the application of –

    (a) any property acquired under any disposition or agreement previously made otherwise than for full consideration in money or money's worth, or any property representing property so acquired,

    (b) any property representing income which has accrued before the alteration is made, or

(c)   the income from any such property as aforesaid.

(2) Where a charity is a company, any alteration by it –

(a)   of the objects clause in its memorandum of association, or

(b)   of any other provision in its memorandum of association, or any provision in its articles of association, which is a provision directing or restricting the manner in which property of the company may be used or applied,

is ineffective without the prior written consent of the Commissioners. ...

[See Appendix, Charities Act 2006, s31(1), (2).]

69   Investigation of accounts

(1) In the case of a charity which is a company the Commission may by order require that the condition and accounts of the charity for such period as the Commission thinks fit shall be investigated and audited by an auditor appointed by the Commission, being a person eligible for appointment as a company auditor under section 25 of the Companies Act 1989. ...

PART IX

MISCELLANEOUS

72   Persons disqualified for being trustees of a charity

(1) Subject to the following provisions of this section, a person shall be disqualified for being a charity trustee or trustee for a charity if –

(a)   he has been convicted of any offence involving dishonesty or deception;

(b)   he has been adjudged bankrupt or sequestration of his estate has been awarded and (in either case) he has not been discharged or he is the subject of a bankruptcy restrictions order or an interim order;

(c)   he has made a composition or arrangement with, or granted a trust deed for, his creditors and has not been discharged in respect of it;

(d)   he has been removed from the office of charity trustee or trustee for a charity by an order made –

(i)   by the Commission or Commissioners under section 18(2)(i) above, or

(ii)   by the Commissioners under section 20(1A)(i) of the Charities Act 1960 (power to act for protection of charities) or under section 20(1)(i) of that Act (as in force before the commencement of section 8 of the Charities Act 1992), or

(iii) by the High Court,

on the grounds of any misconduct or mismanagement in the administration of the charity for which he was responsible or to which he was privy, or which he by his conduct contributed to or facilitated;

(e)   he has been removed, under section 7 of the Law Reform (Miscellaneous Provisions) (Scotland) Act 1990 (powers of Court of Session to deal with management of charities) or section 34(5)(e) of the Charities and Trustee Investment (Scotland) Act 2005 (powers of the Court of Session), from being concerned in the management or control of any body;

(f)   he is subject to a disqualification order or disqualification undertaking under the Company Directors Disqualification Act 1986 ... or to an order made under section 429(2)(b) of the Insolvency Act 1986 (failure to pay under county court administration order).

(2) In subsection (1) above –

(a) paragraph (a) applies whether the conviction occurred before or after the commencement of that subsection, but does not apply in relation to any conviction which is a spent conviction for the purposes of the Rehabilitation of Offenders Act 1974;

(b) paragraph (b) applies whether the adjudication of bankruptcy or the sequestration or the making of a bankruptcy restrictions order or an interim order occurred before or after the commencement of that subsection;

(c) paragraph (c) applies whether the composition or arrangement was made, or the trust deed was granted, before or after the commencement of that subsection; and

(d) paragraphs (d) to (f) apply in relation to orders made and removals effected before or after the commencement of that subsection.

(3) Where (apart from this subsection) a person is disqualified under subsection (1)(b) above for being a charity trustee or trustee for any charity which is a company, he shall not be so disqualified if leave has been granted under section 11 of the Company Directors Disqualification Act 1986 (undischarged bankrupts) for him to act as director of the charity; and similarly a person shall not be disqualified under subsection (1)(f) above for being a charity trustee or trustee for such a charity if –

(a) in the case of a person subject to a disqualification order or disqualification undertaking under the Company Directors Disqualification Act 1986, leave for the purposes of section 1(1)(a) or 1A(1)(a) of that Act has been granted for him to act as director of the charity ..., or

(b) in the case of a person subject to an order under section 429(2)(b) of the Insolvency Act 1986, leave has been granted by the court which made the order for him to so act.

(4) The Commission may, on the application of any person disqualified under subsection (1) above, waive his disqualification either generally or in relation to a particular charity or a particular class of charities; but no such waiver may be granted in relation to any charity which is a company if –

(a) the person concerned is for the time being prohibited, by virtue of –
   (i) a disqualification order or disqualification undertaking under the Company Directors Disqualification Act 1986, or
   (ii) section 11(1), 12(2), 12A or 12B of that Act (undischarged bankrupts; failure to pay under county court administration order ...),
   from acting as director of the charity; and

(b) leave has not been granted for him to act as director of any other company.

(4A) If –

(a) a person disqualified under subsection (1)(d) or (e) makes an application under subsection (4) above five years or more after the date on which his disqualification took effect, and

(b) the Commission is not prevented from granting the application by virtue of paragraphs (a) and (b) of subsection (4),

the Commission must grant the application unless satisfied that, by reason of any special circumstances, it should be refused.

(5) Any waiver under subsection (4) above shall be notified in writing to the person concerned.

(6) For the purposes of this section the Commission shall keep, in such manner as it thinks fit, a register of all persons who have been removed from office as mentioned in subsection (1)(d) above either –

(a) by an order of the Commission or the Commissioners made before or after the commencement of subsection (1) above, or

(b) by an order of the High Court made after the commencement of section 45(1) of the
      Charities Act 1992;

and, where any person is so removed from office by an order of the High Court, the court shall
notify the Commission of his removal.

(7) The entries in the register kept under subsection (6) above shall be available for public
inspection in legible form at all reasonable times.

(8) In this section 'the Commissioners' means the Charity Commissioners for England and Wales.

73   Persons acting as charity trustee while disqualified

(1) Subject to subsection (2) below, any person who acts as a charity trustee or trustee for a charity
while he is disqualified for being such a trustee by virtue of section 72 above shall be guilty of an
offence and liable –

(a) on summary conviction, to imprisonment for a term not exceeding six months or to
      a fine not exceeding the statutory maximum, or both;

(b) on conviction on indictment, to imprisonment for a term not exceeding two years or
      to a fine, or both.

(2) Subsection (1) above shall not apply where –

(a) the charity concerned is a company; and

(b) the disqualified person is disqualified by virtue only of paragraph (b) or (f) of section
      72(1) above.

(3) Any acts done as charity trustee or trustee for a charity by a person disqualified for being
such a trustee by virtue of section 72 above shall not be invalid by reason only of that
disqualification.

(4) Where the Commissioners are satisfied –

(a) that any person has acted as charity trustee or trustee for a charity (other than an
      exempt charity) while disqualified for being such a trustee by virtue of section 72
      above, and

(b) that, while so acting, he has received from the charity any sums by way of remuneration
      or expenses, or any benefit in kind, in connection with his acting as charity trustee or
      trustee for the charity,

they may by order direct him to repay to the charity the whole or part of any such sums, or (as
the case may be) to pay to the charity the whole or part of the monetary value (as determined by
them) of any such benefit.

(5) Subsection (4) above does not apply to any sums received by way of remuneration or expenses
in respect of any time when the person concerned was not disqualified for being a charity trustee
or trustee for the charity.

[See Appendix, Charities Act 2006, Schedule 5, para 9, Schedule 8, paras 96, 157, Schedule 9.]

74   Power to transfer all property, modify objects, etc

(1) This section applies to a charity if –

(a) its gross income in its last financial year did not exceed £5,000, and

(b) it does not hold any land on trusts which stipulate that the land is to be used for the
      purposes, or any particular purposes, of the charity,

and it is neither an exempt charity nor a charitable company.

(2) Subject to the following provisions of this section, the charity trustees of a charity to which
this section applies may resolve for the purposes of this section –

(a) that all the property of the charity should be transferred to such other charity as is specified in the resolution, being either a registered charity or a charity which is not required to be registered;

(b) that all the property of the charity should be divided, in such manner as is specified in the resolution, between such two or more other charities as are so specified, being in each case either a registered charity or a charity which is not required to be registered;

(c) that the trusts of the charity should be modified by replacing all or any of the purposes of the charity with such other purposes, being in law charitable, as are specified in the resolution;

(d) that any provision of the trusts of the charity –
  (i) relating to any of the powers exercisable by the charity trustees in the administration of the charity, or
  (ii) regulating the procedure to be followed in any respect in connection with its administration,

should be modified in such manner as is specified in the resolution.

(3) Any resolution passed under subsection (2) above must be passed by a majority of not less than two-thirds of such charity trustees as vote on the resolution.

(4) The charity trustees of a charity to which this section applies ('the transferor charity') shall not have power to pass a resolution under subsection (2)(a) or (b) above unless they are satisfied –

(a) that the existing purposes of the transferor charity have ceased to be conducive to a suitable and effective application of the charity's resources; and

(b) that the purposes of the charity or charities specified in the resolution are as similar in character to the purposes of the transferor charity as is reasonably practicable;

and before passing the resolution they must have received from the charity trustees of the charity, or (as the case may be) of each of the charities, specified in the resolution written confirmation that those trustees are willing to accept a transfer of property under this section.

(5) The charity trustees of any such charity shall not have power to pass a resolution under subsection (2)(c) above unless they are satisfied –

(a) that the existing purposes of the charity (or, as the case may be, such of them as it is proposed to replace) have ceased to be conducive to a suitable and effective application of the charity's resources; and

(b) that the purposes specified in the resolution are as similar in character to those existing purposes as is practical in the circumstances.

(6) Where charity trustees have passed a resolution under subsection (2) above, they shall –

(a) give public notice of the resolution in such manner as they think reasonable in the circumstances; and

(b) send a copy of the resolution to the Commissioners, together with a statement of their reasons for passing it.

(7) The Commissioners may, when considering the resolution, require the charity trustees to provide additional information or explanation –

(a) as to the circumstances in and by reference to which they have determined to act under this section, or

(b) relating to their compliance with this section in connection with the resolution;

and the Commissioners shall take into account any representations made to them by persons appearing to them to be interested in the charity where those representations are made within the period of six weeks beginning with the date when the Commissioners receive a copy of the resolution by virtue of subsection (6)(b) above.

(8) Where the Commissioners have so received a copy of a resolution from any charity trustees

and it appears to them that the trustees have complied with this section in connection with the resolution, the Commissioners shall, within the period of three months beginning with the date when they receive the copy of the resolution, notify the trustees in writing either –

    (a)   that the Commissioners concur with the resolution; or

    (b)   that they do not concur with it.

(9) Where the Commissioners so notify their concurrence with the resolution, then –

    (a)   if the resolution was passed under subsection (2)(a) or (b) above, the charity trustees shall arrange for all the property of the transferor charity to be transferred in accordance with the resolution and on terms that any property so transferred –

        (i)   shall be held and applied by the charity to which it is transferred ('the transferee charity') for the purposes of that charity, but

        (ii)   shall, as property of the transferee charity, nevertheless be subject to any restrictions on expenditure to which it is subject as property of the transferor charity,

        and those trustees shall arrange for it to be so transferred by such date as may be specified in the notification; and

    (b)   if the resolution was passed under subsection (2)(c) or (d) above, the trusts of the charity shall be deemed, as from such date as may be specified in the notification, to have been modified in accordance with the terms of the resolution.

(10) For the purpose of enabling any property to be transferred to a charity under this section, the Commissioners shall have power, at the request of the charity trustees of that charity, to make orders vesting any property of the transferor charity –

    (a)   in the charity trustees of the first-mentioned charity or in any trustee for that charity, or

    (b)   in any other person nominated by those charity trustees to hold the property in trust for that charity.

(11) The Minister may by order amend subsection (1) above by substituting a different sum for the sum for the time being specified there.

(12) In this section –

    (a)   'charitable company' means a charity which is a company or other body corporate; and

    (b)   references to the transfer of property to a charity are references to its transfer –

        (i)   to the charity trustees, or

        (ii)   to any trustee for the charity, or

        (iii)   to a person nominated by the charity trustees to hold it in trust for the charity,

        as the charity trustees may determine.

[See Appendix, Charities Act 2006, s40.]

75   Power to spend capital

(1) This section applies to a charity if –

    (a)   it has a permanent endowment which does not consist of or comprise any land, and

    (b)   its gross income in its last financial year did not exceed £1,000,

and it is neither an exempt charity nor a charitable company.

(2) Where the charity trustees of a charity to which this section applies are of the opinion that the property of the charity is too small, in relation to its purposes, for any useful purpose to be achieved by the expenditure of income alone, they may resolve for the purposes of this section that the charity ought to be freed from the restrictions with respect to expenditure of capital to which its permanent endowment is subject.

(3) Any resolution passed under subsection (2) above must be passed by a majority of not less than two-thirds of such charity trustees as vote on the resolution.

(4) Before passing such a resolution the charity trustees must consider whether any reasonable possibility exists of effecting a transfer or division of all the charity's property under section 74 above (disregarding any such transfer or division as would, in their opinion, impose on the charity an unacceptable burden of costs).

(5) Where charity trustees have passed a resolution under subsection (2) above, they shall –

    (a) give public notice of the resolution in such manner as they think reasonable in the circumstances; and

    (b) send a copy of the resolution to the Commissioners, together with a statement of their reasons for passing it.

(6) The Commissioners may, when considering the resolution, require the charity trustees to provide additional information or explanation –

    (a) as to the circumstances in and by reference to which they have determined to act under this section, or

    (b) relating to their compliance with this section in connection with the resolution;

and the Commissioners shall take into account any representations made to them by persons appearing to them to be interested in the charity where those representations are made within the period of six weeks beginning with the date when the Commissioners receive a copy of the resolution by virtue of subsection (5)(b) above.

(7) Where the Commissioners have so received a copy of a resolution from any charity trustees and it appears to them that the trustees have complied with this section in connection with the resolution, the Commissioners shall, within the period of three months beginning with the date when they receive the copy of the resolution, notify the trustees in writing either –

    (a) that the Commissioners concur with the resolution; or

    (b) that they do not concur with it.

(8) Where the Commissioners so notify their concurrence with the resolution, the charity trustees shall have, as from such date as may be specified in the notification, power by virtue of this section to expend any property of the charity without regard to any such restrictions as are mentioned in subsection (2) above.

(9) The Minister may by order amend subsection (1) above by substituting a different sum for the sum for the time being specified there.

(10) In this section 'charitable company' means a charity which is a company or other body corporate.

[See Appendix, Charities Act 2006, s43.]

81   Manner of giving notice of charity meetings, etc

(1) All notices which are required or authorised by the trusts of a charity to be given to a charity trustee, member or subscriber may be sent by post, and, if sent by post, may be addressed to any address given as his in the list of charity trustees, members or subscribers for the time being in use at the office or principal office of the charity.

(2) Where any such notice required to be given as aforesaid is given by post, it shall be deemed to have been given by the time at which the letter containing it would be delivered in the ordinary course of post.

(3) No notice required to be given as aforesaid of any meeting or election need be given to any charity trustee, member or subscriber, if in the list above mentioned he has no address in the United Kingdom.

82   Manner of executing instruments

(1) Charity trustees may, subject to the trusts of the charity, confer on any of their body (not being less than two in number) a general authority, or an authority limited in such manner as the trustees think fit, to execute in the names and on behalf of the trustees assurances or other deeds or instruments for giving effect to transactions to which the trustees are a party; and any deed or instrument executed in pursuance of an authority so given shall be of the same effect as if executed by the whole body.

(2) An authority under subsection (1) above –

- (a) shall suffice for any deed or instrument if it is given in writing or by resolution of a meeting of the trustees, notwithstanding the want of any formality that would be required in giving an authority apart from that subsection;
- (b) may be given so as to make the powers conferred exercisable by any of the trustees, or may be restricted to named persons or in any other way;
- (c) subject to any such restriction, and until it is revoked, shall, notwithstanding any change in the charity trustees, have effect as a continuing authority given by the charity trustees from time to time of the charity and exercisable by such trustees.

(3) In any authority under this section to execute a deed or instrument in the names and on behalf of charity trustees there shall, unless the contrary intention appears, be implied authority also to execute it for them in the name and on behalf of the official custodian or of any other person, in any case in which the charity trustees could do so.

(4) Where a deed or instrument purports to be executed in pursuance of this section, then in favour of a person who (then or afterwards) in good faith acquires for money or money's worth an interest in or charge on property or the benefit of any covenant or agreement expressed to be entered into by the charity trustees, it shall be conclusively presumed to have been duly executed by virtue of this section.

(5) The powers conferred by this section shall be in addition to and not in derogation of any other powers.

83   Transfer and evidence of title to property vested in trustees

(1) Where, under the trusts of a charity, trustees of property held for the purposes of the charity may be appointed or discharged by resolution of a meeting of the charity trustees, members or other persons, a memorandum declaring a trustee to have been so appointed or discharged shall be sufficient evidence of that fact if the memorandum is signed either at the meeting by the person presiding or in some other manner directed by the meeting and is attested by two persons present at the meeting.

(2) A memorandum evidencing the appointment or discharge of a trustee under subsection (1) above, if executed as a deed, shall have the like operation under section 40 of the Trustee Act 1925 (which relates to vesting declarations as respects trust property in deeds appointing or discharging trustees) as if the appointment or discharge were effected by the deed.

(3) For the purposes of this section, where a document purports to have been signed and attested as mentioned in subsection (1) above, then on proof (whether by evidence or as a matter of presumption) of the signature the document shall be presumed to have been so signed and attested, unless the contrary is shown.

(4) This section shall apply to a memorandum made at any time, except that subsection (2) shall apply only to those made after the commencement of the Charities Act 1960.

(5) This section shall apply in relation to any institution to which the Literary and Scientific Institutions Act 1854 applies as it applies in relation to a charity.

PART X

SUPPLEMENTARY

84 Supply by Commissioners of copies of documents open to public inspection

The Commissioners shall, at the request of any person, furnish him with copies of, or extracts from, any document in their possession which is for the time being open to inspection under Parts II to VI of this Act.

[See Appendix, Charities Act 2006, Schedule 8, paras 96, 163(1)–(4).]

87 Enforcement of requirements by order of Commission

(1) If a person fails to comply with any requirement imposed by or under this Act then (subject to subsection (2) below) the Commission may by order give him such directions as it considers appropriate for securing that the default is made good.

(2) Subsection (1) above does not apply to any such requirement if –

    (a) a person who fails to comply with, or is persistently in default in relation to, the requirement is liable to any criminal penalty; or

    (b) the requirement is imposed –

        (i) by an order of the Commission to which section 88 below applies, or

        (ii) by a direction of the Commission to which that section applies by virtue of section 90(2) below.

88 Enforcement of orders of Commission

A person guilty of disobedience –

    (a) to an order of the Commissioners under section 9(1), 44(2), 61, 73 or 80 above; or

    (b) to an order of the Commissioners under section 16 or 18 above requiring a transfer of property or payment to be called for or made; or

    (c) to an order of the Commissioners requiring a default under this Act to be made good;

may on the application of the Commissioners to the High Court be dealt with as for disobedience to an order of the High Court.

[See Appendix, Charities Act 2006, Schedule 8, paras 96, 167(1)–(4).]

90 Directions of the Commission

(1) Any direction given by the Commission under any provision contained in this Act –

    (a) may be varied or revoked by a further direction given under that provision; and

    (b) shall be given in writing.

(2) Sections 88 and 89(1), (2) and (4) above shall apply to any such directions as they apply to an order of the Commission.

(3) In subsection (1) above the reference to the Commission includes, in relation to a direction under subsection (3) of section 8 above, a reference to any person conducting an inquiry under that section.

(4) Nothing in this section shall be read as applying to any directions contained in an order made by the Commission under section 87(1) above.

92 Appeals from Commissioners

(1) Provision shall be made by rules of court for regulating appeals to the High Court under this Act against orders or decisions of the Commissioners.

(2) On such an appeal the Attorney General shall be entitled to appear and be heard, and such other persons as the rules allow or as the court may direct.

[See Appendix, Charities Act 2006, Schedule 8, paras 96, 171, Schedule 9.]

95   Offences by bodies corporate

Where any offence under this Act is committed by a body corporate and is proved to have been committed with the consent or connivance of, or to be attributable to any neglect on the part of, any director, manager, secretary or other similar officer of the body corporate, or any person who was purporting to act in any such capacity, he as well as the body corporate shall be guilty of that offence and shall be liable to be proceeded against and punished accordingly. In relation to a body corporate whose affairs are managed by its members, 'director' means a member of the body corporate.

96   Construction of references to a 'charity' or to particular classes of charity

(1) In this Act, except in so far as the context otherwise requires –

'charity' means any institution, corporate or not, which is established for charitable purposes and is subject to the control of the High Court in the exercise of the court's jurisdiction with respect to charities;

'ecclesiastical charity' has the same meaning as in the Local Government Act 1894;

'exempt charity' means (subject to section 24(8) above) a charity comprised in Schedule 2 to this Act;

'local charity' means, in relation to any area, a charity established for purposes which are by their nature or by the trusts of the charity directed wholly or mainly to the benefit of that area or of part of it;

'parochial charity' means, in relation to any parish or (in Wales) community, a charity the benefits of which are, or the separate distribution of the benefits of which is, confined to inhabitants of the parish or community, or of a single ancient ecclesiastical parish which included that parish or community or part of it, or of an area consisting of that parish or community with not more than four neighbouring parishes or communities.

(2) The expression 'charity' is not in this Act applicable –

(a)   to any ecclesiastical corporation (that is to say, any corporation in the Church of England, whether sole or aggregate, which is established for spiritual purposes) in respect of the corporate property of the corporation, except to a corporation aggregate having some purposes which are not ecclesiastical in respect of its corporate property held for those purposes; or

(b)   to any Diocesan Board of Finance (or any subsidiary thereof) within the meaning of the Endowments and Glebe Measure 1976 for any diocese in respect of the diocesan glebe land of that diocese within the meaning of that Measure; or

(c)   to any trust of property for purposes for which the property has been consecrated.

(3) A charity shall be deemed for the purposes of this Act to have a permanent endowment unless all property held for the purposes of the charity may be expended for those purposes without distinction between capital and income, and in this Act 'permanent endowment' means, in relation to any charity, property held subject to a restriction on its being expended for the purposes of the charity.

(4) References in this Act to a charity whose income from all sources does not in aggregate amount to more than a specified amount shall be construed –

(a)   by reference to the gross revenues of the charity, or

(b) if the Commissioners so determine, by reference to the amount which they estimate to be the likely amount of those revenues,

but without (in either case) bringing into account anything for the yearly value of land occupied by the charity apart from the pecuniary income (if any) received from that land; and any question as to the application of any such reference to a charity shall be determined by the Commissioners, whose decision shall be final.

(5) The Commission may direct that for all or any of the purposes of this Act an institution established for any special purposes of or in connection with a charity (being charitable purposes) shall be treated as forming part of that charity or as forming a distinct charity.

(6) The Commission may direct that for all or any of the purposes of this Act two or more charities having the same charity trustees shall be treated as a single charity.

[See Appendix, Charities Act 2006, Schedule 8, paras 96, 173(1)–(3), Schedule 9.]

97 General interpretation

(1) In this Act, except in so far as the context otherwise requires –

'charitable purposes' means purposes which are exclusively charitable according to the law of England and Wales;

'charity trustees' means the persons having the general control and management of the administration of a charity;

'the Commission' means the Charity Commission;

'company' means a company formed and registered under the Companies Act 1985 or to which the provisions of that Act apply as they apply to such a company;

'the court' means the High Court and, within the limits of its jurisdiction, any other court in England and Wales having a jurisdiction in respect of charities concurrent (within any limit of area or amount) with that of the High Court, and includes any judge or officer of the court exercising the jurisdiction of the court; ...

'institution' means an institution whether incorporated or not, and includes any trust or undertaking;

'members', in relation to a charity with a body of members distinct from the charity trustees, means any of those members;

'the Minister' means the Minister for the Cabinet Office;

'the official custodian' means the official custodian for charities;

'the register' means the register of charities kept under section 3 above and

'principal regulator', in relation to an exempt charity, means the charity's principal regulator within the meaning of section 13 of the Charities Act 2006;

'registered' shall be construed accordingly;

'special trust' means property which is held and administered by or on behalf of a charity for any special purposes of the charity, and is so held and administered on separate trusts relating only to that property but a special trust shall not, by itself, constitute a charity for the purposes of Part VI of this Act;

'the Tribunal' means the Charity Tribunal;

'trusts' in relation to a charity, means the provisions establishing it as a charity and regulating its purposes and administration, whether those provisions take effect by way of trust or not, and in relation to other institutions has a corresponding meaning. ...

[See Appendix, Charities Act 2006, Schedule 7, Part 2, paras 3, 7, Schedule 8, paras 96, 174(a).]

SCHEDULE 1A

THE CHARITY COMMISSION

Membership

1. – (1) The Commission shall consist of a chairman and at least four, but not more than eight, other members.

(2) The members shall be appointed by the Minister.

(3) The Minister shall exercise the power in sub-paragraph (2) so as to secure that –

 (a) the knowledge and experience of the members of the Commission (taken together) includes knowledge and experience of the matters mentioned in sub-paragraph (4),

 (b) at least two members have a seven year general qualification within the meaning of section 71 of the Courts and Legal Services Act 1990, and

 (c) at least one member knows about conditions in Wales and has been appointed following consultation with the National Assembly for Wales.

(4) The matters mentioned in this sub-paragraph are –

 (a) the law relating to charities,

 (b) charity accounts and the financing of charities, and

 (c) the operation and regulation of charities of different sizes and descriptions.

(5) In sub-paragraph (3)(c) 'member' does not include the chairman of the Commission.

Terms of appointment and remuneration

2. The members of the Commission shall hold and vacate office as such in accordance with the terms of their respective appointments.

3. – (1) An appointment of a person to hold office as a member of the Commission shall be for a term not exceeding three years.

(2) A person holding office as a member of the Commission –

 (a) may resign that office by giving notice in writing to the Minister, and

 (b) may be removed from office by the Minister on the ground of incapacity or misbehaviour.

(3) Before removing a member of the Commission the Minister shall consult –

 (a) the Commission, and

 (b) if the member was appointed following consultation with the National Assembly for Wales, the Assembly.

(4) No person may hold office as a member of the Commission for more than ten years in total.

(5) For the purposes of sub-paragraph (4), time spent holding office as a Charity Commissioner for England and Wales shall be counted as time spent holding office as a member of the Commission. ...

Annual report

11. – (1) As soon as practicable after the end of each financial year the Commission shall publish a report on –

 (a) the discharge of its functions,

 (b) the extent to which, in its opinion, its objectives (see section 1B of this Act) have been met,

 (c) the performance of its general duties (see section 1D of this Act), and

 (d) the management of its affairs,

during that year.

(2) The Commission shall lay a copy of each such report before Parliament.

(3) In sub-paragraph (1) above, 'financial year' means –

    (a) the period beginning with the date on which the Commission is established and ending with the next 31st March following that date, and

    (b) each successive period of 12 months ending with 31st March.

Annual public meeting

12. – (1) The Commission shall hold a public meeting ('the annual meeting') for the purpose of enabling a report under paragraph 11 above to be considered.

(2) The annual meeting shall be held within the period of three months beginning with the day on which the report is published.

(3) The Commission shall organise the annual meeting so as to allow –

    (a) a general discussion of the contents of the report which is being considered, and

    (b) a reasonable opportunity for those attending the meeting to put questions to the Commission about matters to which the report relates.

(4) But subject to sub-paragraph (3) above the annual meeting is to be organised and conducted in such a way as the Commission considers appropriate.

(5) The Commission shall –

    (a) take such steps as are reasonable in the circumstances to ensure that notice of the annual meeting is given to every registered charity, and

    (b) publish notice of the annual meeting in the way appearing to it to be best calculated to bring it to the attention of members of the public.

(6) Each such notice shall –

    (a) give details of the time and place at which the meeting is to be held,

    (b) set out the proposed agenda for the meeting,

    (c) indicate the proposed duration of the meeting, and

    (d) give details of the Commission's arrangements for enabling persons to attend.

(7) If the Commission proposes to alter any of the arrangements which have been included in notices given or published under sub-paragraph (5) above it shall –

    (a) give reasonable notice of the alteration, and

    (b) publish the notice in the way appearing to it to be best calculated to bring it to the attention of registered charities and members of the public. ...

SCHEDULE 2

EXEMPT CHARITIES

The following institutions, so far as they are charities, are exempt charities within the meaning of this Act, that is to say –

    (a) any institution which, if the Charities Act 1960 had not been passed, would be exempted from the powers and jurisdiction, under the Charitable Trusts Acts 1853 to 1939, of the Commissioners or Minister of Education (apart from any power of the Commissioners or Minister to apply those Acts in whole or in part to charities otherwise exempt) by the terms of any enactment not contained in those Acts other than section 9 of the Places of Worship Registration Act 1855;

    (b) the universities of Oxford, Cambridge, London, Durham and Newcastle, the colleges and halls in the universities of Oxford, Cambridge, Durham and Newcastle, Queen Mary and Westfield College in the University of London and the colleges of Winchester and Eton;

(c) any university, university college, or institution connected with a university or university college, which Her Majesty declares by Order in Council to be an exempt charity for the purposes of this Act;

(da) the Qualifications and Curriculum Authority;

(i) a successor company to a higher education corporation (within the meaning of section 129(5) of the Education Reform Act 1988) at a time when an institution conducted by the company is for the time being designated under that section;

(k) the Board of Trustees of the Victoria and Albert Museum;

(l) the Board of Trustees of the Science Museum;

(m) the Board of Trustees of the Armouries;

(n) the Board of Trustees of the Royal Botanic Gardens, Kew;

(o) the Board of Trustees of the National Museums and Galleries on Merseyside;

(p) the trustees of the British Museum and the trustees of the Natural History Museum;

(q) the Board of Trustees of the National Gallery;

(r) the Board of Trustees of the Tate Gallery;

(s) the Board of Trustees of the National Portrait Gallery;

(t) the Board of Trustees of the Wallace Collection;

(u) the Trustees of the Imperial War Museum;

(v) the Trustees of the National Maritime Museum;

(w) any institution which is administered by or on behalf of an institution included above and is established for the general purposes of, or for any special purpose of or in connection with, the last-mentioned institution;

(x) the Church Commissioners and any institution which is administered by them;

(y) any registered society within the meaning of the Industrial and Provident Societies Act 1965 and any registered society or branch within the meaning of the Friendly Societies Act 1974;

(z) the Board of Governors of the Museum of London;

(za) the British Library Board;

[See Appendix, Charities Act 2006, s11(1)–(9), Schedule 8, paras 96, 177, Schedule 9.]

SCHEDULE 5

MEANING OF 'CONNECTED PERSON' FOR PURPOSES OF SECTION 36(2)

1. – (1) In section 36(2) of this Act 'connected person', in relation to a charity, means any person who falls within sub-paragraph (2) –

(a) at the time of the disposition in question, or

(b) at the time of any contract for the disposition in question.

(2) The persons falling within this sub-paragraph are –

(a) a charity trustee or trustee for the charity;

(b) a person who is the donor of any land to the charity (whether the gift was made on or after the establishment of the charity);

(c) a child, parent, grandchild, grandparent, brother or sister of any such trustee or donor;

(d) an officer, agent or employee of the charity;

(e) the spouse or civil partner of any person falling within any of sub-paragraphs (a) to (d) above;

(ea) a person carrying on business in partnership with any person falling within any of sub-paragraphs (a) to (e) above;

(f) an institution which is controlled –

    (i) by any person failing within any of sub-paragraphs (a) to (ea) above, or

    (ii) by two or more such persons taken together; or

(g) a body corporate in which –

    (i) any connected person falling within any of sub-paragraphs (a) to (f) above has a substantial interest, or

    (ii) two or more such persons, taken together, have a substantial interest.

2. – (1) In paragraph 1(2)(c) above 'child' includes a stepchild and an illegitimate child.

(2) For the purposes of paragraph 1(2)(e) above a person living with another as that person's husband or wife shall be treated as that person's spouse.

(3) Where two persons of the same sex are not civil partners but live together as if they were, each of them shall be treated for those purposes as the civil partner of the other.

3. For the purposes of paragraph 1(2)(f) above a person controls an institution if he is able to secure that the affairs of the institution are conducted in accordance with his wishes.

4. – (1) For the purposes of paragraph 1(2)(g) above any such connected person as is there mentioned has a substantial interest in a body corporate if the person or institution in question –

(a) is interested in shares comprised in the equity share capital of that body of a nominal value of more than one-fifth of that share capital, or

(b) is entitled to exercise, or control the exercise of, more than one-fifth of the voting power at any general meeting of that body. …

As amended by the Charities Act 1993 (Substitution of Sums) Order 1995, art 2(1), (3), (4); Companies Act 1985 (Audit Exemption) Regulations 1994, reg 6; Deregulation and Contracting Out Act 1994, ss28(2), 29(1)–(4), (8), 30(2), (3); Charities (Amendment) Act 1995, s1; Education Act 1997, s57(1), Schedule 7, para 7; School Standards and Framework 1998, s140(1), (3), Schedule 30, para 48, Schedule 31; Teaching and Higher Education Act 1998, s44(1)(2), Schedule 3, para 9, Schedule 4; Trustee Act 2000, s40, Schedule 2, para 2(1), Schedule 4, Pt I; Insolvency Act 2000, s8, Schedule 4, Pt II, para 18; Church of England (Miscellaneous Provisions) Measure 2000, s11; Insolvency Act 2000 (Company Directors Disqualification Undertakings) Order 2004, art 3, Schedule, para 5(c); Civil Partnership Act 2004, s261(1), Schedule 27, para 147; Regulatory Reform (National Health Service Charitable and Non-Charitable Trust Accounts and Audit) Order 2005, art 3(1), (5); Charities Act 2006, ss6, 22–25, 27, 28(1)–(5), 35, 75(1), (2), Schedule 8, paras 96, 97, 98(1)–(4), 99(1), (2), (4)(b), (c), (5)(b), 100(1), (2), 101–103, 106, 107, 109(1)–(11), (13), 110(1)–(3), 111(1)–(6), (8)–(10), 112(1)–(5), (7) 116, 117, 119, 120, 121(1), (6), 122(1)–(3), 123–126, 128, 130, 132, 133, 134(1), (2), 138(1)–(6), 139(1), (2), (5), 141(1), (2), 143(1), (2), 149, 150, 154(1), (2), 156, 166, 167(1), (5), 169, 173(1), (4), 174(b)–(d), 178, Schedule 9 (part); Transfer of Functions (Third Sector, Communities and Equality) Order 2006, art 6, Schedule, para 4 (a), (c), (e), (g), (i), j), (o), (q), (t) (v), (w); Enterprise Act 2002 (Disqualification from Office: General Order 2006, art 2(2), Schedule 2, Part 1, para 4(a), (b); Charities and Trustee Investment (Scotland) Act 2005 (Consequential Provisions and Modifications) Order 2006, art 5, Schedule, Part 1, para 6(1), (2); Charities Act 2006 (Interim Changes in Threshold for Registration of Small Charities) Order 2007, art 2.

DISABILITY DISCRIMINATION ACT 1995
(1995 c 50)

18C Charities and support for particular groups of persons

(1) Nothing in this Part [The Employment Field] –

    (a) affects any charitable instrument which provides for conferring benefits on one or more categories of person determined by reference to any physical or mental capacity; or

    (b) makes unlawful any act done by a charity or recognised body in pursuance of any of its charitable purposes, so far as those purposes are connected with persons so determined.

(2) Nothing in this Part prevents –

    (a) a person who provides supported employment from treating members of a particular group of disabled persons more favourably than other persons in providing such employment; or

    (b) the Secretary of State from agreeing to arrangements for the provision of supported employment which will, or may, have that effect.

(3) In this section –

'charitable instrument' means an enactment or other instrument (whenever taking effect) so far as it relates to charitable purposes;

'charity' has the same meaning as in the Charities Act 1993;

'recognised body' means a body which is a recognised body for the purposes of Part I of the Law Reform (Miscellaneous Provisions) (Scotland) Act 1990; and

'supported employment' means facilities provided, or in respect of which payments are made, under section 15 of the Disabled Persons (Employment) Act 1944.

(4) In the application of this section to England and Wales, 'charitable purposes' means purposes which are exclusively charitable according to the law of England and Wales. …

As amended by the Disability Discrimination Act 1995 (Amendment) Regulations 2003, regs 3(1), 11.

TRUSTS OF LAND AND APPOINTMENT OF TRUSTEES ACT 1996
(1996 c 47)

PART I

TRUSTS OF LAND

1 Meaning of 'trust of land'

(1) In this Act –

    (a) 'trust of land' means (subject to subsection (3)) any trust of property which consists of or includes land, and

    (b) 'trustees of land' means trustees of a trust of land.

(2) The reference in subsection (1)(a) to a trust –

    (a) is to any description of a trust (whether express, implied, resulting or constructive), including a trust for sale and a bare trust, and

(b) includes a trust created, or arising, before the commencement of this Act,

(3) The reference to land in subsection (1)(a) does not include land which (despite section 2) is settled land or which is land to which the Universities and College Estates Act 1925 applies.

2 Trusts in place of settlements

(1) No settlement created after the commencement of this Act is a settlement for the purposes of the Settled Land Act 1925; and no settlement shall be deemed to be made under that Act after that commencement.

(2) Subsection (1) does not apply to a settlement created on the occasion of an alteration in any interest in, or of a person becoming entitled under, a settlement which –

(a) is in existence at the commencement of this Act, or

(b) derives from a settlement within paragraph (a) or this paragraph.

(3) But a settlement created as mentioned in subsection (2) is not a settlement for the purposes of the Settled land Act 1925 if provision to the effect that it is not is made in the instrument, or any of the instruments, by which it is created.

(4) Where at any time after the commencement of this Act there is in the case of any settlement which is a settlement for the purposes of the Settled land Act 1925 no relevant property which is, or is deemed to be, subject to the settlement, the settlement permanently ceases at that time to be a settlement for the purposes of that Act. In this subsection 'relevant property' means land and personal chattels to which section 67(1) of the Settled Land Act 1925 (heirlooms) applies.

(5) No land held on charitable, ecclesiastical or public trusts shall be or be deemed to be settled land after the commencement of this Act, even if it was or was deemed to be settled land before that commencement.

(6) Schedule 1 has effect to make provision consequential on this section (including provision to impose a trust in circumstances in which, apart from this section, there would be a settlement for the purposes of the Settled Land Act 1925 (and there would not otherwise be a trust)).

3 Abolition of doctrine of conversion

(1) Where land is held by trustees subject to a trust for sale, the land is not to be regarded as personal property; and where personal property is subject to a trust for sale in order that the trustees may acquire land, the personal property is not to be regarded as land.

(2) Subsection (1) does not apply to a trust created by a will if the testator died before the commencement of this Act.

(3) Subject to that, subsection (1) applies to a trust whether it is created, or arises, before or after that commencement.

4 Express trusts for sale as trusts of land

(1) In the case of every trust for sale of land created by a disposition there is to be implied, despite any provision to the contrary made by the disposition, a power for the trustees to postpone sale of the land; and the trustees are not liable in any way for postponing sale of the land, in the exercise of their discretion, for an indefinite period.

(2) Subsection (1) applies to a trust whether it is created, or arises, before or after the commencement of this Act

(3) Subsection (1) does not affect any liability incurred by trustees before that commencement.

5 Implied trusts for sale as trusts of land

(1) Schedule 2 has effect in relation to statutory provisions which impose a trust for sale of land in certain circumstances so that in those circumstances there is instead a trust of the land (without a duty to sell).

(2) Section 1 of the Settled Land Act 1925 does not apply to land held on any trust arising by virtue of that Schedule (so that any such land is subject to a trust of land).

6 General powers of trustees

(1) For the purpose of exercising their functions as trustees, the trustees of land have in relation to the land subject to the trust all the powers of an absolute owner.

(2) Where in the case of any land subject to a trust of land each of the beneficiaries interested in the land is a person of full age and capacity who is absolutely entitled to the land, the powers conferred on the trustees by subsection (1) include the power to convey the land to the beneficiaries even though they have not required the trustees to do so; and where land is conveyed by virtue of this subsection –

(a) the beneficiaries shall do whatever is necessary to secure that it vests in them, and

(b) if they fail to do so, the court may make an order requiring them to do so.

(3) The trustees of land have power to acquire land under the power conferred by section 8 of the Trustee Act 2000.

(5) In exercising the powers conferred by this section trustees shall have regard to the rights of the beneficiaries.

(6) The powers conferred by this section shall not be exercised in contravention of, or of any order made in pursuance of, any other enactment or any rule of law or equity.

(7) The reference in subsection (6) to an order includes an order of any court or of the Charity Commission.

(8) Where any enactment other than this section confers on trustees authority to act subject to any restriction, limitation or condition, trustees of land may not exercise the powers conferred by this section to do any act which they are prevented from doing under the other enactment by reason of the restriction, limitation or condition.

(9) The duty of care under section 1 of the Trustee Act 2000 applies to trustees of land when exercising the powers conferred by this section.

7 Partition by trustees

(1) The trustees of land may, where beneficiaries of full age are absolutely entitled in undivided shares to land subject to the trust, partition the land, or any part of it, and provide (by way of mortgage or otherwise) for the payment of any equality money.

(2) The trustees shall give effect to any such partition by conveying the partitioned land in severalty (whether or not subject to any legal mortgage created for raising equality money), either absolutely or in trust, in accordance with the rights of those beneficiaries.

(3) Before exercising their powers under subsection (2) the trustees shall obtain the consent of each of those beneficiaries.

(4) Where a share in the land is affected by an incumbrance, the trustees may either give effect to it or provide for its discharge from the property allotted to that share as they think fit.

(5) If a share in the land is absolutely vested in a minor, subsections (1) to (4) apply as if he were of full age, except that the trustees may act on his behalf and retain land or other property representing his share in trust for him.

(6) Subsection (1) is subject to sections 21 (part-unit: interests) and 22 (part-unit: charging) of the Commonhold and Leasehold Reform Act 2002.

8 Exclusion and restriction of powers

(1) Sections 6 and 7 do not apply in the case of a trust of land created by a disposition in so far as provision to the effect that they do not apply is made by the disposition.

(2) If the disposition creating such a trust makes provision requiring any consent to be obtained

to the exercise of any power conferred by section 6 or 7, the power may not be exercised without that consent.

(3) Subsection (1) does not apply in the case of charitable, ecclesiastical or public trusts.

(4) Subsections (1) and (2) have effect subject to any enactment which prohibits or restricts the effect of provision of the description mentioned in them.

9 Delegation by trustees

(1) The trustees of land may, by power of attorney, delegate to any beneficiary or beneficiaries of full age and beneficially entitled to an interest in possession in land subject to the trust any of their functions as trustees which relate to the land.

(2) Where trustees purport to delegate to a person by a power of attorney under subsection (1) functions relating to any land and another person in good faith deals with him in relation to the land, he shall be presumed in favour of that other person to have been a person to whom the functions could be delegated unless that other person has knowledge at the time of the transaction that he was not such a person. And it shall be conclusively presumed in favour of any purchaser whose interest depends on the validity of that transaction that that other person dealt in good faith and did not have such knowledge if that other person makes a statutory declaration to that effect before or within three months after the completion of the purchase.

(3) A power of attorney under subsection (1) shall be given by all the trustees jointly and (unless expressed to be irrevocable and to be given by way of security) may be revoked by any one or more of them; and such a power is revoked by the appointment as a trustee of a person other than those by whom it is given (though not by any of those persons dying or otherwise ceasing to be a trustee).

(4) Where a beneficiary to whom functions are delegated by a power of attorney under subsection (1) ceases to be a person beneficially entitled to an interest in possession in land subject to the trust —

(a) if the functions are delegated to him alone, the power is revoked,

(b) if the functions are delegated to him and to other beneficiaries to be exercised by them jointly (but not separately), the power is revoked if each of the other beneficiaries ceases to be so entitled (but otherwise functions exercisable in accordance with the power are so exercisable by the remaining beneficiary or beneficiaries), and

(c) if the functions are delegated to him and to other beneficiaries to be exercised by them separately (or either separately or jointly), the power is revoked in so far as it relates to him.

(5) A delegation under subsection (1) may be for any period or indefinite.

(6) A power of attorney under subsection (1) cannot be an enduring power within the meaning of the Enduring Powers of Attorney Act 1985.

(7) Beneficiaries to whom functions have been delegated under subsection (1) are, in relation to the exercise of the functions, in the same position as trustees (with the same duties and liabilities); but such beneficiaries shall not be regarded as trustees for any other purposes (including, in particular, the purposes of any enactment permitting the delegation of functions by trustees or imposing requirements relating to the payment of capital money).

(9) Neither this section nor the repeal by this Act of section 29 of the Law of Property Act 1925 (which is superseded by this section) affects the operation after the commencement of this Act of any delegation effected before that commencement.

9A   Duties of trustees in connection with delegation, etc

(1) The duty of care under section 1 of the Trustee Act 2000 applies to trustees of land in deciding whether to delegate any of their functions under section 9.

(2) Subsection (3) applies if the trustees of land –

  (a)   delegate any of their functions under section 9, and

  (b)   the delegation is not irrevocable.

(3) While the delegation continues, the trustees –

  (a)   must keep the delegation under review,

  (b)   if circumstances make it appropriate to do so, must consider whether there is a need to exercise any power of intervention that they have, and

  (c)   if they consider that there is a need to exercise such a power, must do so.

(4) 'Power of intervention' includes –

  (a)   a power to give directions to the beneficiary;

  (b)   a power to revoke the delegation.

(5) The duty of care under section 1 of the 2000 Act applies to trustees in carrying out any duty under subsection (3).

(6) A trustee of land is not liable for any act or default of the beneficiary, or beneficiaries, unless the trustee fails to comply with the duty of care in deciding to delegate any of the trustees' functions under section 9 or in carrying out any duty under subsection (3).

(7) Neither this section nor the repeal of section 9(8) by the Trustee Act 2000 affects the operation after the commencement of this section of any delegation effected before that commencement.

10   Consents

(1) If a disposition creating a trust of land requires the consent of more than two persons to the exercise by the trustees of any function relating to the land, the consent of any two of them to the exercise of the function is sufficient in favour of a purchaser.

(2) Subsection (1) does not apply to the exercise of a function by trustees of land held on charitable, ecclesiastical or public trusts.

(3) Where at any time a person whose consent is expressed by a disposition creating a trust of land to be required to the exercise by the trustees of any function relating to the land is not of full age –

  (a)   his consent is not, in favour of a purchaser, required to the exercise of the function, but

  (b)   the trustees shall obtain the consent of a parent who has parental responsibility for him (within the meaning of the Children Act 1989) or of a guardian of his.

11   Consultation with beneficiaries

(1) The trustees of land shall in the exercise of any function relating to land subject to the trust –

  (a)   so far as is practicable, consult the beneficiaries of full age and beneficially entitled to an interest in possession in the land, and

  (b)   so far as consistent with the general interest of the trust, give effect to the wishes of those beneficiaries, or (in case of dispute) of the majority (according to the value of their combined interests).

(2) Subsection (1) does not apply –

  (a)   in relation to a trust created by a disposition in so far as provision that it does not apply is made by the disposition,

  (b)   in relation to a trust created or arising under a will made before the commencement of this Act, or

(c) in relation to the exercise of the power mentioned in section 6(2).

(3) Subsection (1) does not apply to a trust created before the commencement of this Act by a disposition, or a trust created after that commencement by reference to such a trust, unless provision to the effect that it is to apply is made by a deed executed –

> (a) in a case in which the trust was created by one person and he is of full capacity, by that person, or
>
> (b) in a case in which the trust was created by more than one person, by such of the persons who created the trust as are alive and of full capacity.

(4) A deed executed for the purposes of subsection (3) is irrevocable.

12 The right to occupy

(1) A beneficiary who is beneficially entitled to an interest in possession in land subject to a trust of land is entitled by reason of his interest to occupy the land at any time if at that time –

> (a) the purposes of the trust include making the land available for his occupation (or for the occupation of beneficiaries of a class of which he is a member or of beneficiaries in general), or
>
> (b) the land is held by the trustees so as to be so available.

(2) Subsection (1) does not confer on a beneficiary a right to occupy land if it is either unavailable or unsuitable for occupation by him.

(3) This section is subject to section 13.

13 Exclusion and restriction of right to occupy

(1) Where two or more beneficiaries are (or apart from this subsection would be) entitled under section 12 to occupy land, the trustees of land may exclude or restrict the entitlement of any one or more (but not all) of them.

(2) Trustees may not under subsection (1) –

> (a) unreasonably exclude any beneficiary's entitlement to occupy land, or
>
> (b) restrict any such entitlement to an unreasonable extent.

(3) The trustees of land may from time to time impose reasonable conditions on any beneficiary in relation to his occupation of land by reason of his entitlement under section 12.

(4) The matters to which trustees are to have regard in exercising the powers conferred by this section include –

> (a) the intentions of the person or persons (if any) who created the trust,
>
> (b) the purposes for which the land is held, and
>
> (c) the circumstances and wishes of each of the beneficiaries who is (or apart from any previous exercise by the trustees of those powers would be) entitled to occupy the land under section 12.

(5) The conditions which may be imposed on a beneficiary under subsection (3) include, in particular, conditions requiring him –

> (a) to pay any outgoings or expenses in respect of the land, or
>
> (b) to assume any other obligation in relation to the land or to any activity which is or is proposed to be conducted there.

(6) Where the entitlement of any beneficiary to occupy land under section 12 has been excluded or restricted, the conditions which may be imposed on any other beneficiary under subsection (3) include, in particular, conditions requiring him to –

> (a) make payments by way of compensation to the beneficiary whose entitlement has been excluded or restricted, or

    (b) forgo any payment or other benefit to which he would otherwise be entitled under the trust so as to benefit that beneficiary.

(7) The powers conferred on trustees by this section may not be exercised –

    (a) so as to prevent any person who is in occupation of land (whether or not by reason of an entitlement under section 12) from continuing to occupy the land, or

    (b) in a manner likely to result in any such person ceasing to occupy the land,

unless he consents or the court has given approval.

(8) The matters to which the court is to have regard in determining whether to give approval under subsection (7) include the matters mentioned in subsection (4)(a) to (c).

14   Applications for order

(1) Any person who is a trustee of land or has an interest in property subject to a trust of land may make an application to the court for an order under this section.

(2) On application for an order under this section the court may make any such order –

    (a) relating to the exercise by the trustees of any of their functions (including an order relieving them of any obligation to obtain the consent of, or to consult, any person in connection with the exercise of any of their functions), or

    (b) declaring the nature or extent of a person's interest in property subject to the trust,

as the court thinks fit.

(3) The court may not under this section make any order as to the appointment or removal of trustees.

(4) The powers conferred on the court by this section are exercisable on an application whether it is made before or after the commencement of this Act.

15   Matters relevant in determining applications

(1) The matters to which the court is to have regard in determining an application for an order under section 14 include –

    (a) the intentions of the person or persons (if any) who created the trust,

    (b) the purposes for which the property subject to the trust is held,

    (c) the welfare of any minor who occupies or might reasonably be expected to occupy any land subject to the trust as his home, and

    (d) the interests of any secured creditor of any beneficiary.

(2) In the case of an application relating to the exercise in relation to any land of the powers conferred on the trustees by section 13, the matters to which the court is to have regard also include the circumstances and wishes of each of the beneficiaries who is (or apart from any previous exercise by the trustees of those powers would be) entitled to occupy the land under section 12.

(3) In the case of any other application, other than one relating to the exercise of the power mentioned in section 6(2), the matters to which the court is to have regard also include the circumstances and wishes of any beneficiaries of full age and entitled to an interest in possession in property subject to the trust or (in case of dispute) of the majority (according to the value of their combined interests).

(4) This section does not apply to an application if section 335A of the Insolvency Act 1986 (which is inserted by Schedule 3 and relates to applications by a trustee of a bankrupt) applies to it.

16   Protection of purchasers

(1) A purchaser of land which is or has been subject to a trust need not be concerned to see that any requirement imposed on the trustees by section 6(5), 7(3) or 11(1) has been complied with.

(2) Where –
   (a)   trustees of land who convey land which (immediately before it is conveyed) is subject
         to the trust contravene section 6(6) or (8), but
   (b)   the purchaser of the land from the trustees has no actual notice of the contravention,
the contravention does not invalidate the conveyance.
(3) Where the powers of trustees of land are limited by virtue of section 8 –
   (a)   the trustees shall take all reasonable steps to bring the limitation to the notice of any
         purchaser of the land from them, but
   (b)   the limitation does not invalidate any conveyance by the trustees to a purchaser who
         has no actual notice of the limitation.
(4) Where trustees of land convey land which (immediately before it is conveyed) is subject to
the trust to persons believed by them to be beneficiaries absolutely entitled to the land under the
trust and of full age and capacity –
   (a)   the trustees shall execute a deed declaring that they are discharged from the trust in
         relation to that land, and
   (b)   if they fail to do so, the court may make an order requiring them to do so.
(5) A purchaser of land to which a deed under subsection (4) relates is entitled to assume that,
as from the date of the deed, the land is not subject to the trust unless he has actual notice that
the trustees were mistaken in their belief that the land was conveyed to beneficiaries absolutely
entitled to the land under the trust and of full age and capacity.
(6) Subsections (2) and (3) do not apply to land held on charitable, ecclesiastical or public trusts.
(7) This section does not apply to registered land.

17   Application of provisions to trusts of proceeds of sale

(2) Section 14 applies in relation to a trust of proceeds of sale of land and trustees of such a trust
as in relation to a trust of land and trustees of land.
(3) In this section 'trust of proceeds of sale of land' means (subject to subsection (5)) any trust of
property (other than a trust of land) which consists of or includes –
   (a)   any proceeds of a disposition of land held in trust (including settled land), or
   (b)   any property representing any such proceeds.
(4) The references in subsection (3) to a trust –
   (a)   are to any description of trust (whether express, implied, resulting or constructive),
         including a trust for sale and a bare trust, and
   (b)   include a trust created, or arising, before the commencement of this Act.
(5) A trust which (despite section 2) is a settlement for the purposes of the Settled Land Act
1925 cannot be a trust of proceeds of sale of land.
(6) In subsection (3) –
   (a)   'disposition' includes any disposition made, or coming into operation, before the
         commencement of this Act, and
   (b)   the reference to settled land includes personal chattels to which section 67(1) of the
         Settled Land Act 1925 (heirlooms) applies.

18   Application of Part to personal representatives

(1) The provisions of this Part relating to trustees, other than sections 10, 11 and 14, apply to
personal representatives, but with appropriate modifications and without prejudice to the
functions of personal representatives for the purposes of administration.
(2) The appropriate modifications include –

(a) the substitution of references to persons interested in the due administration of the estate for references to beneficiaries, and

(b) the substitution of references to the will for references to the disposition creating the trust.

(3) Section 3(1) does not apply to personal representatives if the death occurs before the commencement of this Act.

PART II

APPOINTMENT AND RETIREMENT OF TRUSTEES

19   Appointment and retirement of trustee at instance of beneficiaries

(1) This section applies in the case of a trust where –

(a) there is no person nominated for the purpose of appointing new trustees by the instrument, if any, creating the trust, and

(b) the beneficiaries under the trust are of full age and capacity and (taken together) are absolutely entitled to the property subject to the trust.

(2) The beneficiaries may give a direction or directions of either or both of the following descriptions –

(a) a written direction to a trustee or trustees to retire from the trust, and

(b) a written direction to the trustees or trustee for the time being (or, if there are none, to the personal representative of the last person who was a trustee) to appoint by writing to be a trustee or trustees the person or persons specified in the direction.

(3) Where –

(a) a trustee has been given a direction under subsection (2)(a),

(b) reasonable arrangements have been made for the protection of any rights of his in connection with the trust,

(c) after he has retired there will be either a trust corporation or at least two persons to act as trustees to perform the trust, and

(d) either another person is to be appointed to be a new trustee on his retirement (whether in compliance with a direction under subsection (2)(b) or otherwise) or the continuing trustees by deed consent to his retirement,

he shall make a deed declaring his retirement and shall be deemed to have retired and be discharged from the trust.

(4) Where a trustee retires under subsection (3) he and the continuing trustees (together with any new trustee) shall (subject to any arrangements for the protection of his rights) do anything necessary to vest the trust property in the continuing trustees (or the continuing and new trustees).

(5) This section has effect subject to the restrictions imposed by the Trustee Act 1925 on the number of trustees.

20   Appointment of substitute for incapable trustee

(1) This section applies where –

(a) a trustee is incapable by reason of mental disorder of exercising his functions as trustee,

(b) there is no person who is both entitled and willing and able to appoint a trustee in place of him under section 36(1) of the Trustee Act 1925, and

(c) the beneficiaries under the trust are of full age and capacity and (taken together) are absolutely entitled to the property subject to the trust.

(2) The beneficiaries may give to –

(a) a receiver of the trustee,

(b) an attorney acting for him under the authority of a power of attorney created by an instrument which is registered under section 6 of the Enduring Powers of Attorney Act 1985, or

(c) a person authorised for the purpose by the authority having jurisdiction under Part VII of the Mental Health Act 1983,

a written direction to appoint by writing the person or persons specified in the direction to be a trustee or trustees in place of the incapable trustee.

21 Supplementary

(1) For the purposes of section 19 or 20 a direction is given by beneficiaries if –

(a) a single direction is jointly given by all of them, or

(b) (subject to subsection (2)) a direction is given by each of them (whether solely or jointly with one or more, but not all, of the others),

and none of them by writing withdraws the direction given by him before it has been complied with.

(2) Where more than one direction is given each must specify for appointment or retirement the same person or persons.

(3) Subsection (7) of section 36 of the Trustee Act 1925 (powers of trustees appointed under that section) applies to a trustee appointed under section 19 or 20 as if he were appointed under that section.

(4) A direction under section 19 or 20 must not specify a person or persons for appointment if the appointment of that person or those persons would be in contravention of section 35(1) of the Trustee Act 1925 or section 24(1) of the Law of Property Act 1925 (requirements as to identity of trustees).

(5) Sections 19 and 20 do not apply in relation to a trust created by a disposition in so far as provision that they do not apply is made by the disposition.

(6) Sections 19 and 20 do not apply in relation to a trust created before the commencement of this Act by a disposition in so far as provision to the effect that they do not apply is made by a deed executed –

(a) in a case in which the trust was created by one person and he is of full capacity, by that person, or

(b) in a case in which the trust was created by more than one person, by such of the persons who created the trust as are alive and of full capacity.

(7) A deed executed for the purposes of subsection (6) is irrevocable.

(8) Where a deed is executed for the purposes of subsection (6) –

(a) it does not affect anything done before its execution to comply with a direction under section 19 or 20, but

(b) a direction under section 19 or 20 which has been given but not complied with before its execution shall cease to have effect.

PART III

SUPPLEMENTARY

22 Meaning of 'beneficiary'

(1) In this Act 'beneficiary', in relation to a trust, means any person who under the trust has an interest in property subject to the trust (including a person who has such an interest as a trustee or a personal representative).

(2) In this Act references to a beneficiary who is beneficially entitled do not include a beneficiary who has an interest in property subject to the trust only by reason of being a trustee or personal representative.

(3) For the purposes of this Act a person who is a beneficiary only by reason of being an annuitant is not to be regarded as entitled to an interest in possession in land subject to the trust.

23   Other interpretation provisions

(1) In this Act 'purchaser' has the same meaning as in Part I of the Law of Property Act 1925.

(2) Subject to that, where an expression used in this Act is given a meaning by the Law of Property Act 1925 it has the same meaning as in that Act unless the context otherwise requires.

(3) In this Act 'the court' means –

> (a) the High Court, or
>
> (b) a county court.

24   Application to Crown

(1) Subject to subsection (2), this Act binds the Crown.

(2) This Act (except so far as it relates to undivided shares and joint ownership) does not affect or alter the descent, devolution or nature of the estates and interests of or in –

> (a) land for the time being vested in Her Majesty in right of the Crown or of the Duchy of Lancaster, or
>
> (b) land for the time being belonging to the Duchy of Cornwall and held in right or respect of the Duchy.

25   Amendments, repeals, etc

(1) The enactments mentioned in Schedule 3 have effect subject to the amendments specified in that Schedule (which are minor or consequential on other provisions of this Act).

(2) The enactments mentioned in Schedule 4 are repealed to the extent specified in the third column of that Schedule.

(3) Neither section 2(5) nor the repeal by this Act of section 29 of the Settled Land Act 1925 applies in relation to the deed of settlement set out in the Schedule of the Chequers Estate Act 1918 or the trust instrument set out in the Schedule to the Chevening Estate Act 1959.

(4) The amendments and repeals made by this Act do not affect any entailed interest created before the commencement of this Act.

(5) The amendments and repeals made by this Act in consequence of section 3 –

> (a) do not affect a trust created by a will if the testator died before the commencement of this Act, and
>
> (b) do not affect personal representatives of a person who died before that commencement;

and the repeal of section 22 of the Partnership Act 1890 does not apply in any circumstances involving the personal representatives of a partner who died before that commencement.

27   Short title, commencement and extent …

(2) This Act comes into force on such day as the Lord Chancellor appoints by order made by statutory instrument. …

SCHEDULE 1

PROVISIONS CONSEQUENTIAL ON SECTION 2

1. – (1) Where after commencement of this Act a person purports to convey a legal estate in land to a minor, or two or more minors, alone, the conveyance –

(a) is not effective to pass the legal estate, but
(b) operates as a declaration that the land is held in trust for the minor or minors (or if he purports to convey it to the minor or minors in trust for any persons, for those persons).

(2) Where after the commencement of this Act a person purports to convey a legal estate in land to –

(a) a minor or two or more minors, and
(b) another person who is, or other persons who are, of full age,

the conveyance operates to vest the land in the other person or persons in trust for the minor or minors and the other person or persons (or if he purports to convey it to them in trust for any persons, for those persons).

(3) Where immediately before the commencement of this Act a conveyance is operating (by virtue of section 27 of the Settled Land Act 1925) as an agreement to execute a settlement in favour of a minor or minors –

(a) the agreement ceases to have effect on the commencement of this Act, and
(b) the conveyance subsequently operates instead as a declaration that the land is held in trust for the minor or minors.

2. Where after the commencement of this Act a legal estate in land would, by reason of intestacy or in any other circumstances not dealt with in paragraph 1, vest in a person who is a minor if he were a person of full age, the land is held in trust for the minor.

3. Where by virtue of an instrument coming into operation after the commencement of this Act, land becomes charged voluntarily (or in consideration of marriage or the formation of a civil partnership) or by way of family arrangement, whether immediately or after an interval, with the payment of –

(a)   a rent charge for the life of a person or a shorter period, or
(b) capital, annual or periodical sums for the benefit of a person,

the instrument operates as a declaration that the land is held in trust for giving effect to the charge.

4. – (1) This paragraphs applies in the case of land held on charitable, ecclesiastical or public trusts (other than land to which the Universities and College Estates Act 1925 applies).
(2) Where there is a conveyance of such land –

(a) if neither section 37(1) nor section 39(1) of the Charities Act 1993 applies to the conveyance, it shall state that the land is held on such trusts, and
(b) if neither section 37(2) nor section 39(2) of that Act has been complied with in relation to the conveyance and a purchaser has notice that the land is held on such trusts, he must see that any consents or orders necessary to authorise the transaction have been obtained.

(3) Where any trustees or the majority of any set of trustees have power to transfer or create any legal estate in the land, the estate shall be transferred or created by them in the names and on behalf of the persons in whom it is vested.

5. – (1) Where a person purports by an instrument coming into operation after the commencement of this Act to grant to another person an entailed interest in real or personal property, the instrument –

(a) is not effective to grant an entailed interest, but
(b) operates instead as a declaration that the property is held in trust absolutely for the person to whom an entailed interest in the property was purportedly granted.

(2) Where a person purports by an instrument coming into operation after the commencement of this Act to declare himself a tenant in tail of real or personal property, the instrument is not effective to create an entailed interest.

6. Where a settlement ceases to be a settlement for the purposes of the Settled land Act 1925 because no relevant property (within the meaning of section 2(4)) is, or is deemed to be, subject to the settlement, any property which is or later becomes subject to the settlement is held in trust for the persons interested under the settlement.

SCHEDULE 2

AMENDMENTS OF STATUTORY PROVISIONS IMPOSING TRUST FOR SALE

1. – (1) Section 31 of the Law of Property Act 1925 (implied trust for sale of mortgaged property where right of redemption is barred) as amended as follows. ...
(7) The amendments made by this paragraph –
    (a) apply whether the right of redemption is discharged before or after the commencement of this Act, but
    (b) are without prejudice to any dealings or arrangements made before the commencement of this Act.
2. – (1) Section 32 of the Law of Property Act 1925 (implied trust for sale of land acquired by trustees of personal property or of land held on trust for sale) is omitted.
(2) The repeal made by this paragraph applies in relation to land purchased after the commencement of this Act whether the trust or will in pursuance of which it is purchased comes into operation before or after the commencement of this Act.

3. – (1) Section 34 of the Law of Property Act 1925 is amended as follows. ...
(6) The amendments made by this paragraph apply whether the disposition is made, or comes into operation, before or after the commencement of this Act.

4. – (1) Section 36 of the Law of Property Act 1925 is amended as follows. ...
(4) The amendments made by this paragraph apply whether the legal estate is limited, or becomes held in trust, before or after the commencement of this Act.

5. – (1) Section 33 of the Administration of Estates Act 1925 (implied trust for sale on intestacy is amended as follows. ...
(5) The amendments made by this paragraph apply whether the death occurs before or after the commencement of this Act.

7. Where at the commencement of this Act any land is held on trust for sale, or on the statutory trusts, by virtue of Schedule 1 to the Law of Property Act 1925 (transitional provisions), it shall after that commencement be held in trust for the persons interested in the land; and references in that Schedule to trusts for sale or trustees for sale or to the statutory trusts shall be construed accordingly.

NB. This Act came into force on 1 January 1997.

As amended by the Trustee Act 2000, s40, Schedule 2, Pt II, paras 45–48, Schedule 4, Pt II; Commonhold and Leasehold Reform Act 2002, s68, Schedule 5, para 8; Civil Partnership Act 2004, s261(1), Schedule 27, para 153; Charities Act 2006, s75(1), Schedule 8, para 182.

TRUSTEE DELEGATION ACT 1999
(1999 c 15)

1   Exercise of trustee functions by attorney

(1) The donee of a power of attorney is not prevented from doing an act in relation to –

(a) land,

(b) capital proceeds of a conveyance of land, or

(c) income from land,

by reason only that the act involves the exercise of a trustee function of the donor if, at the time when the act is done, the donor has a beneficial interest in the land, proceeds or income.

(2) In this section –

(a) 'conveyance' has the same meaning as in the Law of Property Act 1925, and

(b) references to a trustee function of the donor are to a function which the donor has as trustee (either alone or jointly with any other person or persons).

(3) Subsection (1) above –

(a) applies only if and so far as a contrary intention is not expressed in the instrument creating the power of attorney, and

(b) has effect subject to the terms of that instrument.

(4) The donor of the power of attorney –

(a) is liable for the acts or defaults of the donee in exercising any function by virtue of subsection (1) above in the same manner as if they were acts or defaults of the donor, but

(b) is not liable by reason only that a function is exercised by the donee by virtue of that subsection.

(5) Subsections (1) and (4) above –

(a) apply only if and so far as a contrary intention is not expressed in the instrument (if any) creating the trust, and

(b) have effect subject to the terms of such an instrument.

(6) The fact that it appears that, in dealing with any shares or stock, the donee of the power of attorney is exercising a function by virtue of subsection (1) above does not affect with any notice of any trust a person in whose books the shares are, or stock is, registered or inscribed.

(7) In any case where (by way of exception to section 3(1) of the Trusts of Land and Appointment of Trustees Act 1996) the doctrine of conversion continues to operate, any person who, by reason of the continuing operation of that doctrine, has a beneficial interest in the proceeds of sale of land shall be treated for the purposes of this section and section 2 below as having a beneficial interest in the land.

(8) The donee of a power of attorney is not to be regarded as exercising a trustee function by virtue of subsection (1) above if he is acting under a trustee delegation power; and for this purpose a trustee delegation power is a power of attorney given under –

(a) a statutory provision, or

(b) a provision of the instrument (if any) creating a trust,

under which the donor of the power is expressly authorised to delegate the exercise of all or any of his trustee functions by power of attorney.

(9) Subject to section 4(6) below, this section applies only to powers of attorney created after the commencement of this Act.

2   Evidence of beneficial interest

(1) This section applies where the interest of a purchaser depends on the donee of a power of

attorney having power to do an act in relation to any property by virtue of section 1(1) above. In this subsection 'purchaser' has the same meaning as in Part I of the Law of Property Act 1925.

(2) Where this section applies an appropriate statement is, in favour of the purchaser, conclusive evidence of the donor of the power having a beneficial interest in the property at the time of the doing of the act.

(3) In this section 'an appropriate statement' means a signed statement made by the donee –

    (a) when doing the act in question, or

    (b) at any other time within the period of three months beginning with the day on which the act is done,

that the donor has a beneficial interest in the property at the time of the donee doing the act.

(4) If an appropriate statement is false, the donee is liable in the same way as he would be if the statement were contained in a statutory declaration.

5   Delegation under section 25 of the Trustee Act 1925

(1), (2) [Substitute s25 of the 1925 Act.]

(2) Subsection (1) above has effect in relation to powers of attorney created after the commencement of this Act. …

6   Section 25 powers as enduring powers

Section 2(8) of the Enduring Powers of Attorney Act 1985 (which prevents a power of attorney under section 25 of the Trustee Act 1925 from being an enduring power) does not apply to powers of attorney created after the commencement of this Act.

7   Two-trustee rules

(1) A requirement imposed by an enactment –

    (a) that capital money be paid to, or dealt with as directed by, at least two trustees or that a valid receipt for capital money be given otherwise than by a sole trustee, or

    (b) that, in order for an interest or power to be overreached, a conveyance or deed be executed by at least two trustees,

is not satisfied by money being paid to or dealt with as directed by, or a receipt for money being given by, a relevant attorney or by a conveyance or deed being executed by such an attorney.

(2) In this section 'relevant attorney' means a person (other than a trust corporation within the meaning of the Trustee Act 1925) who is acting either –

    (a) both as a trustee and as attorney for one or more other trustees, or

    (b) as attorney for two or more trustees,

and who is not acting together with any other person or persons.

(3) This section applies whether a relevant attorney is acting under a power created before or after the commencement of this Act (but in the case of such an attorney acting under an enduring power created before that commencement is without prejudice to any continuing application of section 3(3) of the Enduring Powers of Attorney Act 1985 to the enduring power after that commencement in accordance with section 4 above).

8   Appointment of additional trustee by attorney

(1) [Inserts Trustee Act 1925, s36(6A)–(6D).]

(2) The amendment made by subsection (1) above has effect only where the power, or (where more than one) each of them, is created after the commencement of this Act.

9   Attorney acting for incapable trustee

(1) [Inserts Law of Property Act 1925, s22(3).]

(2) The amendment made by subsection (1) above has effect whether the enduring power was created before or after the commencement of this Act.

10   Extent of attorney's authority to act in relation to land
(1) Where the donee of a power of attorney is authorised by the power to do an act of any description in relation to any land, his authority to do an act of that description at any time includes authority to do it with respect to any estate or interest in the land which is held at that time by the donor (whether alone or jointly with any other person or persons).
(2) Subsection (1) above –
    (a) applies only if and so far as a contrary intention is not expressed in the instrument creating the power of attorney, and
    (b) has effect subject to the terms of that instrument.
(3) This section applies only to powers of attorney created after the commencement of this Act.

11   Interpretation
(1) In this Act –
    'land' has the same meaning as in the Trustee Act 1925, and
    'enduring power' has the same meaning as in [s2, as amended, of] the Enduring Powers of Attorney Act 1985.
(2) References in this Act to the creation of a power of attorney are to the execution by the donor of the instrument creating it.

NB. This Act came into force on 1 March 2000.

LIMITED LIABILITY PARTNERSHIPS ACT 2000
(2000 c 12)

1   Limited liability partnerships
(1) There shall be a new form of legal entity to be known as a limited liability partnership.
(2) A limited liability partnership is a body corporate (with legal personality separate from that of its members) which is formed by being incorporated under this Act; and –
    (a) in the following provisions of this Act (except in the phrase 'oversea limited liability partnership'), and
    (b) in any other enactment (except where provision is made to the contrary or the context otherwise requires),
references to a limited liability partnership are to such a body corporate.
(3) A limited liability partnership has unlimited capacity.
(4) The members of a limited liability partnership have such liability to contribute to its assets in the event of its being wound up as is provided for by virtue of this Act.
(5) Accordingly, except as far as otherwise provided by this Act or any other enactment, the law relating to partnerships does not apply to a limited liability partnership.
(6) The Schedule (which makes provision about the names and registered offices of limited liability partnerships) has effect.

2   Incorporation document, etc
(1) For a limited liability partnership to be incorporated –
    (a) two or more persons associated for carrying on a lawful business with a view to profit

      must have subscribed their names to an incorporation document,

  (b) there must have been delivered to the registrar either the incorporation document or a copy authenticated in a manner approved by him, and

  (c) there must have been so delivered a statement in a form approved by the registrar, made by either a solicitor engaged in the formation of the limited liability partnership or anyone who subscribed his name to the incorporation document, that the requirement imposed by paragraph (a) has been complied with.

(2) The incorporation document must –

  (a) be in a form approved by the registrar (or as near to such a form as circumstances allow),

  (b) state the name of the limited liability partnership,

  (c) state whether the registered office of the limited liability partnership is to be situated in England and Wales, in Wales or in Scotland,

  (d) state the address of that registered office,

  (e) state the name and address of each of the persons who are to be members of the limited liability partnership on incorporation, and

  (f) either specify which of those persons are to be designated members or state that every person who from time to time is a member of the limited liability partnership is a designated member. …

(3) If a person makes a false statement under subsection (1)(c) which he –

  (a) knows to be false, or

  (b) does not believe to be true,

he commits an offence. …

3   Incorporation by registration

(1) When the requirements imposed by paragraphs (b) and (c) of subsection (1) of section 2 have been complied with, the registrar shall retain the incorporation document or copy delivered to him and, unless the requirement imposed by paragraph (a) of that subsection has not been complied with, he shall –

  (a) register the incorporation document or copy, and

  (b) give a certificate that the limited liability partnership is incorporated by the name specified in the incorporation document.

(2) The registrar may accept the statement delivered under paragraph (c) of subsection (1) of section 2 as sufficient evidence that the requirement imposed by paragraph (a) of that subsection has been complied with.

(3) The certificate shall either be signed by the registrar or be authenticated by his official seal.

(4) The certificate is conclusive evidence that the requirements of section 2 are complied with and that the limited liability partnership is incorporated by the name specified in the incorporation document.

4   Members

(1) On the incorporation of a limited liability partnership its members are the persons who subscribed their names to the incorporation document (other than any who have died or been dissolved).

(2) Any other person may become a member of a limited liability partnership by and in accordance with an agreement with the existing members.

(3) A person may cease to be a member of a limited liability partnership (as well as by death or dissolution) in accordance with an agreement with the other members or, in the absence of

agreement with the other members as to cessation of membership, by giving reasonable notice to the other members.

(4) A member of a limited liability partnership shall not be regarded for any purpose as employed by the limited liability partnership unless, if he and the other members were partners in a partnership, he would be regarded for that purpose as employed by the partnership.

5 Relationship of members, etc

(1) Except as far as otherwise provided by this Act or any other enactment, the mutual rights and duties of the members of a limited liability partnership, and the mutual rights and duties of a limited liability partnership and its members, shall be governed –

  (a) by agreement between the members, or between the limited liability partnership and its members, or
  (b) in the absence of agreement as to any matter, by any provision made in relation to that matter by regulations under section 15(c).

(2) An agreement made before the incorporation of a limited liability partnership between the persons who subscribe their names to the incorporation document may impose obligations on the limited liability partnership (to take effect at any time after its incorporation).

6 Members as agents

(1) Every member of a limited liability partnership is the agent of the limited liability partnership.

(2) But a limited liability partnership is not bound by anything done by a member in dealing with a person if –

  (a) the member in fact has no authority to act for the limited liability partnership by doing that thing, and
  (b) the person knows that he has no authority or does not know or believe him to be a member of the limited liability partnership.

(3) Where a person has ceased to be a member of a limited liability partnership, the former member is to be regarded (in relation to any person dealing with the limited liability partnership) as still being a member of the limited liability partnership unless –

  (a) the person has notice that the former member has ceased to be a member of the limited liability partnership, or
  (b) notice that the former member has ceased to be a member of the limited liability partnership has been delivered to the registrar.

(4) Where a member of a limited liability partnership is liable to any person (other than another member of the limited liability partnership) as a result of a wrongful act or omission of his in the course of the business of the limited liability partnership or with its authority, the limited liability partnership is liable to the same extent as the member.

7 Ex-members

(1) This section applies where a member of a limited liability partnership has either ceased to be a member or –

  (a) has died,
  (b) has become bankrupt or had his estate sequestrated or has been wound up,
  (c) has granted a trust deed for the benefit of his creditors, or
  (d) has assigned the whole or any part of his share in the limited liability partnership (absolutely or by way of charge or security).

(2) In such an event the former member or –

  (a) his personal representative,

(b) his trustee in bankruptcy or permanent or interim trustee (within the meaning of the Bankruptcy (Scotland) Act 1985) or liquidator,

(c) his trustee under the trust deed for the benefit of his creditors, or

(d) his assignee,

may not interfere in the management or administration of any business or affairs of the limited liability partnership.

(3) But subsection (2) does not affect any right to receive an amount from the limited liability partnership in that event.

8   Designated members

(1) If the incorporation document specifies who are to be designated members –

(a) they are designated members on incorporation, and

(b) any member may become a designated member by and in accordance with an agreement with the other members,

and a member may cease to be a designated member in accordance with an agreement with the other members.

(2) But if there would otherwise be no designated members, or only one, every member is a designated member.

(3) If the incorporation document states that every person who from time to time is a member of the limited liability partnership is a designated member, every member is a designated member.

(4) A limited liability partnership may at any time deliver to the registrar –

(a) notice that specified members are to be designated members, or

(b) notice that every person who from time to time is a member of the limited liability partnership is a designated member,

and, once it is delivered, subsection (1) (apart from paragraph (a)) and subsection (2), or subsection (3), shall have effect as if that were stated in the incorporation document.

(5) A notice delivered under subsection (4) –

(a) shall be in a form approved by the registrar, and

(b) shall be signed by a designated member of the limited liability partnership or authenticated in a manner approved by the registrar.

(6) A person ceases to be a designated member if he ceases to be a member.

TRUSTEE ACT 2000

(2000 c 29)

PART I

THE DUTY OF CARE

1   The duty of care

(1) Whenever the duty under this subsection applies to a trustee, he must exercise such care and skill as is reasonable in the circumstances, having regard in particular –

(a) to any special knowledge or experience that he has or holds himself out as having, and

(b) if he acts as trustee in the course of a business or profession, to any special knowledge or experience that it is reasonable to expect of a person acting in the course of that kind of business or profession.

(2) In this Act the duty under subsection (1) is called 'the duty of care'.

2   Application of duty of care
Schedule 1 makes provision about when the duty of care applies to a trustee.

PART II

INVESTMENT

3   General power of investment
(1) Subject to the provisions of this Part, a trustee may make any kind of investment that he could make if he were absolutely entitled to the assets of the trust.

(2) In this Act the power under subsection (1) is called 'the general power of investment'.

(3) The general power of investment does not permit a trustee to make investments in land other than in loans secured on land (but see also section 8).

(4) A person invests in a loan secured on land if he has rights under any contract under which –
     (a)   one person provides another with credit, and
     (b)   the obligation of the borrower to repay is secured on land.

(5) 'Credit' includes any cash loan or other financial accommodation.

(6) 'Cash' includes money in any form.

4   Standard investment criteria
(1) In exercising any power of investment, whether arising under this Part or otherwise, a trustee must have regard to the standard investment criteria.

(2) A trustee must from time to time review the investments of the trust and consider whether, having regard to the standard investment criteria, they should be varied.

(3) The standard investment criteria, in relation to a trust, are –
     (a)   the suitability to the trust of investments of the same kind as any particular investment proposed to be made or retained and of that particular investment as an investment of that kind, and
     (b)   the need for diversification of investments of the trust, in so far as is appropriate to the circumstances of the trust.

5   Advice
(1) Before exercising any power of investment, whether arising under this Part or otherwise, a trustee must (unless the exception applies) obtain and consider proper advice about the way in which, having regard to the standard investment criteria, the power should be exercised.

(2) When reviewing the investments of the trust, a trustee must (unless the exception applies) obtain and consider proper advice about whether, having regard to the standard investment criteria, the investments should be varied.

(3) The exception is that a trustee need not obtain such advice if he reasonably concludes that in all the circumstances it is unnecessary or inappropriate to do so.

(4) Proper advice is the advice of a person who is reasonably believed by the trustee to be qualified to give it by his ability in and practical experience of financial and other matters relating to the proposed investment.

6   Restriction or exclusion of this Part, etc
(1) The general power of investment is –
     (a)   in addition to powers conferred on trustees otherwise than by this Act, but
     (b)   subject to any restriction or exclusion imposed by the trust instrument or by any enactment or any provision of subordinate legislation.

(2) For the purposes of this Act, an enactment or a provision of subordinate legislation is not to

be regarded as being, or as being part of, a trust instrument.

(3) In this Act 'subordinate legislation' has the same meaning as in the Interpretation Act 1978.

7   Existing trusts

(1) This Part applies in relation to trusts whether created before or after its commencement.

(2) No provision relating to the powers of a trustee contained in a trust instrument made before 3rd August 1961 is to be treated (for the purposes of section 6(1)(b)) as restricting or excluding the general power of investment.

(3) A provision contained in a trust instrument made before the commencement of this Part which –

    (a)   has effect under section 3(2) of the Trustee Investments Act 1961 as a power to invest under that Act, or

    (b)   confers power to invest under that Act,

is to be treated as conferring the general power of investment on a trustee.

PART III

ACQUISITION OF LAND

8   Power to acquire freehold and leasehold land

(1) A trustee may acquire freehold or leasehold land in the United Kingdom –

    (a)   as an investment,

    (b)   for occupation by a beneficiary, or

    (c)   for any other reason.

(2) 'Freehold or leasehold land' means –

    (a)   in relation to England and Wales, a legal estate in land,

    (b)   in relation to Scotland –

        (i)   the estate or interest of the proprietor of the dominium utile or, in the case of land not held on feudal tenure, the estate or interest of the owner, or

        (ii)   a tenancy, and

    (c)   in relation to Northern Ireland, a legal estate in land, including land held under a fee farm grant.

(3) For the purpose of exercising his functions as a trustee, a trustee who acquires land under this section has all the powers of an absolute owner in relation to the land.

9   Restriction or exclusion of this Part, etc

The powers conferred by this Part are –

    (a)   in addition to powers conferred on trustees otherwise than by this Part, but

    (b)   subject to any restriction or exclusion imposed by the trust instrument or by any enactment or any provision of subordinate legislation.

10   Existing trusts

(1) This Part does not apply in relation to –

    (a)   a trust of property which consists of or includes land which (despite section 2 of the Trusts of Land and Appointment of Trustees Act 1996) is settled land, or

    (b)   a trust to which the Universities and College Estates Act 1925 applies.

(2) Subject to subsection (1), this Part applies in relation to trusts whether created before or after its commencement.

PART IV

AGENTS, NOMINEES AND CUSTODIANS

11   Power to employ agents

(1) Subject to the provisions of this Part, the trustees of a trust may authorise any person to exercise any or all of their delegable functions as their agent.

(2) In the case of a trust other than a charitable trust, the trustees' delegable functions consist of any function other than –

    (a) any function relating to whether or in what way any assets of the trust should be distributed,

    (b) any power to decide whether any fees or other payment due to be made out of the trust funds should be made out of income or capital,

    (c) any power to appoint a person to be a trustee of the trust, or

    (d) any power conferred by any other enactment or the trust instrument which permits the trustees to delegate any of their functions or to appoint a person to act as a nominee or custodian.

(3) In the case of a charitable trust, the trustees' delegable functions are –

    (a) any function consisting of carrying out a decision that the trustees have taken;

    (b) any function relating to the investment of assets subject to the trust (including, in the case of land held as an investment, managing the land and creating or disposing of an interest in the land);

    (c) any function relating to the raising of funds for the trust otherwise than by means of profits of a trade which is an integral part of carrying out the trust's charitable purpose;

    (d) any other function prescribed by an order made by the Secretary of State.

(4) For the purposes of subsection (3)(c) a trade is an integral part of carrying out a trust's charitable purpose if, whether carried on in the United Kingdom or elsewhere, the profits are applied solely to the purposes of the trust and either –

    (a) the trade is exercised in the course of the actual carrying out of a primary purpose of the trust, or

    (b) the work in connection with the trade is mainly carried out by beneficiaries of the trust.

(5) The power to make an order under subsection (3)(d) is exercisable by statutory instrument which shall be subject to annulment in pursuance of a resolution of either House of Parliament.

12   Persons who may act as agents

(1) Subject to subsection (2), the persons whom the trustees may under section 11 authorise to exercise functions as their agent include one or more of their number.

(2) The trustees may not authorise two (or more) persons to exercise the same function unless they are to exercise the function jointly.

(3) The trustees may not under section 11 authorise a beneficiary to exercise any function as their agent (even if the beneficiary is also a trustee).

(4) The trustees may under section 11 authorise a person to exercise functions as their agent even though he is also appointed to act as their nominee or custodian (whether under section 16, 17 or 18 or any other power).

13   Linked functions, etc

(1) Subject to subsections (2) and (5), a person who is authorised under section 11 to exercise a

function is (whatever the terms of the agency) subject to any specific duties or restrictions attached to the function.

For example, a person who is authorised under section 11 to exercise the general power of investment is subject to the duties under section 4 in relation to that power.

(2) A person who is authorised under section 11 to exercise a power which is subject to a requirement to obtain advice is not subject to the requirement if he is the kind of person from whom it would have been proper for the trustees, in compliance with the requirement, to obtain advice.

(3) Subsections (4) and (5) apply to a trust to which section 11(1) of the Trusts of Land and Appointment of Trustees Act 1996 (duties to consult beneficiaries and give effect to their wishes) applies.

(4) The trustees may not under section 11 authorise a person to exercise any of their functions on terms that prevent them from complying with section 11(1) of the 1996 Act.

(5) A person who is authorised under section 11 to exercise any function relating to land subject to the trust is not subject to section 11(1) of the 1996 Act.

14 Terms of agency

(1) Subject to subsection (2) and sections 15(2) and 29 to 32, the trustees may authorise a person to exercise functions as their agent on such terms as to remuneration and other matters as they may determine.

(2) The trustees may not authorise a person to exercise functions as their agent on any of the terms mentioned in subsection (3) unless it is reasonably necessary for them to do so.

(3) The terms are –

    (a) a term permitting the agent to appoint a substitute;

    (b) a term restricting the liability of the agent or his substitute to the trustees or any beneficiary;

    (c) a term permitting the agent to act in circumstances capable of giving rise to a conflict of interest.

15 Asset management: special restrictions

(1) The trustees may not authorise a person to exercise any of their asset management functions as their agent except by an agreement which is in or evidenced in writing.

(2) The trustees may not authorise a person to exercise any of their asset management functions as their agent unless –

    (a) they have prepared a statement that gives guidance as to how the functions should be exercised ('a policy statement'), and

    (b) the agreement under which the agent is to act includes a term to the effect that he will secure compliance with –

        (i) the policy statement, or

        (ii) if the policy statement is revised or replaced under section 22, the revised or replacement policy statement.

(3) The trustees must formulate any guidance given in the policy statement with a view to ensuring that the functions will be exercised in the best interests of the trust.

(4) The policy statement must be in or evidenced in writing.

(5) The asset management functions of trustees are their functions relating to –

    (a) the investment of assets subject to the trust,

    (b) the acquisition of property which is to be subject to the trust, and

    (c) managing property which is subject to the trust and disposing of, or creating or disposing of an interest in, such property.

16   Power to appoint nominees

(1) Subject to the provisions of this Part, the trustees of a trust may –

    (a)   appoint a person to act as their nominee in relation to such of the assets of the trust as they determine (other than settled land), and

    (b)   take such steps as are necessary to secure that those assets are vested in a person so appointed.

(2) An appointment under this section must be in or evidenced in writing.

(3) This section does not apply to any trust having a custodian trustee or in relation to any assets vested in the official custodian for charities.

17   Power to appoint custodians

(1) Subject to the provisions of this Part, the trustees of a trust may appoint a person to act as a custodian in relation to such of the assets of the trust as they may determine.

(2) For the purposes of this Act a person is a custodian in relation to assets if he undertakes the safe custody of the assets or of any documents or records concerning the assets.

(3) An appointment under this section must be in or evidenced in writing.

(4) This section does not apply to any trust having a custodian trustee or in relation to any assets vested in the official custodian for charities.

18   Investment in bearer securities

(1) If trustees retain or invest in securities payable to bearer, they must appoint a person to act as a custodian of the securities.

(2) Subsection (1) does not apply if the trust instrument or any enactment or provision of subordinate legislation contains provision which (however expressed) permits the trustees to retain or invest in securities payable to bearer without appointing a person to act as a custodian.

(3) An appointment under this section must be in or evidenced in writing.

(4) This section does not apply to any trust having a custodian trustee or in relation to any securities vested in the official custodian for charities.

19   Persons who may be appointed as nominees or custodians

(1) A person may not be appointed under section 16, 17 or 18 as a nominee or custodian unless one of the relevant conditions is satisfied.

(2) The relevant conditions are that –

    (a)   the person carries on a business which consists of or includes acting as a nominee or custodian;

    (b   the person is a body corporate which is controlled by the trustees;

    (c)   the person is a body corporate recognised under section 9 of the Administration of Justice Act 1985.

(3) The question whether a body corporate is controlled by trustees is to be determined in accordance with section 840 of the Income and Corporation Taxes Act 1988.

(4) The trustees of a charitable trust which is not an exempt charity must act in accordance with any guidance given by the Charity Commission concerning the selection of a person for appointment as a nominee or custodian under section 16, 17 or 18.

(5) Subject to subsections (1) and (4), the persons whom the trustees may under section 16, 17 or 18 appoint as a nominee or custodian include –

    (a)   one of their number, if that one is a trust corporation, or

    (b)   two (or more) of their number, if they are to act as joint nominees or joint custodians.

(6) The trustees may under section 16 appoint a person to act as their nominee even though he is also –

(a) appointed to act as their custodian (whether under section 17 or 18 or any other power), or

(b) authorised to exercise functions as their agent (whether under section 11 or any other power).

(7) Likewise, the trustees may under section 17 or 18 appoint a person to act as their custodian even though he is also –

(a) appointed to act as their nominee (whether under section 16 or any other power), or

(b) authorised to exercise functions as their agent (whether under section 11 or any other power).

20   Terms of appointment of nominees and custodians

(1) Subject to subsection (2) and sections 29 to 32, the trustees may under section 16, 17 or 18 appoint a person to act as a nominee or custodian on such terms as to remuneration and other matters as they may determine.

(2) The trustees may not under section 16, 17 or 18 appoint a person to act as a nominee or custodian on any of the terms mentioned in subsection (3) unless it is reasonably necessary for them to do so.

(3) The terms are –

(a) a term permitting the nominee or custodian to appoint a substitute;

(b) a term restricting the liability of the nominee or custodian or his substitute to the trustees or to any beneficiary;

(c) a term permitting the nominee or custodian to act in circumstances capable of giving rise to a conflict of interest.

21   Application of sections 22 and 23

(1) Sections 22 and 23 apply in a case where trustees have, under section 11, 16, 17 or 18 –

(a) authorised a person to exercise functions as their agent, or

(b) appointed a person to act as a nominee or custodian.

(2) Subject to subsection (3), sections 22 and 23 also apply in a case where trustees have, under any power conferred on them by the trust instrument or by any enactment or any provision of subordinate legislation –

(a) authorised a person to exercise functions as their agent, or

(b) appointed a person to act as a nominee or custodian.

(3) If the application of section 22 or 23 is inconsistent with the terms of the trust instrument or the enactment or provision of subordinate legislation, the section in question does not apply.

22   Review of agents, nominees and custodians, etc

(1) While the agent, nominee or custodian continues to act for the trust, the trustees –

(a) must keep under review the arrangements under which the agent, nominee or custodian acts and how those arrangements are being put into effect,

(b) if circumstances make it appropriate to do so, must consider whether there is a need to exercise any power of intervention that they have, and

(c) if they consider that there is a need to exercise such a power, must do so.

(2) If the agent has been authorised to exercise asset management functions, the duty under subsection (1) includes, in particular –

(a) a duty to consider whether there is any need to revise or replace the policy statement made for the purposes of section 15,

(b) if they consider that there is a need to revise or replace the policy statement, a duty to do so, and

(c) a duty to assess whether the policy statement (as it has effect for the time being) is being complied with.

(3) Subsections (3) and (4) of section 15 apply to the revision or replacement of a policy statement under this section as they apply to the making of a policy statement under that section.

(4) 'Power of intervention' includes –

(a) a power to give directions to the agent, nominee or custodian;

(b) a power to revoke the authorisation or appointment.

23   Liability for agents, nominees and custodians, etc

(1) A trustee is not liable for any act or default of the agent, nominee or custodian unless he has failed to comply with the duty of care applicable to him, under paragraph 3 of Schedule 1 –

(a) when entering into the arrangements under which the person acts as agent, nominee or custodian, or

(b) when carrying out his duties under section 22.

(2) If a trustee has agreed a term under which the agent, nominee or custodian is permitted to appoint a substitute, the trustee is not liable for any act or default of the substitute unless he has failed to comply with the duty of care applicable to him, under paragraph 3 of Schedule 1 –

(a) when agreeing that term, or

(b) when carrying out his duties under section 22 in so far as they relate to the use of the substitute.

24   Effect of trustees exceeding their powers

A failure by the trustees to act within the limits of the powers conferred by this Part –

(a) in authorising a person to exercise a function of theirs as an agent, or

(b) in appointing a person to act as a nominee or custodian,

does not invalidate the authorisation or appointment.

25   Sole trustees

(1) Subject to subsection (2), this Part applies in relation to a trust having a sole trustee as it applies in relation to other trusts (and references in this Part to trustees –except in sections 12(1) and (3) and 19(5) –are to be read accordingly).

(2) Section 18 does not impose a duty on a sole trustee if that trustee is a trust corporation.

26   Restriction or exclusion of this Part, etc

The powers conferred by this Part are –

(a) in addition to powers conferred on trustees otherwise than by this Act, but

(b) subject to any restriction or exclusion imposed by the trust instrument or by any enactment or any provision of subordinate legislation.

27   Existing trusts

This Part applies in relation to trusts whether created before or after its commencement.

PART V

REMUNERATION

28   Trustee's entitlement to payment under trust instrument

(1) Except to the extent (if any) to which the trust instrument makes inconsistent provision, subsections (2) to (4) apply to a trustee if –

    (a) there is a provision in the trust instrument entitling him to receive payment out of trust funds in respect of services provided by him to or on behalf of the trust, and

    (b) the trustee is a trust corporation or is acting in a professional capacity.

(2) The trustee is to be treated as entitled under the trust instrument to receive payment in respect of services even if they are services which are capable of being provided by a lay trustee.

(3) Subsection (2) applies to a trustee of a charitable trust who is not a trust corporation only –

    (a) if he is not a sole trustee, and

    (b) to the extent that a majority of the other trustees have agreed that it should apply to him.

(4) Any payments to which the trustee is entitled in respect of services are to be treated as remuneration for services (and not as a gift) for the purposes of –

    (a) section 15 of the Wills Act 1837 (gifts to an attesting witness to be void), and

    (b) section 34(3) of the Administration of Estates Act 1925 (order in which estate to be paid out).

(5) For the purposes of this Part, a trustee acts in a professional capacity if he acts in the course of a profession or business which consists of or includes the provision of services in connection with –

    (a) the management or administration of trusts generally or a particular kind of trust, or

    (b) any particular aspect of the management or administration of trusts generally or a particular kind of trust,

and the services he provides to or on behalf of the trust fall within that description.

(6) For the purposes of this Part, a person acts as a lay trustee if he –

    (a) is not a trust corporation, and

    (b) does not act in a professional capacity.

29   Remuneration of certain trustees

(1) Subject to subsection (5), a trustee who –

    (a) is a trust corporation, but

    (b) is not a trustee of a charitable trust,

is entitled to receive reasonable remuneration out of the trust funds for any services that the trust corporation provides to or on behalf of the trust.

(2) Subject to subsection (5), a trustee who –

    (a) acts in a professional capacity, but

    (b) is not a trust corporation, a trustee of a charitable trust or a sole trustee,

is entitled to receive reasonable remuneration out of the trust funds for any services that he provides to or on behalf of the trust if each other trustee has agreed in writing that he may be remunerated for the services.

(3) 'Reasonable remuneration' means, in relation to the provision of services by a trustee, such remuneration as is reasonable in the circumstances for the provision of those services to or on behalf of that trust by that trustee and for the purposes of subsection (1) includes, in relation to the provision of services by a trustee who is an authorised institution under the Banking Act 1987 and provides the services in that capacity, the institution's reasonable charges for the provision of such services.

(4) A trustee is entitled to remuneration under this section even if the services in question are capable of being provided by a lay trustee.

(5) A trustee is not entitled to remuneration under this section if any provision about his entitlement to remuneration has been made –

    (a) by the trust instrument, or

(b) by any enactment or any provision of subordinate legislation.

(6) This section applies to a trustee who has been authorised under a power conferred by Part IV or the trust instrument –

    (a) to exercise functions as an agent of the trustees, or

    (b) to act as a nominee or custodian,

as it applies to any other trustee.

30   Remuneration of trustees of charitable trusts

(1) The Secretary of State may by regulations make provision for the remuneration of trustees of charitable trusts who are trust corporations or act in a professional capacity.

(2) The power under subsection (1) includes power to make provision for the remuneration of a trustee who has been authorised under a power conferred by Part IV or any other enactment or any provision of subordinate legislation, or by the trust instrument –

    (a) to exercise functions as an agent of the trustees, or

    (b) to act as a nominee or custodian.

(3) Regulations under this section may –

    (a) make different provision for different cases;

    (b) contain such supplemental, incidental, consequential and transitional provision as the Secretary of State considers appropriate.

(4) The power to make regulations under this section is exercisable by statutory instrument, but no such instrument shall be made unless a draft of it has been laid before Parliament and approved by a resolution of each House of Parliament.

31   Trustees' expenses

(1) A trustee –

    (a) is entitled to be reimbursed from the trust funds, or

    (b) may pay out of the trust funds,

expenses properly incurred by him when acting on behalf of the trust.

(2) This section applies to a trustee who has been authorised under a power conferred by Part IV or any other enactment or any provision of subordinate legislation, or by the trust instrument –

    (a) to exercise functions as an agent of the trustees, or

    (b) to act as a nominee or custodian,

as it applies to any other trustee.

32   Remuneration and expenses of agents, nominees and custodians

(1) This section applies if, under a power conferred by Part IV or any other enactment or any provision of subordinate legislation, or by the trust instrument, a person other than a trustee has been –

    (a) authorised to exercise functions as an agent of the trustees, or

    (b) appointed to act as a nominee or custodian.

(2) The trustees may remunerate the agent, nominee or custodian out of the trust funds for services if –

    (a) he is engaged on terms entitling him to be remunerated for those services, and

    (b) the amount does not exceed such remuneration as is reasonable in the circumstances for the provision of those services by him to or on behalf of that trust.

(3) The trustees may reimburse the agent, nominee or custodian out of the trust funds for any expenses properly incurred by him in exercising functions as an agent, nominee or custodian.

33   Application

(1) Subject to subsection (2), sections 28, 29, 31 and 32 apply in relation to services provided to or on behalf of, or (as the case may be) expenses incurred on or after their commencement on behalf of, trusts whenever created.

(2) Nothing in section 28 or 29 is to be treated as affecting the operation of –

    (a)   section 15 of the Wills Act 1837, or

    (b)   section 34(3) of the Administration of Estates Act 1925,

in relation to any death occurring before the commencement of section 28 or (as the case may be) section 29.

PART VI

MISCELLANEOUS AND SUPPLEMENTARY

34   Power to insure

(1) [Substitutes section 19 of the Trustee Act 1925.]

(2) [Amends section 20(1) of the Trustee Act 1925.]

(3) The amendments made by this section apply in relation to trusts whether created before or after its commencement.

35   Personal representatives

(1) Subject to the following provisions of this section, this Act applies in relation to a personal representative administering an estate according to the law as it applies to a trustee carrying out a trust for beneficiaries.

(2) For this purpose this Act is to be read with the appropriate modifications and in particular –

    (a)   references to the trust instrument are to be read as references to the will,

    (b)   references to a beneficiary or to beneficiaries, apart from the reference to a beneficiary in section 8(1)(b), are to be read as references to a person or the persons interested in the due administration of the estate, and

    (c)   the reference to a beneficiary in section 8(1)(b) is to be read as a reference to a person who under the will of the deceased or under the law relating to intestacy is beneficially interested in the estate.

(3) Remuneration to which a personal representative is entitled under section 28 or 29 is to be treated as an administration expense for the purposes of –

    (a)   section 34(3) of the Administration of Estates Act 1925 (order in which estate to be paid out), and

    (b)   any provision giving reasonable administration expenses priority over the preferential debts listed in Schedule 6 to the Insolvency Act 1986.

(4) Nothing in subsection (3) is to be treated as affecting the operation of the provisions mentioned in paragraphs (a) and (b) of that subsection in relation to any death occurring before the commencement of this section.

38   Common investment schemes for charities, etc

Parts II to IV do not apply to –

    (a)   trustees managing a fund under a common investment scheme made, or having effect as if made, under section 24 of the Charities Act 1993, other than such a fund the trusts of which provide that property is not to be transferred to the fund except by or on behalf of a charity the trustees of which are the trustees appointed to manage the fund, or

(b) trustees managing a fund under a common deposit scheme made, or having effect as if made, under section 25 of that Act.

39   Interpretation

(1) In this Act –

'asset' includes any right or interest;

'charitable trust' means a trust under which property is held for charitable purposes and 'charitable purposes' has the same meaning as in the Charities Act 1993;

'custodian trustee' has the same meaning as in the Public Trustee Act 1906;

'enactment' includes any provision of a Measure of the Church Assembly or of the General Synod of the Church of England;

'exempt charity' has the same meaning as in the Charities Act 1993;

'functions' includes powers and duties;

'legal mortgage' has the same meaning as in the Law of Property Act 1925;

'personal representative' has the same meaning as in the Trustee Act 1925;

'settled land' has the same meaning as in the Settled Land Act 1925;

'trust corporation' has the same meaning as in the Trustee Act 1925;

'trust funds' means income or capital funds of the trust. ...

40   Minor and consequential amendments, etc ...

(2) Schedule 3 (transitional provisions and savings) shall have effect. ...

41   Power to amend other Acts

(1) A Minister of the Crown may by order make such amendments of any Act, including an Act extending to places outside England and Wales, as appear to him appropriate in consequence of or in connection with Part II or III.

(2) Before exercising the power under subsection (1) in relation to a local, personal or private Act, the Minister must consult any person who appears to him to be affected by any proposed amendment.

(3) An order under this section may –

(a) contain such transitional provisions and savings as the Minister thinks fit;

(b) make different provision for different purposes.

(4) The power to make an order under this section is exercisable by statutory instrument which shall be subject to annulment in pursuance of a resolution of either House of Parliament.

(5) 'Minister of the Crown' has the same meaning as in the Ministers of the Crown Act 1975.

SCHEDULE 1

APPLICATION OF DUTY OF CARE

Investment

1. The duty of care applies to a trustee –

(a) when exercising the general power of investment or any other power of investment, however conferred;

(b) when carrying out a duty to which he is subject under section 4 or 5 (duties relating to the exercise of a power of investment or to the review of investments).

Acquisition of land

2. The duty of care applies to a trustee –

(a) when exercising the power under section 8 to acquire land;

(b) when exercising any other power to acquire land, however conferred;

(c) when exercising any power in relation to land acquired under a power mentioned in sub-paragraph (a) or (b).

Agents, nominees and custodians

3. – (1) The duty of care applies to a trustee –

(a) when entering into arrangements under which a person is authorised under section 11 to exercise functions as an agent;

(b) when entering into arrangements under which a person is appointed under section 16 to act as a nominee;

(c) when entering into arrangements under which a person is appointed under section 17 or 18 to act as a custodian;

(d) when entering into arrangements under which, under any other power, however conferred, a person is authorised to exercise functions as an agent or is appointed to act as a nominee or custodian;

(e) when carrying out his duties under section 22 (review of agent, nominee or custodian, etc).

(2) For the purposes of sub-paragraph (1), entering into arrangements under which a person is authorised to exercise functions or is appointed to act as a nominee or custodian includes, in particular –

(a) selecting the person who is to act,

(b) determining any terms on which he is to act, and

(c) if the person is being authorised to exercise asset management functions, the preparation of a policy statement under section 15.

Compounding of liabilities

4. The duty of care applies to a trustee –

(a) when exercising the power under section 15 of the Trustee Act 1925 to do any of the things referred to in that section;

(b) when exercising any corresponding power, however conferred.

Insurance

5. The duty of care applies to a trustee –

(a) when exercising the power under section 19 of the Trustee Act 1925 to insure property;

(b) when exercising any corresponding power, however conferred.

Reversionary interests, valuations and audit

6. The duty of care applies to a trustee –

(a) when exercising the power under section 22(1) or (3) of the Trustee Act 1925 to do any of the things referred to there;

(b) when exercising any corresponding power, however conferred.

Exclusion of duty of care

7. The duty of care does not apply if or in so far as it appears from the trust instrument that the duty is not meant to apply.

NB. This Act came into force on 1 February 2001.

As amended by the Charities Act 2006, s75(1), Schedule 8, para 197.

COMPANIES (AUDIT, INVESTIGATIONS AND COMMUNITY ENTERPRISE) ACT 2004
(2004 c 27)

PART 2

COMMUNITY INTEREST COMPANIES

26   Community interest companies

(1) There is to be a new type of company to be known as the community interest company.

(2) In accordance with this Part –

    (a) a company limited by shares or a company limited by guarantee and not having a share capital may be formed as or become a community interest company, and

    (b) a company limited by guarantee and having a share capital may become a community interest company.

(3) A community interest company established for charitable purposes is to be treated as not being so established and accordingly –

    (a) is not a charity ...

27   Regulator

(1) There is to be an officer known as the Regulator of Community Interest Companies (referred to in this Part as 'the Regulator').

(2) The Secretary of State must appoint a person to be the Regulator. ...

30   Cap on distributions and interest

(1) Community interest companies must not distribute assets to their members unless regulations make provision authorising them to do so. ...

33   Names

(1) The name of a community interest company which is not a public company must end with –

    (a) 'community interest company', or

    (b) 'c.i.c.'.

(2) But the name of such a company may (instead) end with –

    (a) 'cwmni buddiant cymunedol', or

    (b) 'c.b.c.',

if the memorandum of the company states that the company's registered office is to be situated in Wales.

(3) The name of a community interest company which is a public company must end with –

    (a) 'community interest public limited company', or

    (b) 'community interest plc'.

(4) But the name of such a company may (instead) end with –

    (a) 'cwmni buddiant cymunedol cyhoeddus cyfyngedig', or

    (b) 'cwmni buddiant cymunedol c.c.c.',

if the memorandum of the company states that the company's registered office is to be situated in Wales.

(5) Section 25 of the Companies Act 1985 (company name to end with 'public limited company' or 'limited' or equivalent) does not apply to community interest companies.

(6) Schedule 6 (further provisions about names) has effect.

35   Community interest test and excluded companies

(1) This section has effect for the purposes of this Part.

(2) A company satisfies the community interest test if a reasonable person might consider that its activities are being carried on for the benefit of the community.

(3) An object stated in the memorandum of a company is a community interest object of the company if a reasonable person might consider that the carrying on of activities by the company in furtherance of the object is for the benefit of the community.

(4) Regulations may provide that activities of a description prescribed by the regulations are to be treated as being, or as not being, activities which a reasonable person might consider are activities carried on for the benefit of the community.

(5) 'Community' includes a section of the community (whether in Great Britain or anywhere else); and regulations may make provision about what does, does not or may constitute a section of the community.

(6) A company is an excluded company if it is a company of a description prescribed by regulations.

36   New companies

(1) If a company is to be formed as a community interest company, the documents delivered to the registrar of companies under section 10 of the Companies Act 1985 (memorandum, articles and statement of names and particulars of directors and secretary) must be accompanied by the prescribed formation documents.

(2) 'The prescribed formation documents' means such statutory declarations or other declarations or statements as are required by regulations to accompany the documents delivered under that section, in such form as may be approved in accordance with the regulations.

(3) On receiving the documents delivered under that section and the prescribed formation documents the registrar of companies must (instead of registering the memorandum and articles) –

    (a)   forward a copy of each of the documents to the Regulator, and

    (b)   retain the documents pending the Regulator's decision.

(4) The Regulator must decide whether the company is eligible to be formed as a community interest company.

(5) A company is eligible to be formed as a community interest company if –

    (a)   the memorandum and articles comply with the requirements imposed by and by virtue of section 32 and the company's name complies with section 33, and

    (b)   the Regulator, having regard to the documents delivered under section 10 of the Companies Act 1985 (c 6), the prescribed formation documents and any other relevant considerations, considers that the company will satisfy the community interest test and is not an excluded company.

(6) The Regulator must give notice of the decision to the registrar of companies (but the registrar is not required to record it).

(7) If the Regulator gives notice of a decision that the company is eligible to be formed as a community interest company, section 12 of the Companies Act 1985 (registration of memorandum and articles) applies; and if the registrar registers the memorandum and articles he must also retain and record the prescribed formation documents.

(8) The certificate of incorporation under section 13 of the Companies Act 1985 (effect of registration) is to contain a statement that the company is a community interest company.

(9) The fact that the certificate of incorporation contains such a statement is conclusive evidence that the company is a community interest company.

(10) If the Regulator decides that the company is not eligible to be formed as a community interest company, any subscriber to the memorandum may appeal to the Appeal Officer against the decision.

37 Existing companies: requirements

(1) If a company is to become a community interest company, the company must –

    (a) by special resolution alter its memorandum to state that it is to be a community interest company,

    (b) by special resolutions under the Companies Act 1985 make such alterations of its memorandum and articles as it considers necessary to comply with requirements imposed by and by virtue of section 32 or otherwise appropriate in connection with becoming a community interest company, and

    (c) by special resolution change its name to comply with section 33.

(2) Section 380(1) of the Companies Act 1985 (forwarding of copies of special resolutions to registrar of companies) must be complied with in relation to each of the special resolutions at the same time.

(3) If the special resolutions include one under section 4 or 17 of the Companies Act 1985 (alterations of memorandum) –

    (a) copies of the special resolutions must not be forwarded to the registrar of companies before the relevant date, and

    (b) section 380(1) has effect in relation to them as if it referred to 15 days after the relevant date.

(4) If an application is made under section 5 of the Companies Act 1985 (c 6) (objection to alteration of memorandum under section 4 or 17), the relevant date is –

    (a) the date on which the court determines the application (or, if there is more than one application, the date on which the last to be determined by the court is determined), or

    (b) such later date as the court may order.

(5) If there is no application under section 5 of that Act, the relevant date is the end of the period for making such an application.

(6) The copies of the special resolutions forwarded to the registrar of companies must be accompanied by –

    (a) a copy of the memorandum and articles of the company as altered by the special resolutions, and

    (b) the prescribed conversion documents.

(7) 'The prescribed conversion documents' means such statutory declarations or other declarations or statements as are required by regulations to accompany the copies of the special resolutions, in such form as may be approved in accordance with the regulations.

39 Existing companies: charities

(1) A charitable company may not by special resolution change its name to comply with section 33 without the prior written consent of the Charity Commission.

(2) If a charitable company contravenes subsection (1), the Charity Commission may apply to the High Court for an order quashing any altered certificate of incorporation issued under section 28(6) of the Companies Act 1985.

(3) If a charitable company becomes a community interest company, that does not affect the application of –

    (a) any property acquired under any disposition or agreement previously made otherwise than for full consideration in money or money's worth, or any property representing property so acquired,

    (b) any property representing income which has previously accrued, or

    (c) the income from any such property.

(4) 'Charitable company' means a company which is a charity, other than one to which section 40 [Existing companies: Scottish charities] applies.

45   Appointment of director

(1) The Regulator may by order appoint a director of a community interest company.

(2) The person appointed may be anyone whom the Regulator thinks appropriate, other than a member of the Regulator's staff.

(3) A person may be appointed as a director of a company under this section –

    (a) whether or not the person is a member of the company, and

    (b) irrespective of any provision made by the memorandum or articles of the company or a resolution of the company in general meeting.

(4) An order appointing a person to be a director of a company under this section must specify the terms on which the director is to hold office; and those terms have effect as if contained in a contract between the director and the company.

(5) The terms specified must include the period for which the director is to hold office, and may include terms as to the remuneration of the director by the company.

(6) A director appointed under this section has all the powers of the directors appointed by the company (including powers exercisable only by a particular director or class of directors).

(7) A director appointed under this section may not be removed by the company, but may be removed by the Regulator at any time.

(8) Where –

    (a) a person is appointed to be a director of the company under this section, or

    (b) a person so appointed ceases to be a director of the company,

the obligation which would otherwise be imposed on the company under section 288(2) of the Companies Act 1985 (c 6) (requirement that company notify change among directors to registrar) is instead an obligation of the Regulator.

(9) But if subsection (10) applies, section 288(2) applies as if the period within which the Regulator must send a notification to the registrar of companies is 14 days from the date on which the Regulator receives notification under that subsection.

(10) Where a person appointed to be a director of the company under this section ceases to be a director of the company (otherwise than by removal under subsection (7)), the company must give notification of that fact to the Regulator in a form approved by the Regulator before the end of the period of 14 days beginning with the date on which the person ceases to be a director.

(11) If the company fails to comply with subsection (10) it commits an offence.

(12) A person guilty of an offence under subsection (11) is liable on summary conviction to a fine not exceeding level 5 on the standard scale.

(13) The company may appeal to the Appeal Officer against an order under this section.

46   Removal of director

(1) The Regulator may by order remove a director of a community interest company.

(2) If a person has been removed under subsection (1) –

(a) the company may not subsequently appoint him a director of the company, and

(b) any assignment to the person of the office of director of the company is of no effect (even if approved by special resolution of the company).

(3) The Regulator may by order suspend a director of the company pending a decision whether to remove him.

(4) The maximum period for which a director may be suspended under subsection (3) is one year.

(5) If the Regulator suspends a director under subsection (3) the Regulator may give directions in relation to the performance of the director's functions.

(6) The Regulator may discharge an order made under subsection (1).

(7) The discharge of an order made under subsection (1) does not reinstate the person removed by the order as a director of the company, but on the discharge of the order subsection (2) ceases to apply to the person.

(8) The Regulator must from time to time review any order made under subsection (3) and, if it is appropriate to do so, discharge the order.

(9) Before making an order under subsection (1) or (3) in relation to a director, the Regulator must give at least 14 days' notice to –

(a) the director, and

(b) the company.

(10) Where an order is made in relation to a director under subsection (1) or (3) the director may appeal against the order –

(a) in England and Wales, to the High Court …

(11) The Regulator must, before the end of the period of 14 days beginning with the date on which –

(a) an order under subsection (1) is made or discharged,

(b) an order under subsection (3) is made or discharged or expires, or

(c) an order under subsection (1) or (3) is quashed on appeal,

give notification of that event to the registrar of companies in a form approved by the registrar of companies.

(12) Where subsection (11) imposes an obligation to notify the registrar of companies of an event, section 288(2) of the Companies Act 1985 (c 6) (requirement that company notify change among directors to registrar) does not apply in respect of the event.

47   Appointment of manager

(1) The Regulator may by order appoint a manager in respect of the property and affairs of a community interest company.

(2) The person appointed may be anyone whom the Regulator thinks appropriate, other than a member of the Regulator's staff.

(3) An order under subsection (1) may make provision as to the functions to be exercised by, and the powers of, the manager.

(4) The order may in particular provide –

(a) for the manager to have such of the functions of the company's directors as are specified in the order, and

(b) for the company's directors to be prevented from exercising any of those functions.

(5) In carrying out his functions the manager acts as the company's agent; and a person dealing with the manager in good faith and for value need not inquire whether the manager is acting within his powers.

(6) The appointment of the manager does not affect –

(a)　any right of any person to appoint a receiver or manager of the company's property (including any right under section 51 of the Insolvency Act 1986 (c 45)), or

(b)　the rights of a receiver or manager appointed by a person other than the Regulator.

(7) The manager's functions are to be discharged by him under the supervision of the Regulator; and the Regulator must from time to time review the order by which the manager is appointed and, if it is appropriate to do so, discharge it in whole or in part.

(8) In particular, the Regulator must discharge the order on the appointment of a person to act as administrative receiver, administrator, provisional liquidator or liquidator of the company.

(9) The Regulator may apply to the court for directions in relation to any matter arising in connection with the manager's functions or powers.

(10) On an application under subsection (9) the court may give such directions or make such orders as it thinks fit.

(11) The costs of any application under subsection (9) are to be paid by the company.

(12) Regulations may authorise the Regulator –

(a)　to require a manager to make reports,

(b)　to require a manager to give security (or, in Scotland, to find caution) for the due exercise of the manager's functions, and

(c)　to remove a manager in circumstances prescribed by the regulations.

(13) Regulations may –

(a)　provide for a manager's remuneration to be payable from the property of the company, and

(b)　authorise the Regulator to determine the amount of a manager's remuneration and to disallow any amount of remuneration in circumstances prescribed by the regulations.

(14) The company may appeal to the Appeal Officer against an order under this section.

53　Ceasing to be a community interest company

A community interest company may not cease to be a community interest company except by dissolution or as provided –

(a)　by sections 54 and 55 (becoming a charity or a Scottish charity), or

(b)　if regulations are made under section 56 (becoming an industrial and provident society), by the regulations.

54　Becoming a charity or a Scottish charity: requirements

(1) If a community interest company is to cease being a community interest company and become a charity or a Scottish charity, the company must –

(a)　by special resolution alter its memorandum so that it does not state that it is to be a community interest company,

(b)　by special resolutions under the Companies Act 1985 make such alterations of its memorandum and articles as it considers appropriate, and

(c)　by special resolution change its name so that it does not comply with section 33.

(2) Section 380(1) of the Companies Act 1985 (forwarding of copies of special resolutions to registrar of companies) must be complied with in relation to each of the special resolutions at the same time.

(3) If the special resolutions include one under section 4 or 17 of the Companies Act 1985 (alterations of memorandum) –

(a)　copies of the special resolutions must not be forwarded to the registrar of companies before the relevant date, and

(b) section 380(1) has effect in relation to them as if it referred to 15 days after the relevant date.

(4) If an application is made under section 5 of the Companies Act 1985 (objection to alteration of memorandum under section 4 or 17), the relevant date is –

(a) the date on which the court determines the application (or, if there is more than one application, the date on which the last to be determined by the court is determined), or

(b) such later date as the court may order.

(5) If there is no application under section 5 of that Act, the relevant date is the end of the period for making such an application.

(6) The copies of the special resolutions forwarded to the registrar of companies must be accompanied by –

(a) a copy of the memorandum and articles of the company as altered by the special resolutions, and

(b) a statement under subsection (7) or, if the company's registered office is situated in Scotland and the company is to become a Scottish charity, a statement under subsection (8).

(7) A statement under this subsection is a statement by the Charity Commission that in its opinion, if the special resolutions take effect and the company ceases to be a community interest company the company will be a charity and will not be an exempt charity.

(8) A statement under this subsection is a statement by the Scottish Charity Regulator that, if the special resolutions take effect and the company ceases to be a community interest company, the company will be entered in the Scottish Charity Register.

(9) 'Exempt charity' has the same meaning as in the Charities Act 1993 (c 10) (see section 96 of that Act).

55   Becoming a charity or a Scottish charity: decisions, etc

(1) On receiving under section 54 the copies of the special resolutions, the memorandum and articles as altered by the special resolutions and the statement, the registrar must (instead of recording the special resolutions and entering a new name on the register) –

(a) forward a copy of each of the documents to the Regulator, and

(b) retain them pending the Regulator's decision.

(2) The alterations of the memorandum and articles made by the special resolutions are to take effect only as provided by this section.

(3) The Regulator must decide whether the company is eligible to cease being a community interest company.

(4) The company is eligible to cease being a community interest company if it has complied with section 54 and none of the following applies –

(a) the Regulator has under section 43 appointed an auditor to audit the company's annual accounts and the audit has not been completed,

(b) civil proceedings instituted by the Regulator in the name of the company under section 44 have not been determined or discontinued,

(c) a director of the company holds office by virtue of an order under section 45,

(d) a director of the company is suspended under section 46(3),

(e) there is a manager in respect of the property and affairs of the company appointed under section 47,

(f) the Official Property Holder holds property as trustee for the company,

(g) an order under section 48(2) or (3) is in force in relation to the company,

(h) a petition has been presented for the company to be wound up.

(5) The Regulator must give notice of the decision to the registrar of companies (but the registrar is not required to record it).

(6) If the Regulator gives notice of a decision that the company is eligible to cease being a community interest company, section 28(6) of the Companies Act 1985 (c 6) (registration of new name) applies; and if the registrar of companies enters the new name of the company on the register he must also retain and record the special resolutions and the statement.

(7) On the date on which the certificate of incorporation is issued the alterations to the company's articles and memorandum made by the special resolutions take effect and the company ceases to be a community interest company.

(8) If the Regulator decides that the company is not eligible to cease being a community interest company, the company may appeal to the Appeal Officer against the decision.

56 Becoming an industrial and provident society

(1) Unless regulations make provision to the contrary, a community interest company may not convert itself into a registered society under section 53 of the Industrial and Provident Societies Act 1965 (c 12).

(2) If regulations make provision allowing the conversion of community interest companies under that section they may include provision modifying that section in its application by virtue of the regulations.

63 Interpretation

(1) In this Part –

'administrative receiver' has the meaning given by section 251 of the Insolvency Act 1986 (c 45),

'the Appeal Officer' has the meaning given by section 28(1),

'charity' (except in the phrase 'Scottish charity') has the same meaning as in the Charities Act 1993 (c 10) (see section 96 of that Act),

'community interest object' is to be construed in accordance with section 35(3),

'the community interest test' is to be construed in accordance with section 35(2),

'enactment' includes an Act of the Scottish Parliament,

'excluded company' is to be construed in accordance with section 35(6),

'the Official Property Holder' has the meaning given by section 29(1),

'the Regulator' has the meaning given by section 27(1), and

'Scottish charity' means a body entered in the Scottish Charity Register.

(2) Any expression used in this Part and in the Companies Act 1985 (c 6) has the same meaning in this Part as in that Act.

As amended by the Charities and Trustee Investment (Scotland) Act 2005 (Consequential Provisions and Modifications) Order 2006, art 5, Schedule, Pt 1, para 8(1), (4), (5); Charities Act 2006, s75(1), Schedule 8, paras 200, 201, 203.

CIVIL PARTNERSHIP ACT 2004
(2004 c 33)

PART 1

INTRODUCTION

1 Civil partnership

(1) A civil partnership is a relationship between two people of the same sex ('civil partners') –
  (a) which is formed when they register as civil partners of each other –
    (i) in England or Wales (under Part 2) …

(2) Subsection (1) is subject to the provisions of this Act under or by virtue of which a civil partnership is void.

(3) A civil partnership ends only on death, dissolution or annulment.

(4) The references in subsection (3) to dissolution and annulment are to dissolution and annulment having effect under or recognised in accordance with this Act. …

PART 2

CIVIL PARTNERSHIP: ENGLAND AND WALES

CHAPTER 3

PROPERTY AND FINANCIAL ARRANGEMENTS

65 Contribution by civil partner to property improvement

(1) This section applies if –
  (a) a civil partner contributes in money or money's worth to the improvement of real or personal property in which or in the proceeds of sale of which either or both of the civil partners has or have a beneficial interest, and
  (b) the contribution is of a substantial nature.

(2) The contributing partner is to be treated as having acquired by virtue of the contribution a share or an enlarged share (as the case may be) in the beneficial interest of such an extent –
  (a) as may have been then agreed, or
  (b) in default of such agreement, as may seem in all the circumstances just to any court before which the question of the existence or extent of the beneficial interest of either of the civil partners arises (whether in proceedings between them or in any other proceedings).

(3) Subsection (2) is subject to any agreement (express or implied) between the civil partners to the contrary.

66 Disputes between civil partners about property

(1) In any question between the civil partners in a civil partnership as to title to or possession of property, either civil partner may apply to –
  (a) the High Court, or
  (b) such county court as may be prescribed by rules of court.

(2) On such an application, the court may make such order with respect to the property as it thinks fit (including an order for the sale of the property).

(3) Rules of court made for the purposes of this section may confer jurisdiction on county courts whatever the situation or value of the property in dispute.

67   Applications under section 66 where property not in possession, etc

(1) The right of a civil partner ('A') to make an application under section 66 includes the right to make such an application where A claims that the other civil partner ('B') has had in his possession or under his control –

    (a) money to which, or to a share of which, A was beneficially entitled, or

    (b) property (other than money) to which, or to an interest in which, A was beneficially entitled,

and that either the money or other property has ceased to be in B's possession or under B's control or that A does not know whether it is still in B's possession or under B's control.

(2) For the purposes of subsection (1)(a) it does not matter whether A is beneficially entitled to the money or share –

    (a) because it represents the proceeds of property to which, or to an interest in which, A was beneficially entitled, or

    (b) for any other reason.

(3) Subsections (4) and (5) apply if, on such an application being made, the court is satisfied that B –

    (a) has had in his possession or under his control money or other property as mentioned in subsection (1)(a) or (b), and

    (b) has not made to A, in respect of that money or other property, such payment or disposition as would have been appropriate in the circumstances.

(4) The power of the court to make orders under section 66 includes power to order B to pay to A –

    (a) in a case falling within subsection (1)(a), such sum in respect of the money to which the application relates, or A's s share of it, as the court considers appropriate, or

    (b) in a case falling within subsection (1)(b), such sum in respect of the value of the property to which the application relates, or A's interest in it, as the court considers appropriate.

(5) If it appears to the court that there is any property which –

    (a) represents the whole or part of the money or property, and

    (b) is property in respect of which an order could (apart from this section) have been made under section 66,

the court may (either instead of or as well as making an order in accordance with subsection (4)) make any order which it could (apart from this section) have made under section 66.

(6) Any power of the court which is exercisable on an application under section 66 is exercisable in relation to an application made under that section as extended by this section.

68   Applications under section 66 by former civil partners

(1) This section applies where a civil partnership has been dissolved or annulled.

(2) Subject to subsection (3), an application may be made under section 66 (including that section as extended by section 67) by either former civil partner despite the dissolution or annulment (and references in those sections to a civil partner are to be read accordingly).

(3) The application must be made within the period of 3 years beginning with the date of the dissolution or annulment.

EQUALITY ACT 2006
(2006 c 3)

PART 2

DISCRIMINATION ON GROUNDS OF RELIGIOUS BELIEF

44   Religion and belief

In this Part –
- (a) 'religion' means any religion,
- (b) 'belief' means any religious or philosophical belief,
- (c) a reference to religion includes a reference to lack of religion, and
- (d) a reference to belief includes a reference to lack of belief.

45   Discrimination

(1) A person ('A') discriminates against another ('B') for the purposes of this Part if on grounds of the religion or belief of B or of any other person except A (whether or not it is also A's religion or belief) A treats B less favourably than he treats or would treat others (in cases where there is no material difference in the relevant circumstances).

(2) In subsection (1) a reference to a person's religion or belief includes a reference to a religion or belief to which he is thought to belong or subscribe.

(3) A person ('A') discriminates against another ('B') for the purposes of this Part if A applies to B a provision, criterion or practice –
- (a) which he applies or would apply equally to persons not of B's religion or belief,
- (b) which puts persons of B's religion or belief at a disadvantage compared to some or all others (where there is no material difference in the relevant circumstances),
- (c) which puts B at a disadvantage compared to some or all persons who are not of his religion or belief (where there is no material difference in the relevant circumstances), and
- (d) which A cannot reasonably justify by reference to matters other than B's religion or belief.

(4) A person ('A') discriminates against another ('B') if A treats B less favourably than he treats or would treat another and does so by reason of the fact that, or by reason of A's knowledge or suspicion that, B –
- (a) has brought or intended to bring, or intends to bring, proceedings under this Part,
- (b) has given or intended to give, or intends to give, evidence in proceedings under this Part,
- (c) has provided or intended to provide, or intends to provide, information in connection with proceedings under this Part,
- (d) has done or intended to do, or intends to do, any other thing under or in connection with this Part, or
- (e) has alleged or intended to allege, or intends to allege, that a person contravened this Part.

(5) Subsection (4) does not apply where A's treatment of B relates to B's making or intending to make, not in good faith, a false allegation.

57   Organisations relating to religion or belief

(1) This section applies to an organisation the purpose of which is –
- (a) to practice a religion or belief,

(b) to advance a religion or belief,

(c) to teach the practice or principles of a religion or belief,

(d) to enable persons of a religion or belief to receive any benefit, or to engage in any activity, within the framework of that religion or belief, or

(e) to improve relations, or maintain good relations, between persons of different religions or beliefs.

(2) But this section does not apply to an organisation whose sole or main purpose is commercial.

(3) Nothing in this Part shall make it unlawful for an organisation to which this section applies or anyone acting on behalf of or under the auspices of an organisation to which this section applies –

(a) to restrict membership of the organisation,

(b) to restrict participation in activities undertaken by the organisation or on its behalf or under its auspices,

(c) to restrict the provision of goods, facilities or services in the course of activities undertaken by the organisation or on its behalf or under its auspices, or

(d)   to restrict the use or disposal of premises owned or controlled by the organisation.

(4) Nothing in this Part shall make it unlawful for a minister –

(a) to restrict participation in activities carried on in the performance of his functions in connection with or in respect of an organisation to which this section relates, or

(b) to restrict the provision of goods, facilities or services in the course of activities carried on in the performance of his functions in connection with or in respect of an organisation to which this section relates.

(5) But subsections (3) and (4) permit a restriction only if imposed –

(a) by reason of or on the grounds of the purpose of the organisation, or

(b) in order to avoid causing offence, on grounds of the religion or belief to which the organisation relates, to persons of that religion or belief.

(6) In subsection (4) the reference to a minister is a reference to a minister of religion, or other person, who –

(a) performs functions in connection with a religion or belief to which an organisation, to which this section applies, relates, and

(b) holds an office or appointment in, or is accredited, approved or recognised for purposes of, an organisation to which this section applies.

58   Charities relating to religion or belief

(1) Nothing in this Part shall make it unlawful for a person to provide benefits only to persons of a particular religion or belief, if –

(a) he acts in pursuance of a charitable instrument, and

(b) the restriction of benefits to persons of that religion or belief is imposed by reason of or on the grounds of the provisions of the charitable instrument.

(2) Nothing in this Part shall make it unlawful for the Charity Commission or the holder of the Office of the Scottish Charity Regulator to exercise a function in relation to a charity in a manner which appears to the Commission or to the holder to be expedient in the interests of the charity, having regard to the provisions of the charitable instrument.

(3) In this section 'charitable instrument' –

(a) means an instrument establishing or governing a charity, and

(b) includes a charitable instrument made before the commencement of this section.

59   Faith schools, etc.

(1) Nothing in this Part shall make it unlawful for an educational institution established or conducted for the purpose of providing education relating to, or within the framework of, a specified religion or belief –

    (a) to restrict the provision of goods, facilities or services, or

    (b) to restrict the use or disposal of premises.

(2) But subsection (1) permits a restriction only if imposed –

    (a) by reason of or on the grounds of the purpose of the institution, or

    (b) in order to avoid causing offence, on grounds of the religion or belief to which the institution relates, to persons connected with the institution.

(3) In this Part a reference to the provision of facilities or services shall not, in so far as it applies to an educational institution, include a reference to educational facilities or educational services provided to students of the institution.

60   Membership requirement

(1) Nothing in this Part shall make it unlawful for a charity to require members, or persons wishing to become members, to make a statement which asserts or implies membership or acceptance of a religion or belief.

(2) Subsection (1) shall apply to the imposition of a requirement by a charity only if –

    (a) the charity, or an organisation of which the charity is part, first imposed a requirement of the kind specified in subsection (1) before 18th May 2005, and

    (b) the charity or organisation has not ceased since that date to impose a requirement of that kind.

61   Education, training and welfare

Nothing in this Part shall make it unlawful to do anything by way of –

    (a) meeting special needs for education, training or welfare of persons of a religion or belief, or

    (b) providing ancillary benefits in connection with meeting the needs mentioned in paragraph (a).

79   Interpretation

(1) In this Part 'charity' –

    (a) in relation to England and Wales, has the meaning given by section 1(1) of the Charities Act 2006, and

    (b) in relation to Scotland, means a body entered in the Scottish Charity Register. ...

NB. The insertion, in s79(1)(a), above, of the words 'section 1(1) of' was not in force on 1 June 2007.

As amended by the Charities Act 2006, s75(1), Schedule 8, para 212.

APPENDIX

Provisions of the Charities Act 2006 which were not in force, or fully in force, on 1 June 2007. For the precise position as at that date, see section 79 of the 2006 Act and the Charities Act 2006 (Commencement No 1, Transitional Provisions and Savings) Order 2007 (SI 2007/309).

CHARITIES ACT 2006
(2006 c 50)

PART 1

MEANING OF 'CHARITY' AND 'CHARITABLE PURPOSE'

1   Meaning of 'charity'
(1) For the purposes of the law of England and Wales, 'charity' means an institution which –
    (a) is established for charitable purposes only, and
    (b) falls to be subject to the control of the High Court in the exercise of its jurisdiction with respect to charities.
(2) The definition of 'charity' in subsection (1) does not apply for the purposes of an enactment if a different definition of that term applies for those purposes by virtue of that or any other enactment.
(3) A reference in any enactment or document to a charity within the meaning of the Charitable Uses Act 1601 (c. 4) or the preamble to it is to be construed as a reference to a charity as defined by subsection (1).

2   Meaning of 'charitable purpose'
(1) For the purposes of the law of England and Wales, a charitable purpose is a purpose which –
    (a) falls within subsection (2), and
    (b) is for the public benefit (see section 3).
(2) A purpose falls within this subsection if it falls within any of the following descriptions of purposes –
    (a) the prevention or relief of poverty;
    (b) the advancement of education;
    (c) the advancement of religion;
    (d) the advancement of health or the saving of lives;
    (e) the advancement of citizenship or community development;
    (f) the advancement of the arts, culture, heritage or science;
    (g) the advancement of amateur sport;

(h) the advancement of human rights, conflict resolution or reconciliation or the promotion of religious or racial harmony or equality and diversity;

(i) the advancement of environmental protection or improvement;

(j) the relief of those in need by reason of youth, age, ill-health,disability, financial hardship or other disadvantage;

(k) the advancement of animal welfare;

(l) the promotion of the efficiency of the armed forces of the Crown, or of the efficiency of the police, fire and rescue services or ambulance services;

(m) any other purposes within subsection (4).

(3) In subsection (2) –

(a) in paragraph (c) 'religion' includes –
    (i) a religion which involves belief in more than one god, and
    (ii) a religion which does not involve belief in a god;

(b) in paragraph (d) 'the advancement of health' includes the prevention or relief of sickness, disease or human suffering;

(c) paragraph (e) includes –
    (i) rural or urban regeneration, and
    (ii) the promotion of civic responsibility, volunteering, the voluntary sector or the effectiveness or efficiency of charities;

(d) in paragraph (g) 'sport' means sports or games which promote health by involving physical or mental skill or exertion;

(e) paragraph (j) includes relief given by the provision of accommodation or care to the persons mentioned in that paragraph; and

(f) in paragraph (l) 'fire and rescue services' means services provided by fire and rescue authorities under Part 2 of the Fire and Rescue Services Act 2004 (c 21).

(4) The purposes within this subsection (see subsection (2)(m)) are –

(a) any purposes not within paragraphs (a) to (l) of subsection (2) but recognised as charitable purposes under existing charity law or by virtue of section 1 of the Recreational Charities Act 1958 (c 17);

(b) any purposes that may reasonably be regarded as analogous to, or within the spirit of, any purposes falling within any of those paragraphs or paragraph (a) above; and

(c) any purposes that may reasonably be regarded as analogous to, or within the spirit of, any purposes which have been recognised under charity law as falling within paragraph (b) above or this paragraph.

(5) Where any of the terms used in any of paragraphs (a) to (l) of subsection (2), or in subsection (3), has a particular meaning under charity law, the term is to be taken as having the same meaning where it appears in that provision.

(6) Any reference in any enactment or document (in whatever terms) –

(a) to charitable purposes, or

(b) to institutions having purposes that are charitable under charity law,

is to be construed in accordance with subsection (1).

(7) Subsection (6) –

(a) applies whether the enactment or document was passed or made before or after the passing of this Act, but

(b) does not apply where the context otherwise requires.

(8) In this section –

'charity law' means the law relating to charities in England and Wales; and 'existing charity law' means charity law as in force immediately before the day on which this section comes into force.

3   The 'public benefit' test

(1) This section applies in connection with the requirement in section 2(1)(b) that a purpose falling within section 2(2) must be for the public benefit if it is to be a charitable purpose.

(2) In determining whether that requirement is satisfied in relation to any such purpose, it is not to be presumed that a purpose of a particular description is for the public benefit.

(3) In this Part any reference to the public benefit is a reference to the public benefit as that term is understood for the purposes of the law relating to charities in England and Wales.

(4) Subsection (3) applies subject to subsection (2).

4   Guidance as to operation of public benefit requirement

(1) The Charity Commission for England and Wales (see section 6 of this Act) must issue guidance in pursuance of its public benefit objective.

(2) That objective is to promote awareness and understanding of the operation of the requirement mentioned in section 3(1) (see section 1B(3) and (4) of the Charities Act 1993 (c. 10), as inserted by section 7 of this Act).

(3) The Commission may from time to time revise any guidance issued under this section.

(4) The Commission must carry out such public and other consultation as it considers appropriate –

   (a) before issuing any guidance under this section, or

   (b) (unless it considers that it is unnecessary to do so) before revising any such guidance.

(5) The Commission must publish any guidance issued or revised under this section in such manner as it considers appropriate.

(6) The charity trustees of a charity must have regard to any such guidance when exercising any powers or duties to which the guidance is relevant.

5   Special provisions about recreational charities, sports clubs etc

(1) The Recreational Charities Act 1958 (c. 17) is amended in accordance with subsections (2) and (3).

(2) In section 1 (certain recreational and similar purposes deemed to be charitable) for subsection (2) substitute –

   '(2) The requirement in subsection (1) that the facilities are provided in the interests of social welfare cannot be satisfied if the basic conditions are not met.

   (2A) The basic conditions are –

      (a) that the facilities are provided with the object of improving the conditions of life for the persons for whom the facilities are primarily intended; and

      (b) that either –

         (i)   those persons have need of the facilities by reason of their youth, age, infirmity or disability, poverty, or social and economic circumstances, or

         (ii) the facilities are to be available to members of the public at large or to male, or to female, members of the public at large.' ...

PART 2

REGULATION OF CHARITIES

CHAPTER 1

THE CHARITY COMMISSION …

7   **The Commission's objectives, general functions and duties**
After section 1A of the 1993 Act (inserted by section 6 above) insert –

'1B The Commission's objectives

(1) The Commission has the objectives set out in subsection (2).
(2) The objectives are –
    1.   The public confidence objective.
    2.   The public benefit objective.
    3.   The compliance objective.
    4.   The charitable resources objective.
    5.   The accountability objective.
(3) Those objectives are defined as follows –
    1.   The public confidence objective is to increase public trust and confidence in charities.
    2.   The public benefit objective is to promote awareness and understanding of the operation of the public benefit requirement.
    3.   The compliance objective is to promote compliance by charity trustees with their legal obligations in exercising control and management of the administration of their charities.
    4.   The charitable resources objective is to promote the effective use of charitable resources.
    5.   The accountability objective is to enhance the accountability of charities to donors, beneficiaries and the general public.
(4) In this section "the public benefit requirement" means the requirement in section 2(1)(b) of the Charities Act 2006 that a purpose falling within section 2(2) of that Act must be for the public benefit if it is to be a charitable purpose.

1C The Commission's general functions

(1) The Commission has the general functions set out in subsection (2).
(2) The general functions are –
    1.   Determining whether institutions are or are not charities.
    2.   Encouraging and facilitating the better administration of charities.
    3.   Identifying and investigating apparent misconduct or mismanagement in the administration of charities and taking remedial or protective action in connection with misconduct or mismanagement therein.
    4.   Determining whether public collections certificates should be issued, and remain in force, in respect of public charitable collections.
    5.   Obtaining, evaluating and disseminating information in connection with the performance of any of the Commission's functions or meeting any of its objectives.
    6.   Giving information or advice, or making proposals, to any Minister of the Crown on matters relating to any of the Commission's functions or meeting any of its objectives.

(3) The Commission's fifth general function includes (among other things) the maintenance of an accurate and up-to-date register of charities under section 3 below.

(4) The Commission's sixth general function includes (among other things) complying, so far as is reasonably practicable, with any request made by a Minister of the Crown for information or advice on any matter relating to any of its functions.

(5) In this section "public charitable collection" and "public collections certificate" have the same meanings as in Chapter 1 of Part 3 of the Charities Act 2006.

1D The Commission's general duties

(1) The Commission has the general duties set out in subsection (2).

(2) The general duties are –

1. So far as is reasonably practicable the Commission must, in performing its functions, act in a way –
    (a) which is compatible with its objectives, and
    (b) which it considers most appropriate for the purpose of meeting those objectives.

2. So far as is reasonably practicable the Commission must, in performing its functions, act in a way which is compatible with the encouragement of –
    (a) all forms of charitable giving, and
    (b) voluntary participation in charity work.

3. In performing its functions the Commission must have regard to the need to use its resources in the most efficient, effective and economic way.

4. In performing its functions the Commission must, so far as relevant, have regard to the principles of best regulatory practice (including the principles under which regulatory activities should be proportionate, accountable, consistent, transparent and targeted only at cases in which action is needed).

5. In performing its functions the Commission must, in appropriate cases, have regard to the desirability of facilitating innovation by or on behalf of charities.

6. In managing its affairs the Commission must have regard to such generally accepted principles of good corporate governance as it is reasonable to regard as applicable to it.

1E The Commission's incidental powers

(1) The Commission has power to do anything which is calculated to facilitate, or is conducive or incidental to, the performance of any of its functions or general duties.

(2) However, nothing in this Act authorises the Commission –
    (a) to exercise functions corresponding to those of a charity trustee in relation to a charity, or
    (b) otherwise to be directly involved in the administration of a charity.

(3) Subsection (2) does not affect the operation of section 19A or 19B below (power of Commission to give directions as to action to be taken or as to application of charity property).'

CHAPTER 2

THE CHARITY TRIBUNAL

8   The Charity Tribunal
(1) After section 2 of the 1993 Act insert –

'PART 1A

THE CHARITY TRIBUNAL

2A The Charity Tribunal
(1) There shall be a tribunal to be known as the Charity Tribunal (in this Act referred to as "the Tribunal").

(2) In Welsh the Tribunal shall be known as "Tribiwnlys Elusennau".

(3) The provisions of Schedule 1B to this Act shall have effect with respect to the constitution of the Tribunal and other matters relating to it.

(4) The Tribunal shall have jurisdiction to hear and determine –
- (a) such appeals and applications as may be made to the Tribunal in accordance with Schedule 1C to this Act, or any other enactment, in respect of decisions, orders or directions of the Commission, and
- (b) such matters as may be referred to the Tribunal in accordance with Schedule 1D to this Act by the Commission or the Attorney General.

(5) Such appeals, applications and matters shall be heard and determined by the Tribunal in accordance with those Schedules, or any such enactment, taken with section 2B below and rules made under that section.

2B Practice and procedure
(1) The Lord Chancellor may make rules –
- (a) regulating the exercise of rights to appeal or to apply to the Tribunal and matters relating to the making of references to it;
- (b) about the practice and procedure to be followed in relation to proceedings before the Tribunal. ...

2C Appeal from Tribunal
(1) A party to proceedings before the Tribunal may appeal to the High Court against a decision of the Tribunal.

(2) Subject to subsection (3) below, an appeal may be brought under this section against a decision of the Tribunal only on a point of law.

(3) In the case of an appeal under this section against a decision of the Tribunal which determines a question referred to it by the Commission or the Attorney General, the High Court –
- (a) shall consider afresh the question referred to the Tribunal, and
- (b) may take into account evidence which was not available to the Tribunal.

(4) An appeal under this section may be brought only with the permission of –
- (a) the Tribunal, or
- (b) if the Tribunal refuses permission, the High Court.

(5) For the purposes of subsection (1) above –

(a) the Commission and the Attorney General are to be treated as parties to all proceedings before the Tribunal, and

(b) rules under section 2B(1) above may include provision as to who else is to be treated as being (or not being) a party to proceedings before the Tribunal.

2D Intervention by Attorney General

(1) This section applies to any proceedings –

    (a) before the Tribunal, or

    (b) on an appeal from the Tribunal,

to which the Attorney General is not a party.

(2) The Tribunal or, in the case of an appeal from the Tribunal, the court may at any stage of the proceedings direct that all the necessary papers in the proceedings be sent to the Attorney General.

(3) A direction under subsection (2) may be made by the Tribunal or court –

    (a) of its own motion, or

    (b) on the application of any party to the proceedings.

(4) The Attorney General may –

    (a) intervene in the proceedings in such manner as he thinks necessary or expedient, and

    (b) argue before the Tribunal or court any question in relation to the proceedings which the Tribunal or court considers it necessary to have fully argued.

(5) Subsection (4) applies whether or not the Tribunal or court has given a direction under subsection (2).'

(2) Schedule 3 [The Charity Tribunal] (which inserts the new Schedule 1B into the 1993 Act) has effect.

(3) Schedule 4 [Appeals and Applications to Charity Tribunal] (which inserts the new Schedules 1C and 1D into the 1993 Act) has effect.

CHAPTER 3

REGISTRATION OF CHARITIES

9   Registration of charities

For section 3 of the 1993 Act substitute –

'3   Register of charities

(1) There shall continue to be a register of charities, which shall be kept by the Commission.

(2) The register shall be kept by the Commission in such manner as it thinks fit.

(3) The register shall contain –

    (a) the name of every charity registered in accordance with section 3A below (registration), and

    (b) such other particulars of, and such other information relating to, every such charity as the Commission thinks fit.

(4) The Commission shall remove from the register –

    (a) any institution which it no longer considers is a charity, and

    (b) any charity which has ceased to exist or does not operate.

(5) If the removal of an institution under subsection (4)(a) above is due to any change in its trusts, the removal shall take effect from the date of that change.

(6) A charity which is for the time being registered under section 3A(6) below (voluntary registration) shall be removed from the register if it so requests.

(7) The register (including the entries cancelled when institutions are removed from the register) shall be open to public inspection at all reasonable times.

(8) Where any information contained in the register is not in documentary form, subsection (7) above shall be construed as requiring the information to be available for public inspection in legible form at all reasonable times.

(9) If the Commission so determines, subsection (7) shall not apply to any particular information contained in the register that is specified in the determination.

(10) Copies (or particulars) of the trusts of any registered charity as supplied to the Commission under section 3B below (applications for registration etc.) shall, so long as the charity remains on the register –

    (a) be kept by the Commission, and

    (b) be open to public inspection at all reasonable times.

3A Registration of charities

(1) Every charity must be registered in the register of charities unless subsection (2) below applies to it.

(2) The following are not required to be registered –

    (a) any exempt charity (see Schedule 2 to this Act);

    (b) any charity which for the time being –

        (i)   is permanently or temporarily excepted by order of the Commission, and

        (ii) complies with any conditions of the exception,

        and whose gross income does not exceed £100,000;

    (c) any charity which for the time being –

        (i)   is, or is of a description, permanently or temporarily excepted by regulations made by the Minister, and

        (ii) complies with any conditions of the exception,

        and whose gross income does not exceed £100,000; and

    (d) any charity whose gross income does not exceed £5,000.

(3) For the purposes of subsection (2)(b) above –

    (a) any order made or having effect as if made under section 3(5)(b) of this Act (as originally enacted) and in force immediately before the appointed day has effect as from that day as if made under subsection (2)(b) (and may be varied or revoked accordingly); and

    (b) no order may be made under subsection (2)(b) so as to except on or after the appointed day any charity that was not excepted immediately before that day.

(4) For the purposes of subsection (2)(c) above –

    (a) any regulations made or having effect as if made under section 3(5)(b) of this Act (as originally enacted) and in force immediately before the appointed day have effect as from that day as if made under subsection (2)(c) (and may be varied or revoked accordingly);

    (b) such regulations shall be made under subsection (2)(c) as are necessary to secure that all of the formerly specified institutions are excepted under that provision (subject to compliance with any conditions of the exception and the financial limit mentioned in that provision); but

(c) otherwise no regulations may be made under subsection (2)(c) so as to except on or after the appointed day any description of charities that was not excepted immediately before that day.

(5) In subsection (4)(b) above "formerly specified institutions" means –

    (a) any institution falling within section 3(5B)(a) or (b) of this Act as in force immediately before the appointed day (certain educational institutions); or

    (b) any institution ceasing to be an exempt charity by virtue of section 11 of the Charities Act 2006 or any order made under that section.

(6) A charity within –

    (a) subsection (2)(b) or (c) above, or

    (b) subsection (2)(d) above,

must, if it so requests, be registered in the register of charities.

(7) The Minister may by order amend –

    (a) subsection (2)(b) and (c) above, or

    (b) subsection (2)(d) above,

by substituting a different sum for the sum for the time being specified there.

(8) The Minister may only make an order under subsection (7) above –

    (a) so far as it amends subsection (2)(b) and (c), if he considers it expedient to so with a view to reducing the scope of the exception provided by those provisions;

    (b) so far as it amends subsection (2)(d), if he considers it expedient to do so in consequence of changes in the value of money or with a view to extending the scope of the exception provided by that provision,

and no order may be made by him under subsection (7)(a) unless a copy of a report under section 73 of the Charities Act 2006 (report on operation of that Act) has been laid before Parliament in accordance with that section.

(9) In this section "the appointed day" means the day on which subsections (1) to (5) above come into force by virtue of an order under section 79 of the Charities Act 2006 relating to section 9 of that Act (registration of charities).

(10) In this section any reference to a charity's "gross income" shall be construed, in relation to a particular time –

    (a) as a reference to the charity's gross income in its financial year immediately preceding that time, or

    (b) if the Commission so determines, as a reference to the amount which the Commission estimates to be the likely amount of the charity's gross income in such financial year of the charity as is specified in the determination.

(11) The following provisions of this section –

    (a) subsection (2)(b) and (c),

    (b) subsections (3) to (5), and

    (c) subsections (6)(a), (7)(a), (8)(a) and (9),

shall cease to have effect on such day as the Minister may by order appoint for the purposes of this subsection.

3B Duties of trustees in connection with registration

(1) Where a charity required to be registered by virtue of section 3A(1) above is not registered, it is the duty of the charity trustees –

    (a) to apply to the Commission for the charity to be registered, and

    (b) to supply the Commission with the required documents and information.

(2) The "required documents and information" are –

(a) copies of the charity's trusts or (if they are not set out in any extant document) particulars of them,

(b) such other documents or information as may be prescribed by regulations made by the Minister, and

(c) such other documents or information as the Commission may require for the purposes of the application.

(3) Where an institution is for the time being registered, it is the duty of the charity trustees (or the last charity trustees) –

(a) to notify the Commission if the institution ceases to exist, or if there is any change in its trusts or in the particulars of it entered in the register, and

(b) (so far as appropriate), to supply the Commission with particulars of any such change and copies of any new trusts or alterations of the trusts.

(4) Nothing in subsection (3) above requires a person –

(a) to supply the Commission with copies of schemes for the administration of a charity made otherwise than by the court,

(b) to notify the Commission of any change made with respect to a registered charity by such a scheme, or

(c) if he refers the Commission to a document or copy already in the possession of the Commission, to supply a further copy of the document.

(5) Where a copy of a document relating to a registered charity –

(a) is not required to be supplied to the Commission as the result of subsection (4) above, but

(b) is in the possession of the Commission,

a copy of the document shall be open to inspection under section 3(10) above as if supplied to the Commission under this section.' ...

11   Changes in exempt charities

(1) Schedule 2 to the 1993 Act (exempt charities) is amended as follows.

(2) In paragraph (a) (general exemption by reference to law existing prior to Charities Act 1960 (c 58)) after '1855' insert '(*but see Note 1*)'.

(3) In paragraph (b) (certain specified universities, colleges and schools) –

(a) before 'Queen Mary and Westfield College' insert 'and'; and

(b) omit 'and the colleges of Winchester and Eton'.

(4) Before paragraph (i) insert –

'(h) a higher education corporation;'.

(5) After paragraph (i) insert –

'(j) a further education corporation;'.

(6) In paragraph (w) (exemption for institutions administered by or on behalf of institutions exempted under preceding provisions) after 'last-mentioned institution' insert '(*but see Note 2*)'.

(7) Omit paragraph (x) (Church Commissioners and institutions administered by them).

(8) In paragraph (y) (industrial and provident societies etc.) for the words from 'and any' onwards substitute 'and which is also registered in the register of social landlords under Part 1 of the Housing Act 1996;'.

(9) At the end insert –

> *'Notes*
> 1. Paragraph (a) above does not include –
>> (a) any Investment Fund or Deposit Fund within the meaning of the Church Funds Investment Measure 1958,
>> (b) any investment fund or deposit fund within the meaning of the Methodist Church Funds Act 1960, or
>> (c) he representative body of the Welsh Church or property administered by it.
> 2. Paragraph (w) above does not include any students' union.'

(10) In section 24 of the 1993 Act (schemes to establish common investment funds), in subsection (8) (fund is to be a charity and, if the scheme admits only exempt charities, an exempt charity) omit the words from '; and if the scheme' onwards.

(11) The Minister may by order make such further amendments of Schedule 2 to the 1993 Act as he considers appropriate for securing –

(a) that (so far as they are charities) institutions of a particular description become or (as the case may be) cease to be exempt charities, or

(b) that (so far as it is a charity) a particular institution becomes or (as the case may be) ceases to be an exempt charity,

or for removing from that Schedule an institution that has ceased to exist.

(12) An order under subsection (11) may only be made for the purpose mentioned in paragraph (a) or (b) of that subsection if the Minister is satisfied that the order is desirable in the interests of ensuring appropriate or effective regulation of the charities or charity concerned in connection with compliance by the charity trustees of the charities or charity with their legal obligations in exercising control and management of the administration of the charities or charity.

(13) The Minister may by order make such amendments or other modifications of any enactment as he considers appropriate in connection with –

(a) charities of a particular description becoming, or ceasing to be, exempt charities, or

(b) a particular charity becoming, or ceasing to be, an exempt charity,

by virtue of any provision made by or under this section.

(14) In this section 'exempt charity' has the same meaning as in the 1993 Act.

12   Increased regulation of exempt charities under 1993 Act
The 1993 Act is amended in accordance with Schedule 5 (which has effect for increasing the extent to which exempt charities are subject to regulation under that Act). ...

CHAPTER 4

APPLICATION OF PROPERTY CY-PRÈS

15   Application cy-près by reference to current circumstances
(1) Section 13 of the 1993 Act (occasions for applying property cy-près) is amended as follows.
(2) In subsection (1)(c), (d) and (e)(iii), for 'the spirit of the gift' substitute 'the appropriate considerations'.
(3) After subsection (1) insert –

> '(1A) In subsection (1) above "the appropriate considerations" means –
>> (a) (on the one hand) the spirit of the gift concerned, and

(b) (on the other) the social and economic circumstances prevailing at the time of the proposed alteration of the original purposes.'

16 Application cy-près of gifts by donors unknown or disclaiming

(1) Section 14 of the 1993 Act (application cy-près of gifts of donors unknown or disclaiming) is amended as follows.

(2) In subsection (4) (power of court to direct that property is to be treated as belonging to donors who cannot be identified) after 'court', in both places, insert 'or the Commission'.

17 Application cy-près of gifts made in response to certain solicitations

After section 14 of the 1993 Act insert –

'14A Application cy-près of gifts made in response to certain solicitations

(1) This section applies to property given –
    (a) for specific charitable purposes, and
    (b) in response to a solicitation within subsection (2) below.

(2) A solicitation is within this subsection if –
    (a) it is made for specific charitable purposes, and
    (b) it is accompanied by a statement to the effect that property given in response to it will, in the event of those purposes failing, be applicable cy-près as if given for charitable purposes generally, unless the donor makes a relevant declaration at the time of making the gift.

(3) A "relevant declaration" is a declaration in writing by the donor to the effect that, in the event of the specific charitable purposes failing, he wishes the trustees holding the property to give him the opportunity to request the return of the property in question (or a sum equal to its value at the time of the making of the gift).

(4) Subsections (5) and (6) below apply if –
    (a) a person has given property as mentioned in subsection (1) above,
    (b) the specific charitable purposes fail, and
    (c) the donor has made a relevant declaration.

(5) The trustees holding the property must take the prescribed steps for the purpose of –
    (a) informing the donor of the failure of the purposes,
    (b) enquiring whether he wishes to request the return of the property (or a sum equal to its value), and
    (c) if within the prescribed period he makes such a request, returning the property (or such a sum) to him.

(6) If those trustees have taken all appropriate prescribed steps but –
    (a) they have failed to find the donor, or
    (b) the donor does not within the prescribed period request the return of the property (or a sum equal to its value),
section 14(1) above shall apply to the property as if it belonged to a donor within paragraph (b) of that subsection (application of property where donor has disclaimed right to return of property).

(7) If –
    (a) a person has given property as mentioned in subsection (1) above,
    (b) the specific charitable purposes fail, and
    (c) the donor has not made a relevant declaration,
section 14(1) above shall similarly apply to the property as if it belonged to a donor within paragraph (b) of that subsection.

(8) For the purposes of this section –

   (a) "solicitation"means a solicitation made in any manner and however communicated to the persons to whom it is addressed,

   (b) it is irrelevant whether any consideration is or is to be given in return for the property in question, and

   (c) where any appeal consists of both solicitations that are accompanied by statements within subsection (2)(b) and solicitations that are not so accompanied, a person giving property as a result of the appeal is to be taken to have responded to the former solicitations and not the latter, unless he proves otherwise.

(9) In this section "prescribed" means prescribed by regulations made by the Commission, and any such regulations shall be published by the Commission in such manner as it thinks fit.

(10) Subsections (7) and (10) of section 14 shall apply for the purposes of this section as they apply for the purposes of section 14.'

18   Cy-près schemes

After section 14A of the 1993 Act (inserted by section 17 above) insert –

'14B Cy-près schemes

(1) The power of the court or the Commission to make schemes for the application of property cy-près shall be exercised in accordance with this section.

(2) Where any property given for charitable purposes is applicable cy-près, the court or the Commission may make a scheme providing for the property to be applied –

   (a) for such charitable purposes, and

   (b) (if the scheme provides for the property to be transferred to another charity) by or on trust for such other charity,

as it considers appropriate, having regard to the matters set out in subsection (3).

(3) The matters are –

   (a) the spirit of the original gift,

   (b) the desirability of securing that the property is applied for charitable purposes which are close to the original purposes, and

   (c) the need for the relevant charity to have purposes which are suitable and effective in the light of current social and economic circumstances.

The "relevant charity" means the charity by or on behalf of which the property is to be applied under the scheme.

(4) If a scheme provides for the property to be transferred to another charity, the scheme may impose on the charity trustees of that charity a duty to secure that the property is applied for purposes which are, so far as is reasonably practicable, similar in character to the original purposes.

(5) In this section references to property given include the property for the time being representing the property originally given or property derived from it.

(6) In this section references to the transfer of property to a charity are references to its transfer –

   (a) to the charity, or

   (b) to the charity trustees, or

   (c) to any trustee for the charity, or

   (d) to a person nominated by the charity trustees to hold it in trust for the charity,

as the scheme may provide.' …

CHAPTER 6

AUDIT OR EXAMINATION OF ACCOUNTS WHERE CHARITY IS NOT A COMPANY

29   Duty of auditor etc of charity which is not a company to report matters to Commission ...
(2) In section 46 of the 1993 Act (special provisions as respects accounts and annual reports of exempt and excepted charities) –
    (a) in subsection (1) for 'sections 41 to 45' substitute 'sections 41 to 44 or section 45'; and
    (b) after subsection (2) insert –

'(2A) Section 44A(2) to (7) above shall apply in relation to a person appointed to audit, or report on, the accounts of an exempt charity which is not a company as they apply in relation to a person such as is mentioned in section 44A(1).
(2B) But section 44A(2) to (7) so apply with the following modifications –
    (a) any reference to a person acting in the capacity mentioned in section 44A(1) is to be read as a reference to his acting as a person appointed as mentioned in subsection (2A) above; and
    (b) any reference to the Commission or to any of its functions is to be read as a reference to the charity's principal regulator or to any of that person's functions in relation to the charity as such.' ...

CHAPTER 7

CHARITABLE COMPANIES

31   Relaxation of restriction on altering memorandum etc. of charitable company
(1) Section 64 of the 1993 Act (alteration of objects clause etc) is amended as follows.
(2) For subsection (2) substitute –

'(2) Where a charity is a company, any regulated alteration by the company –
    (a) requires the prior written consent of the Commission, and
    (b) is ineffective if such consent has not been obtained.
(2A) The following are "regulated alterations" –
    (a) any alteration of the objects clause in the company's memorandum of association,
    (b) any alteration of any provision of its memorandum or articles of association directing the application of property of the company on its dissolution, and
    (c) any alteration of any provision of its memorandum or articles of association where the alteration would provide authorisation for any benefit to be obtained by directors or members of the company or persons connected with them.
(2B) For the purposes of subsection (2A) above –
    (a) "benefit" means a direct or indirect benefit of any nature, except that it does not include any remuneration (within the meaning of section 73A below) whose receipt may be authorised under that section; and
    (b) the same rules apply for determining whether a person is connected with a director or member of the company as apply, in accordance with section 73B(5) and (6) below, for determining whether a person is connected with a charity trustee for the purposes of section 73A.' ...

CHAPTER 9

CHARITY TRUSTEES ETC …

38 Power of Commission to relieve trustees, auditors etc. from liability for breach of trust or duty

After section 73C of the 1993 Act (inserted by section 37 above) insert –

'73D Power to relieve trustees, auditors etc. from liability for breach of trust or duty

(1) This section applies to a person who is or has been –

    (a) a charity trustee or trustee for a charity,

    (b) a person appointed to audit a charity's accounts (whether appointed under an enactment or otherwise), or

    (c) an independent examiner, reporting accountant or other person appointed to examine or report on a charity's accounts (whether appointed under an enactment or otherwise).

(2) If the Commission considers –

    (a) that a person to whom this section applies is or may be personally liable for a breach of trust or breach of duty committed in his capacity as a person within paragraph (a), (b) or (c) of subsection (1) above, but

    (b) that he has acted honestly and reasonably and ought fairly to be excused for the breach of trust or duty,

the Commission may make an order relieving him wholly or partly from any such liability.

(3) An order under subsection (2) above may grant the relief on such terms as the Commission thinks fit.

(4) Subsection (2) does not apply in relation to any personal contractual liability of a charity trustee or trustee for a charity.

(5) For the purposes of this section and section 73E below –

    (a) subsection (1)(b) above is to be read as including a reference to the Auditor General for Wales acting as auditor under section 43B above, and

    (b) subsection (1)(c) above is to be read as including a reference to the Auditor General for Wales acting as examiner under that section;

and in subsection (1)(b) and (c) any reference to a charity's accounts is to be read as including any group accounts prepared by the charity trustees of a charity.

(6) This section does not affect the operation of –

    (a) section 61 of the Trustee Act 1925 (power of court to grant relief to trustees),

    (b) section 727 of the Companies Act 1985 (power of court to grant relief to officers or auditors of companies), or

    (c) section 73E below (which extends section 727 to auditors etc. of charities which are not companies).

73E Court's power to grant relief to apply to all auditors etc. of charities which are not companies

(1) Section 727 of the Companies Act 1985 (power of court to grant relief to officers or auditors of companies) shall have effect in relation to a person to whom this section applies as it has effect in relation to a person employed as an auditor by a company.

(2) This section applies to –

    (a) a person acting in a capacity within section 73D(1)(b) or (c) above in a case where, apart from this section, section 727 would not apply in relation to him as a person so acting, and

(b)   a charity trustee of a CIO.' …

CHAPTER 10

POWERS OF UNINCORPORATED CHARITIES

40   Power to transfer all property
For section 74 of the 1993 Act substitute –

'74   Power to transfer all property of unincorporated charity

(1) This section applies to a charity if –
  (a)   its gross income in its last financial year did not exceed £10,000,
  (b)   it does not hold any designated land, and
  (c)   it is not a company or other body corporate.
"Designated land" means land held on trusts which stipulate that it is to be used for the purposes, or any particular purposes, of the charity.

(2) The charity trustees of such a charity may resolve for the purposes of this section –
  (a)   that all the property of the charity should be transferred to another charity specified in the resolution, or
  (b)   that all the property of the charity should be transferred to two or more charities specified in the resolution in accordance with such division of the property between them as is so specified.

(3) Any charity so specified may be either a registered charity or a charity which is not required to be registered.

(4) But the charity trustees of a charity ("the transferor charity") do not have power to pass a resolution under subsection (2) above unless they are satisfied –
  (a)   that it is expedient in the interests of furthering the purposes for which the property is held by the transferor charity for the property to be transferred in accordance with the resolution, and
  (b)   that the purposes (or any of the purposes) of any charity to which property is to be transferred under the resolution are substantially similar to the purposes (or any of the purposes) of the transferor charity.

(5) Any resolution under subsection (2) above must be passed by a majority of not less than two-thirds of the charity trustees who vote on the resolution.

(6) Where charity trustees have passed a resolution under subsection (2), they must send a copy of it to the Commission, together with a statement of their reasons for passing it.

(7) Having received the copy of the resolution, the Commission –
  (a)   may direct the charity trustees to give public notice of the resolution in such manner as is specified in the direction, and
  (b)   if it gives such a direction, must take into account any representations made to it by persons appearing to it to be interested in the charity, where those representations are made to it within the period of 28 days beginning with the date when public notice of the resolution is given by the charity trustees.

(8) The Commission may also direct the charity trustees to provide the Commission with additional information or explanations relating to –

(a) the circumstances in and by reference to which they have decided to act under this section, or

(b) their compliance with any obligation imposed on them by or under this section in connection with the resolution.

(9) Subject to the provisions of section 74A below, a resolution under subsection (2) above takes effect at the end of the period of 60 days beginning with the date on which the copy of it was received by the Commission.

(10) Where such a resolution has taken effect, the charity trustees must arrange for all the property of the transferor charity to be transferred in accordance with the resolution, and on terms that any property so transferred –

(a) is to be held by the charity to which it is transferred ('the transferee charity') in accordance with subsection (11) below, but

(b) when so held is nevertheless to be subject to any restrictions on expenditure to which it was subject as property of the transferor charity;

and the charity trustees must arrange for the property to be so transferred by such date after the resolution takes effect as they agree with the charity trustees of the transferee charity or charities concerned.

(11) The charity trustees of any charity to which property is transferred under this section must secure, so far as is reasonably practicable, that the property is applied for such of its purposes as are substantially similar to those of the transferor charity.

But this requirement does not apply if those charity trustees consider that complying with it would not result in a suitable and effective method of applying the property.

(12) For the purpose of enabling any property to be transferred to a charity under this section, the Commission may, at the request of the charity trustees of that charity, make orders vesting any property of the transferor charity –

(a) in the transferee charity, in its charity trustees or in any trustee for that charity, or

(b) in any other person nominated by those charity trustees to hold property in trust for that charity.

(13) The Minister may by order amend subsection (1) above by substituting a different sum for the sum for the time being specified there.

(14) In this section references to the transfer of property to a charity are references to its transfer –

(a) to the charity, or

(b) to the charity trustees, or

(c) to any trustee for the charity, or

(d) to a person nominated by the charity trustees to hold it in trust for the charity,

as the charity trustees may determine.

(15) Where a charity has a permanent endowment, this section has effect in accordance with section 74B.

74A Resolution not to take effect or to take effect at later date

(1) This section deals with circumstances in which a resolution under section 74(2) above either –

(a) does not take effect under section 74(9) above, or

(b) takes effect at a time later than that mentioned in section 74(9).

(2) A resolution does not take effect under section 74(9) above if before the end of –

(a) the period of 60 days mentioned in section 74(9) ('the 60-day period'), or

(b) that period as modified by subsection (3) or (4) below,

the Commission notifies the charity trustees in writing that it objects to the resolution, either on procedural grounds or on the merits of the proposals contained in the resolution. "On procedural grounds" means on the grounds that any obligation imposed on the charity trustees by or under section 74 above has not been complied with in connection with the resolution.

(3) If under section 74(7) above the Commission directs the charity trustees to give public notice of a resolution, the running of the 60-day period is suspended by virtue of this subsection –

> (a) as from the date on which the direction is given to the charity trustees, and
> (b) until the end of the period of 42 days beginning with the date on which public notice of the resolution is given by the charity trustees.

(4) If under section 74(8) above the Commission directs the charity trustees to provide any information or explanations, the running of the 60-day period is suspended by virtue of this subsection –

> (a) as from the date on which the direction is given to the charity trustees, and
> (b) until the date on which the information or explanations is or are provided to the Commission.

(5) Subsection (6) below applies once the period of time, or the total period of time, during which the 60-day period is suspended by virtue of either or both of subsections (3) and (4) above exceeds 120 days.

(6) At that point the resolution (if not previously objected to by the Commission) is to be treated as if it had never been passed.

74B   Transfer where charity has permanent endowment

(1) This section provides for the operation of section 74 above where a charity within section 74(1) has a permanent endowment (whether or not the charity's trusts contain provision for the termination of the charity).

(2) In such a case section 74 applies as follows –

> (a) if the charity has both a permanent endowment and other property ('unrestricted property') –
> > (i) a resolution under section 74(2) must relate to both its permanent endowment and its unrestricted property, and
> > (ii) that section applies in relation to its unrestricted property in accordance with subsection (3) below and in relation to its permanent endowment in accordance with subsections (4) to (11) below;
> (b) if all of the property of the charity is comprised in its permanent endowment, that section applies in relation to its permanent endowment in accordance with subsections (4) to (11) below.

(3) Section 74 applies in relation to unrestricted property of the charity as if references in that section to all or any of the property of the charity were references to all or any of its unrestricted property.

(4) Section 74 applies in relation to the permanent endowment of the charity with the following modifications.

(5) References in that section to all or any of the property of the charity are references to all or any of the property comprised in its permanent endowment.

(6) If the property comprised in its permanent endowment is to be transferred to a single charity, the charity trustees must (instead of being satisfied as mentioned in section

74(4)(b)) be satisfied that the proposed transferee charity has purposes which are substantially similar to all of the purposes of the transferor charity.

(7) If the property comprised in its permanent endowment is to be transferred to two or more charities, the charity trustees must (instead of being satisfied as mentioned in section 74(4)(b)) be satisfied –

> (a) that the proposed transferee charities, taken together, have purposes which are substantially similar to all of the purposes of the transferor charity, and
>
> (b) that each of the proposed transferee charities has purposes which are substantially similar to one or more of the purposes of the transferor charity.

(8) In the case of a transfer to which subsection (7) above applies, the resolution under section 74(2) must provide for the property comprised in the permanent endowment of the charity to be divided between the transferee charities in such a way as to take account of such guidance as may be given by the Commission for the purposes of this section.

(9) The requirement in section 74(11) shall apply in the case of every such transfer, and in complying with that requirement the charity trustees of a transferee charity must secure that the application of property transferred to the charity takes account of any such guidance.

(10) Any guidance given by the Commission for the purposes of this section may take such form and be given in such manner as the Commission considers appropriate.

(11) For the purposes of sections 74 and 74A above, any reference to any obligation imposed on the charity trustees by or under section 74 includes a reference to any obligation imposed on them by virtue of any of subsections (6) to (8) above.

(12) Section 74(14) applies for the purposes of this section as it applies for the purposes of section 74.' …

CHAPTER 11
POWERS TO SPEND CAPITAL AND MERGERS

43 Power to spend capital
For section 75 of the 1993 Act substitute –

'75 Power of unincorporated charities to spend capital: general
(1) This section applies to any available endowment fund of a charity which is not a company or other body corporate.

(2) But this section does not apply to a fund if section 75A below (power of larger charities to spend capital given for particular purpose) applies to it.

(3) Where the condition in subsection (4) below is met in relation to the charity, the charity trustees may resolve for the purposes of this section that the fund, or a portion of it, ought to be freed from the restrictions with respect to expenditure of capital that apply to it.

(4) The condition in this subsection is that the charity trustees are satisfied that the purposes set out in the trusts to which the fund is subject could be carried out more effectively if the capital of the fund, or the relevant portion of the capital, could be expended as well as income accruing to it, rather than just such income.

(5) Once the charity trustees have passed a resolution under subsection (3) above, the fund or portion may by virtue of this section be expended in carrying out the purposes set out in the trusts to which the fund is subject without regard to the restrictions mentioned in that subsection.

(6) The fund or portion may be so expended as from such date as is specified for this purpose in the resolution.

(7) In this section "available endowment fund", in relation to a charity, means –
  (a) the whole of the charity's permanent endowment if it is all subject to the same trusts, or
  (b) any part of its permanent endowment which is subject to any particular trusts that are different from those to which any other part is subject.

75A   Power of larger unincorporated charities to spend capital given for particular purpose

(1) This section applies to any available endowment fund of a charity which is not a company or other body corporate if –
  (a) the capital of the fund consists entirely of property given –
       (i)   by a particular individual,
       (ii) by a particular institution (by way of grant or otherwise), or
       (iii) by two or more individuals or institutions in pursuit of a common purpose, and
  (b) the financial condition in subsection (2) below is met.
(2) The financial condition in this subsection is met if –
  (a) the relevant charity's gross income in its last financial year exceeded £1,000, and
  (b) the market value of the endowment fund exceeds £10,000.
(3) Where the condition in subsection (4) below is met in relation to the charity, the charity trustees may resolve for the purposes of this section that the fund, or a portion of it, ought to be freed from the restrictions with respect to expenditure of capital that apply to it.
(4) The condition in this subsection is that the charity trustees are satisfied that the purposes set out in the trusts to which the fund is subject could be carried out more effectively if the capital of the fund, or the relevant portion of the capital, could be expended as well as income accruing to it, rather than just such income.
(5) The charity trustees –
  (a) must send a copy of any resolution under subsection (3) above to the Commission, together with a statement of their reasons for passing it, and
  (b) may not implement the resolution except in accordance with the following provisions of this section.
(6) Having received the copy of the resolution the Commission may –
  (a) direct the charity trustees to give public notice of the resolution in such manner as is specified in the direction, and
  (b) if it gives such a direction, must take into account any representations made to it by persons appearing to it to be interested in the charity, where those representations are made to it within the period of 28 days beginning with the date when public notice of the resolution is given by the charity trustees.
(7) The Commission may also direct the charity trustees to provide the Commission with additional information or explanations relating to –
  (a) the circumstances in and by reference to which they have decided to act under this section, or
  (b) their compliance with any obligation imposed on them by or under this section in connection with the resolution.
(8) When considering whether to concur with the resolution the Commission must take into account –
  (a) any evidence available to it as to the wishes of the donor or donors mentioned in subsection (1)(a) above, and

(b) any changes in the circumstances relating to the charity since the making of the gift or gifts (including, in particular, its financial position, the needs of its beneficiaries, and the social, economic and legal environment in which it operates).

(9) The Commission must not concur with the resolution unless it is satisfied –

(a) that its implementation would accord with the spirit of the gift or gifts mentioned in subsection (1)(a) above (even though it would be inconsistent with the restrictions mentioned in subsection (3) above), and

(b) that the charity trustees have complied with the obligations imposed on them by or under this section in connection with the resolution.

(10) Before the end of the period of three months beginning with the relevant date, the Commission must notify the charity trustees in writing either –

(a) that the Commission concurs with the resolution, or

(b) that it does not concur with it.

(11) In subsection (10) "the relevant date" means –

(a) in a case where the Commission directs the charity trustees under subsection (6) above to give public notice of the resolution, the date when that notice is given, and

(b) in any other case, the date on which the Commission receives the copy of the resolution in accordance with subsection (5) above.

(12) Where –

(a) the charity trustees are notified by the Commission that it concurs with the resolution, or

(b) the period of three months mentioned in subsection (10) above has elapsed without the Commission notifying them that it does not concur with the resolution,

the fund or portion may, by virtue of this section, be expended in carrying out the purposes set out in the trusts to which the fund is subject without regard to the restrictions mentioned in subsection (3).

(13) The Minister may by order amend subsection (2) above by substituting a different sum for any sum specified there.

(14) In this section –

(a) "available endowment fund" has the same meaning as in section 75 above,

(b) "market value", in relation to an endowment fund, means –

(i) the market value of the fund as recorded in the accounts for the last financial year of the relevant charity, or

(ii) if no such value was so recorded, the current market value of the fund as determined on a valuation carried out for the purpose, and

(c) the reference in subsection (1) to the giving of property by an individual includes his giving it under his will.

75B   Power to spend capital subject to special trusts

(1) This section applies to any available endowment fund of a special trust which, as the result of a direction under section 96(5) below, is to be treated as a separate charity ("the relevant charity") for the purposes of this section.

(2) Where the condition in subsection (3) below is met in relation to the relevant charity, the charity trustees may resolve for the purposes of this section that the fund, or a portion

of it, ought to be freed from the restrictions with respect to expenditure of capital that apply to it.

(3) The condition in this subsection is that the charity trustees are satisfied that the purposes set out in the trusts to which the fund is subject could be carried out more effectively if the capital of the fund, or the relevant portion of the capital, could be expended as well as income accruing to it, rather than just such income.

(4) Where the market value of the fund exceeds £10,000 and the capital of the fund consists entirely of property given –

    (a) by a particular individual,

    (b) by a particular institution (by way of grant or otherwise), or

    (c) by two or more individuals or institutions in pursuit of a common purpose,

subsections (5) to (11) of section 75A above apply in relation to the resolution and that gift or gifts as they apply in relation to a resolution under section 75A(3) and the gift or gifts mentioned in section 75A(1)(a).

(5) Where –

    (a) the charity trustees have passed a resolution under subsection (2) above, and

    (b) (in a case where section 75A(5) to (11) above apply in accordance with subsection (4) above) either –

        (i)   the charity trustees are notified by the Commission that it concurs with the resolution, or

        (ii) the period of three months mentioned in section 75A(10) has elapsed without the Commission notifying them that it does not concur with the resolution,

the fund or portion may, by virtue of this section, be expended in carrying out the purposes set out in the trusts to which the fund is subject without regard to the restrictions mentioned in subsection (2).

(6) The fund or portion may be so expended as from such date as is specified for this purpose in the resolution.

(7) The Minister may by order amend subsection (4) above by substituting a different sum for the sum specified there.

(8) In this section –

    (a) "available endowment fund" has the same meaning as in section 75 above,

    (b) "market value" has the same meaning as in section 75A above, and

    (c) the reference in subsection (4) to the giving of property by an individual includes his giving it under his will.' ...

PART 4

MISCELLANEOUS AND GENERAL ...

75   Amendments, repeals, revocations and transitional provisions

(1) Schedule 8 contains minor and consequential amendments.

(2) Schedule 9 makes provision for the repeal and revocation of enactments (including enactments which are spent).

(3) Schedule 10 contains transitional provisions and savings. ...

78   Interpretation

(1) In this Act –

    'the 1992 Act' means the Charities Act 1992 (c 41);

'the 1993 Act' means the Charities Act 1993 (c 10).

(2) In this Act –

    (a) 'charity' has the meaning given by section 1(1);

    (b) 'charitable purposes' has (in accordance with section 2(6)) the meaning given by section 2(1); and

    (c) 'charity trustees' has the same meaning as in the 1993 Act;

but (subject to subsection (3) below) the exclusions contained in section 96(2) of the 1993 Act (ecclesiastical corporations etc.) have effect in relation to references to a charity in this Act as they have effect in relation to such references in that Act.

(3) Those exclusions do not have effect in relation to references in section 1 or any reference to the law relating to charities in England and Wales.

(4) In this Act 'enactment' includes –

    (a) any provision of subordinate legislation (within the meaning of the Interpretation Act 1978 (c 30)),

    (b) a provision of a Measure of the Church Assembly or of the General Synod of the Church of England, and

    (c) (in the context of section 6(5) or 75(5)) any provision made by or under an Act of the Scottish Parliament or Northern Ireland legislation,

and references to enactments include enactments passed or made after the passing of this Act.

(5) In this Act 'institution' means an institution whether incorporated or not, and includes a trust or undertaking.

(6) In this Act 'the Minister' means the Minister for the Cabinet Office.

(7) Subsections (2) to (5) apply except where the context otherwise requires.

79   Commencement

(1) The following provisions come into force on the day on which this Act is passed –

    (a) section 13(4) and (5),

    (b) section 74,

    (c) section 75(4) and (5),

    (d) section 78,

    (e) section 77,

    (f) this section and section 80, and

    (g) the following provisions of Schedule 8 –

        paragraph 90(2),

        paragraph 104 so far as it confers power to make regulations, and

        paragraph 174(d),and section 75(1) so far as relating to those provisions.

(2) Otherwise, this Act comes into force on such day as the Minister may by order appoint.

(3) An order under subsection (2) –

    (a) may appoint different days for different purposes or different areas;

    (b) make such provision as the Minister considers necessary or expedient for transitory, transitional or saving purposes in connection with the coming into force of any provision of this Act. ...

SCHEDULE 3

THE CHARITY TRIBUNAL

1. After Schedule 1A to the 1993 Act (inserted by Schedule 1 to this Act) insert –

'SCHEDULE 1B

THE CHARITY TRIBUNAL

Membership

1. – (1) The Tribunal shall consist of the President and its other members.

(2) The Lord Chancellor shall appoint –

   (a) a President of the Tribunal,
   (b) legal members of the Tribunal, and
   (c) ordinary members of the Tribunal.

(3) A person may be appointed as the President or a legal member of the Tribunal only if he has a seven year general qualification within the meaning of section 71 of the Courts and Legal Services Act 1990.

(4) A person may be appointed as an ordinary member of the Tribunal only if he appears to the Lord Chancellor to have appropriate knowledge or experience relating to charities.

Deputy President

2. – (1) The Lord Chancellor may appoint a legal member as deputy President of the Tribunal.

(2) The deputy President –

   (a) may act for the President when he is unable to act or unavailable, and
   (b) shall perform such other functions as the President may delegate or assign to him.

Terms of appointment

3. – (1) The members of the Tribunal shall hold and vacate office as such in accordance with the terms of their respective appointments.

(2) A person holding office as a member of the Tribunal –

   (a) may resign that office by giving notice in writing to the Lord Chancellor, and
   (b) may be removed from office by the Lord Chancellor on the ground of incapacity or misbehaviour.

(3) A previous appointment of a person as a member of the Tribunal does not affect his eligibility for re-appointment as a member of the Tribunal.

Retirement etc.

4. – (1) A person shall not hold office as a member of the Tribunal after reaching the age of 70.

(2) Section 26(5) and (6) of the Judicial Pensions and Retirement Act 1993 (extension to age 75) apply in relation to a member of the Tribunal as they apply in relation to a holder of a relevant office.' ...

SCHEDULE 5

EXEMPT CHARITIES: INCREASED REGULATION UNDER 1993 ACT

1. In section 6 of the 1993 Act (power of Commission to require charity's name to be changed) omit subsection (9) (exclusion of exempt charities).

2. In section 8(1) of the 1993 Act (power of Commission to institute inquiries with regard to charities but not in relation to any exempt charity) after 'any exempt charity' insert 'except where this has been requested by its principal regulator.'

3. In section 9 of the 1993 Act (power of Commission to call for documents and search records) omit subsection (4) (exclusion of documents relating only to exempt charities).

4. – (1) Section 16 of the 1993 Act (concurrent jurisdiction of Commission with High Court for certain purposes) is amended as follows.
(2) In subsection (4)(c) (application for Commission to exercise powers may be made by Attorney General except in case of exempt charity) omit 'in the case of a charity other than an exempt charity,'.
(3) In subsection (5) (jurisdiction exercisable in case of charity which is not an exempt charity and whose annual income does not exceed £500) omit 'which is not an exempt charity and'. …

6. In section 18 of the 1993 Act (power of Commission to act for protection of charities) for subsection (16) substitute –

'(16) In this section –
    (a) subsections (1) to (3) apply in relation to an exempt charity, and
    (b) subsections (4) to (6) apply in relation to such a charity at any time after the Commission have instituted an inquiry under section 8 with respect to it,
  and the other provisions of this section apply accordingly.'

7. In section 28 of the 1993 Act (power of Commission to give directions about dormant bank accounts of charities), omit subsection (10) (exclusion of accounts held by or on behalf of exempt charity).

8. – (1) Section 33 of the 1993 Act (charity proceedings by persons other than Commission) is amended as follows.
(2) In subsection (2) (proceedings relating to a charity other than an exempt charity must be authorised by the Commission) omit '(other than an exempt charity)'.
(3) In subsection (7) (participation by Attorney General in proceedings relating to charity other than exempt charity) omit '(other than an exempt charity)'.

9. In section 73 of the 1993 Act (consequences of person acting as charity trustee while disqualified), in subsection (4) (power of Commission to order disqualified person to repay sums received from a charity other than an exempt charity) omit '(other than an exempt charity)'. …

SCHEDULE 7

CHARITABLE INCORPORATED ORGANISATIONS …

PART 2

OTHER AMENDMENTS OF 1993 ACT

3. The 1993 Act is further amended as follows.

4. In section 45 (annual reports), after subsection (3A) insert –

'(3B) But in the case of a charity which is constituted as a CIO –
    (a) the requirement imposed by subsection (3) applies whatever the charity's gross income is, and
    (b) subsection (3A) does not apply.'

5. In section 48 (annual returns), in subsection (1A), at the end add '(but this subsection does not apply if the charity is constituted as a CIO)'. ...

7. In section 97 (general interpretation), in subsection (1), at the appropriate place insert –

'"CIO" means charitable incorporated organisation;'.

SCHEDULE 8

MINOR AND CONSEQUENTIAL AMENDMENTS ...

Charities Act 1993 (c 10)
96. The 1993 Act has effect subject to the following amendments. ...

99. – (1) Section 4 (claims and objections to registration) is amended as follows. ...
(3) Omit subsection (3).
(4) In subsection (4) –
      (a) for 'High Court' substitute 'Tribunal', ...
(5) In subsection (5) –
      (a) for 'subsection (3) above' substitute 'Schedule 1C to this Act', ...
      (c) omit ', whether given on such an appeal or not'.

100. – (1) Section 6 (power to require charity's name to be changed) is amended as follows. ...
(3) In subsection (5) for 'section 3(7)(b) above' substitute 'section 3B(3)'. ...

109. – (1) Section 16 (concurrent jurisdiction of Commissioners with High Court) is amended as follows. ...
(12) Omit subsections (11) to (14). ...

111. – (1) Section 18 (power to act for protection of charities) is amended as follows....
(7) Omit subsections (8) to (10). ...

133. – (1) Section 42 (annual statements of accounts) is amended as follows.
(2) After subsection (2) insert –

'(2A) Such regulations may, however, not impose on the charity trustees of a charity that is a charitable trust created by any person ("the settlor") any requirement to disclose, in any statement of accounts prepared by them under subsection (1) –
      (a) the identities of recipients of grants made out of the funds of the charity, or
      (b) the amounts of any individual grants so made,
if the disclosure would fall to be made at a time when the settlor or any spouse or civil partner of his was still alive.'

(3) After subsection (7) add –

'(8) Provisions about the preparation of accounts in respect of groups consisting of certain charities and their subsidiary undertakings, and about other matters relating to such groups, are contained in Schedule 5A to this Act (see section 49A below).' ...

139. – (1) Section 46 (special provisions as respects accounts etc of excepted charities) is amended as follows. ...
(3) For subsection (3) substitute –

'(3) Except in accordance with subsections (3A) and (3B) below, nothing in section 43, 44, 44A or 45 applies to any charity which –

    (a)   falls within section 3A(2)(d) above (whether or not it also falls within section 3A(2)(b) or (c)), and

    (b) is not registered.

(3A) Section 44A above applies in accordance with subsections (2A) and (2B) above to a charity mentioned in subsection (3) above which is also an exempt charity.

(3B) Sections 44 and 44A above apply to a charity mentioned in subsection (3) above which is also an English National Health Service charity or a Welsh National Health Service charity (as defined in sections 43A and 43B above).'

(4) In subsection (4) for the words from '(other than' onwards substitute

'which –

    (a)   falls within section 3A(2)(b) or (c) above but does not fall within section 3A(2)(d), and

    (b) is not registered.' …

140. – (1) Section 47 (public inspection of annual reports etc) is amended as follows.

(2) In subsection (1) –

    (a)   for 'Any annual report or other document kept by the Commissioners' substitute 'Any document kept by the Commission',

    (b) for 'the Commissioners so determine' substitute 'the Commission so determines', and

    (c) for 'they may' substitute 'it may'.

(3) In subsection (2)(a) after 'accounts' insert 'or (if subsection (4) below applies) of its most recent annual report'. …

141. – (1) Section 48 (annual returns by registered charities) is amended as follows. …

(3) In subsection (1A) for the words from 'neither' to 'exceeds' substitute 'the charity's gross income does not exceed'.

(4) In subsection (2) –

    (a)   for 'the Commissioners' substitute 'the Commission', and

    (b) for 'to them' substitute 'to the Commission'. …

143. – (1) Section 50 (incorporation of trustees of charity) is amended as follows. …

(3) In subsection (2) –

    (a)   for 'The Commissioners' substitute 'The Commission',

    (b) for 'to them' substitute 'to the Commission', and

    (c) for 'under section 3' substitute 'in accordance with section 3A'. …

157. In section 73(4) (person acting as charity trustee while disqualified) –

    (a)   for 'the Commissioners are' substitute 'the Commission is',

    (b) for 'they may by order' substitute 'the Commission may by order', and

    (c) for '(as determined by them)' substitute '(as determined by the Commission)'. …

163. – (1) Section 84 (supply by Commissioners of copies of documents open to public inspection) is amended as follows.

(2) For 'The Commissioners' substitute 'The Commission'.

(3) For 'their possession' substitute 'the Commission's possession'.

(4) At the end add 'or section 75D'. …

167. – (1) Section 88 (enforcement of orders of Commissioners) is amended as follows.
(2) For paragraph (a) substitute –

'(a) to an order of the Commission under section 9(1), 19A, 19B, 44(2), 61, 73, 73C or
80 above; or'.

(3) In paragraphs (b) and (c) for 'the Commissioners' substitute 'the Commission'.
(4) For 'the Commissioners to' substitute 'the Commission to'. ...

171. Omit section 92 (appeals from Commissioners). ...

173. – (1) Section 96 (construction of references to a 'charity' etc) is amended as follows.
(2) In subsection (1) for the definition of 'charity' substitute –

'charity' has the meaning given by section 1(1) of the Charities Act 2006;'.

(3) Omit –
  (a) in the definition of 'exempt charity' in subsection (1), the words '(subject to section
       24(8) above)', and
  (b) subsection (4). ...

174. In section 97(1) (interpretation) –
  (a) in the definition of 'charitable purposes', for 'charitable according to the law of England
       and Wales;' substitute 'charitable purposes as defined by section 2(1) of the Charities
       Act 2006;'; ...

177. In paragraph (a) of Schedule 2 (exempt charities) for 'the Commissioners' (in the first place)
substitute 'the Charity Commissioners for England and Wales'. ...

SCHEDULE 9

REPEALS AND REVOCATIONS

Short title and chapter or title and number	*Extent of repeal or revocation*
...	
Charities Act 1993 (c 10)	Section 1.
	In section 2(7), the words from ', and the report' onwards.
	In section 4, subsection (3) and, in subsection (5), the words ', whether given on such an appeal or not'.
	Section 6(9).
	Section 9(4).
	In section 16, in subsection (4)(c) the words 'in the case of a charity other than an exempt charity,', in subsection (5) the words 'which is not an exempt charity and', and subsections (11) to (14).
	In section 17(7), the words from 'but this subsection' onwards.

Section 18(8) to (10).

In section 23(2), the words 'or them'.

In section 24(8), the words from '; and if the scheme' onwards.

Section 28(10).

In section 33, in each of subsections (2) and (7) the words '(other than an exempt charity)'.

Section 44(3).

Section 46(8).

Section 61(7).

In section 73(4), the words '(other than an exempt charity)'.

Section 92.

In section 96, in the definition of 'exempt charity' in subsection (1) the words '(subject to section 24(8) above)', and subsection (4).

Schedule 1.

In Schedule 2, in paragraph (b) the words 'and the colleges of Winchester and Eton', and paragraph (x).

In Schedule 6, paragraphs 1(2), 26, 28 and 29(2) to (4), (7) and (8). …

SCHEDULE 10

TRANSITIONAL PROVISIONS AND SAVINGS …

2. Where section 2 of the Recreational Charities Act 1958 (c 17) applies to any trusts immediately before the day on which subsection (3) of section 5 of this Act comes into force, that subsection does not prevent the trusts from continuing to be charitable if they constitute a charity in accordance with section 1(1) of this Act. …

7. The amendments made by section 28 apply in relation to any financial year of a charity which begins on or after the day on which that section comes into force. …

NB. Sections 78 and 79, above, came into force on Royal Assent, ie, on 8 November 2006.

As amended by the Transfer of Functions (Third Sector, Communities and Equality) Order 2006, art 6, Schedule, para 4(d).

INDEX